Barbara H. Foley

Elizabeth R. Neblett

Australia • Brazil • Japan • Korea • Mexico • Singapore • Spain • United Kingdom • United States

English in Action 3
Barbara H. Foley, and Elizabeth R. Neblett

Publisher, Adult and Academic ESL: James W. Brown

Acquisitions Editor: Sherrise Roehr

Senior Developmental Editor: Sarah Barnicle

Editorial Assistant: Audra Longert

Marketing Manager: Eric Bredenberg

Director, Global ESL Training & Development: Evelyn Nelson

Senior Production Editor: Maryellen Killeen

Senior Print Buyer: Mary Beth Hennebury

Project Manager: Tünde A. Dewey

Compositor: Pre-Press PMG

Text Printer/Binder: Transcontinental Printing

Text Designer: Sue Gerould

Cover Designer: Gina Petti/ Rotunda Design House

Cover Art: Zita Asbaghi

Unit Opener Art: Zita Asbaghi

Photo Researcher: Jill Engebretson

Photography Manager: Sheri Blaney

Illustrators: Scott MacNeill; Ray Medici; Glen Giron, Roger Acaya, Ibarra Cristostomo, Leo Cultura of Raketshop Design Studio, Philippines

Library of Congress Control Number: 2004117882

ISBN-13: 978-0-8384-2829-0
ISBN-10: 0-8384-2829-0

Heinle
25 Thomson Place,
Boston, MA 02210
USA

Cengage Learning is a leading provider of customized learning solutions with office locations around the globe, including Singapore, the United Kingdom, Australia, Mexico, Brazil, and Japan. Locate your local office at: **international.cengage.com/region**

Cengage Learning products are represented in Canada by Nelson Education, Ltd.

Visit Heinle online at **elt.heinle.com**

Visit our corporate website at **cengage.com**

International Division List

ASIA
Cengage Learning
Tel: 65-6410-1200
Fax: 65-6410-1208

AUSTRALIA / NEW ZEALAND
Nelson Cengage Learning
Tel: 61-(0)3-9685-4111
Fax: 61-(0)3-9685-4199

BRAZIL
Cengage Pioneira Ltda
Tel: 55 11 3665-9900
Fax: 55 11 3665-9901

CANADA
Nelson Cengage Learning
Tel: 416-752-9448
Fax: 416-752-8102

JAPAN
Cengage Learning
Tel: 81-3-3511-4390
Fax: 81-3-3511-4391

KOREA
Cengage Learning
Tel: 82-2-322-4926
Fax: 82-2-322-4927

LATIN AMERICA
Cengage Learning
Tel: 52-55-5281-2906
Fax: 52-55-5281-2656

SPAIN / PORTUGAL
Paraninfo Cengage Learning
Tel: 34-(0)91-446-3350
Fax: 34-(0)91-445-6218

TAIWAN
Cengage Learning
Tel: 886-2-2375-1118
Fax: 886-2-2375-1119

EUROPE / MIDDLE EAST/ AFRICA
Cengage Learning
Tel: 44-20-7067-2500
Fax: 44-20-7067-2600

Printed in China
9 10 10 09 08

We would like to acknowledge the many individuals who helped, encouraged, and supported us during the writing and production of this series. In keeping with an open-ended format, we would like to offer a matching exercise. Please be advised, there is more than one correct "match" for each person. Thank you all!

Jim Brown	• for your creative eye for art and design.
Eric Bredenberg	• for your enthusiasm and support.
Sherrise Roehr	• for your support, patience, and humor while guiding this project.
Maryellen Killeen	• for your faith in the authors.
Audra Longert	• for your smiles and your stories.
Sarah Barnicle	• for your encouragement, comments, and suggestions.
Tünde A. Dewey	• for putting up with us!
All the Heinle sales reps	• for your understanding of the needs of teachers and programs.
The students at Union County College	• for your keeping us all on schedule.
The faculty and staff at UCC	• for your help with research.
Our families	

The authors and publisher would like to thank the following reviewers and consultants:

Linda Boice
Elk Grove Unified School District, Sacramento, CA

Rocio Castiblanco
Seminole Community College, Sanford, FL

Jared Erfle
Antelope Valley High School, Lancaster, CA

Rob Kustusch
Triton Community College, River Grove, IL

Patricia Long
Old Marshall Adult School, Sacramento, CA

Kathleen Newton
New York City Board of Education, Bronx, NY

Alberto Panizo
Miami-Dade Community College, Miami, FL

Eric Rosenbaum
Bronx Community College, Bronx, NY

Michaela Safadi
South Gate Community, South Gate, CA

Armando Valdez
Huantes Learning and Leadership Development Center, San Antonio, TX

Contents

Contents

Many years ago, I attended an ESL workshop in which the presenter asked a full audience, "How many of you read the **To the Teacher** at the front of the text?" Two participants raised their hands. Since that time, I have begged my publishers to release me from this responsibility, but have always been overruled.

As a teacher, you can form a clear first impression of this book. Flip through the pages. Will the format appeal to your students? Look carefully through the table of contents. Are most of the structures and contexts that your program has established included in the text? Thumb slowly through a few units. Will the activities and exercises, the support, the pace be appropriate for your students? If you wish, you can even read the rest of **To the Teacher** below.

English in Action is a four-level core language series for ESL/EFL students. It is a comprehensive revision and expansion of *The New Grammar in Action*. The popularity of the original edition delighted us, but we heard the same requests over and over: "Please include more readings and pronunciation," and "Could you add a workbook?" In planning the revision, our publisher threw budgetary concerns to the wind and decided to produce a four color, redesigned version. The revision also allowed us, the authors, an opportunity to refine the text. We are writers, but we are also teachers. We wrote a unit, then immediately tried it out in the classroom. Activities, tasks, and exercises were added, deleted, and changed in an ongoing process. Students provided daily and honest feedback.

This third book is designed for intermediate level students. These students have been introduced to the basic tenses, and they can apply them in everyday situations. The units in this text present them with more challenging contexts and encourage them to expand their use of English while discussing topics such as geography, natural disasters, health, crime, and working parents. At this level, students can be expected to use the basic structures of English and to become more comfortable using a variety of tenses.

The units build gradually, developing an interesting context. As students move through each unit, they engage in situations and activities in which they can see, hear, and practice the language. Throughout each unit, there is support in the form of clearly illustrated situations, grammer notes, examples, and vocabulary boxes.

Active Grammar

Each unit opens with an illustration or photo and discussion questions to introduce the topic and to draw the students into the unit. The following six to seven pages of exercises integrate the context and the new grammar. As students progress through this section, they will find a wide variety of activities. There are pictures to discuss, opportunities to interview their teachers and their classmates, conversations to develop, stories to enjoy, dictations for students to present to a partner, and even a few traditional fill-in-the-blank exercises to complete. We encourage you to try them all.

The directions are clear and there are examples for each exercise. Artwork and photos illustrate the context clearly. For many of the exercises, the entire class will be working together with your direction and explainations. Other exercises show a pairwork icon —students can try these with a partner or in a small group. You should walk around the classroom, listening to students and answering questions. With this variety of activities, this book should appeal to every learning style.

Pronunciation

Within the **Active Grammar** section is an exercise that focuses on pronunciation. These are specific pronunciation points that complement the grammar or vocabulary of the lesson, such as contractions, syllables, word stress, and intonation.

The Big Picture

This is our favorite section, integrating listening, vocabulary, and structure. A large, lively picture shows a particular setting, such as an accident, wedding, or hurricane. After listening to a short narrative or conversation, students answer questions, fill in information, review structures, or complete conversations.

Reading

In the third book, the reading feature has been significantly expanded and is now a two-page spread. Each reading is longer and is directly related to the context of the unit. We did not manipulate the selections so that sentences fit into the structure presented in the unit.

There are new vocabulary words and structures that have never been introduced. Teachers can help ESL readers learn that understanding meaning is primary. It is not necessary to master or look up every new word. Each reading is followed by exercises that help to develop reading skills, such as scanning for information, understanding vocabulary in context, looking at the wording of true-false questions, and understanding an author's point of view.

Writing Our Stories

The writing section has also grown into a two-page format. The first page provides a writing model and some form of brainstorming, such as a checklist, discussion questions, fill-in sentences, or a chart. The writing tasks usually ask students to write about their lives or opinions. For variety, other units may direct students to complete an accident report, write a short report from notes, or complete a résumé. Each section also practices one writing point, such as the use of commas, choosing between *but* and *however*, or organizing ideas before writing. Several teachers have told us about the creative ways they share student writing, including publishing student magazines, designing a class Web page, and displaying stories and photos taken by their students. Included at the end of the writing page is a new feature entitled *Looking at the Internet*. If your school has a lab or students have Internet access at home, these short suggestions will give a starting point for follow-up activities on the Internet.

Practicing on Your Own

This is simple: It's a homework section. Some teachers ask students to do the exercises in class. Another suggestion for homework is the audio component. Ask students to listen to it three or four more times, reviewing the vocabulary and the exercises they did in class. Our students tell us that they often write the story from the Big Picture as a dictation activity.

Grammar Summary

Some teachers wanted this summary at the beginning of the unit; others were pleased to see it at the end. Use this section if and when you wish. Some students like to see the grammar up front, having a clear map of the developing grammar. We have found, though, that many of our students at the intermediate level are confused with a clump of grammar explanations at the beginning of a unit. There are small grammar charts as needed throughout the unit. The ending summary brings them together.

I am sure we will be revising the text again in three or four years. We will be gathering your input during that time. You can always e-mail us at www.heinle.com with your comments, complaints, and suggestions.

About the Authors

Liz and I both work at Union County College in Elizabeth, New Jersey. We teach at the Institute for Intensive English, a large English as a Second Language program. Students from over 70 different countries study in our classes. Between us, Liz and I have been teaching at the college for over 40 years! When Liz isn't writing, she spends her time traveling, taking pictures, and watching her favorite baseball team, the New York Mets. Liz took many of the pictures in the texts, for which our students eagerly posed. In the warm weather, I can't start my day without a 15- or 20-mile bicycle ride. My idea of a good time always involves the outdoors: hiking, kayaking, or simply working in my garden.

Barbara H. Foley
Elizabeth R. Neblett

Photo Credits

This page constitutes an extension of the copyright page. We have made every effort to trace the ownership of all copyrighted material and to secure permission from copyright holders. In the event of any question arising as to the use of any material, we will be pleased to make the necessary corrections in future printings. Thanks are due to the following authors, publishers, and agents for permission to use the material indicated.

All photos courtesy of Elizabeth R. Neblett with the following exceptions:

p. 10, top: Jeff Greenberg/Index Stock Imagery
p. 16, top right: AP Photo/Ahn Young-Joon
p. 16, top left: PhotoDisc/Getty Images
p. 16, center: Spencer Grant/Photo Edit
p. 32, bottom center: Chris Luneski/Index Stock Imagery
p. 32, bottom left: David Bitters/Index Stock Imagery
p. 32, center: Frank Siteman/Index Stock Imagery
p. 32, bottom right: Frank Siteman/Index Stock Imagery
p. 32, top right: Ralph Reinhold/Index Stock Imagery
p. 32, top left: Roger Leo/Index Stock Imagery
p. 35, center left: ElektraVision/Index Stock Imagery
p. 37, bottom right, Chris Luneski/Index Stock Imagery
p. 37, bottom left, ElektraVision/Index Stock Imagery
p. 37, bottom center: Ralph Reinhold/Index Stock Imagery
p. 38, top right: Roger Leo/Index Stock Imagery
p. 38, center: Shoot Pty. Ltd./Index Stock Imagery
p. 44, center right: David Bitters/Index Stock Imagery
p. 46, top, Roger Leo/Index Stock Imagery
p. 62, center right: Bruce Clarke/Index Stock Imagery
p. 66, center left: Getty Images
p. 66, center left: Mark Gibson/Index Stock Imagery
p. 71, center left: Cooperphoto/CORBIS
p. 71, bottom left: David Shopper/Index Stock Imagery
p. 90, top right: BSIP Agency/Index Stock Imagery
p. 99, top right: CORBIS SYGMA
p. 99, top left: Rufus F. Folkks/CORBIS
p. 100, top right, Walter Bibikow/Index Stock Imagery
p. 106, center left: John Warden/Stone
p. 106, center right: Mark E. Gibson/CORBIS
p. 112, center: Digital Vision/Getty
p. 115, bottom right: Todd Bigelow/AURORA
p. 120, top: Bonnie Kamin/Photo Edit
p. 122, top right: Erv Schowengerdt
p. 132, top right: PhotoDisc/Getty Images
p. 135: top right, Christopher J. Morris/CORBIS
p. 138, top right: PhotoDisc/Getty Images
p. 140, bottom right: AFP/CORBIS
p. 142, top right: HMS Group Inc./Index Stock Imagery
p. 150, top left: Yang Liu/CORBIS
p. 154, center left: Tom Carter/Photo Edit
p. 160, bottom left: AP Photo/Max Nash
p. 160, center: Bruce Leighty/Index Stock Imagery
p. 160, top right: CORBIS
p. 160, bottom right: Jacob Halaska/Index Stock Imagery
p. 160, center left: Mike Johnson/earthwindow.com
p. 160, top left: PhotoDisc/Getty Images
p. 164, bottom left: NOVASTOCK/Photo Edit
p. 165, top right: Barbara Haynor/Index Stock Imagery
p. 170, center left: Jack Boyd/Index Stock Imagery
p. 170, bottom left: Peter Schulz/Image Stock Imagery
p. 171, top left, Tami Chappell/Reuters/TimePix
p. 176, top right: Gary Conner/Index Stock Imagery
p. 176, center right: Grantpic/Index Stock Imagery
p. 176, top left: Mauritius/Index Stock Imagery
p. 176, center left: SW Production/Index Stock Imagery
p. 177, top left: Michael Newman/Photo Edit
p. 177, center: Michael Newman/Photo Edit
p. 177, center right: Michael Newman/Photo Edit
p. 177, center left: Michael Newman/Photo Edit
p. 177, top: Michael Newman/Photo Edit
p. 177, top right: Michael Newman/Photo Edit
p. 208, bottom left: Benelux Press/Index Stock Imagery
p. 208, top right: Chuck Savage/CORBIS
p. 208, top left: Grantpix/Index Stock Imagery
p. 208, bottom right: Michael Brennen/CORBIS
p. 208, bottom center: Robert Finken/Index Stock Imagery
p. 208, top: Sally Moskol/Index Stock Imagery
p. 234, center left: H & Dielske/Laif/AURORA
p. 236, center: Steve Dunwell/Index Stock Imagery

1 The First Week

A. Read.

Hi. My name is Kenji and I'm a student at the University of California, San Diego. I'm taking Listening and Pronunciation in Room 142. There are 10 students in my class, four men and six women. We are from five different countries. Our class meets on Mondays, Wednesdays, and Fridays, from 10:30 to 12:30. My teacher is Ms. Burak. Her office is in Room 12.

B. Read and complete about yourself.

My name is Ricardo.

I'm a student at S S college.

I'm taking english listening class in Room 202.

There are 14 students in my class, 5 men and 9 women.

I have class on 15,
(days)

from 3:45 to 5:15.

My teacher is dalia.

His/Her office is in Room 15.

Active Grammar: Simple Present Tense Statements

A. Listen as Gloria interviews Kenji about his life in the United States. Take notes as you listen. Then, talk about Kenji.

Notes: Japan
six months

Simple Present Tense Statements

I live in New York.	She lives in New York.
I have a computer.	She **has** a computer.
I work part time.	She works part time.

B. Interview a student in your class. Ask these questions. Take a few notes so that you can introduce your partner to another student.

1. What's your name?
2. What country are you from?
3. Is your family here in the United States?
4. Where do you live?
5. How long have you been in the United States?
6. Are you a new student at this school?
7. Do you work? Where do you work? What do you do?
8. Are you married or single? Do you have any children? If yes, how many?
9. What are your interests?
10. What kind of music do you like?
11. Do you have a computer?

Culture Note

Americans usually do not ask about age, marriage, religion, and salary when they first meet a person.

C. Sit with another pair of students. Introduce your partner to the group.

I'd like to introduce ________________________.
I'd like you to meet ________________________.

Active Grammar: *There is/There are*

A. The school. Circle the rooms and facilities you have in your school.

rest rooms	computer labs	theater	bookstore
cafeteria	water fountains	nurse's office	tutoring center
day care center	library	counselor's office	student center
copy machine	swimming pool	gym	ATM

Talk about the facilities at your school. If you do not know if your school has one of the rooms or facilities, ask another student or your teacher.

There is

There is a ___________ in this building. / in this school. / on this floor.

Is there a library in this school?

There are

There are some ___________ in this building. / in this school. / on this floor.

Are there any rest rooms on this floor?

B. Answer these questions about your school.

1. Is this school in a city?
2. Is this school large?
3. Is this school open in the evening?
4. Are there many students in this school?
5. Are there any computers in this classroom?
6. Is there a library in this building?
7. Is the library open today?
8. Is there a water fountain on this floor?
9. Are there any rest rooms on this floor?
10. Is there a cafeteria in this building?
11. Is the food good?
12. Is there a bookstore in this building?
13. Are the books expensive?
14. Are there many students in this school?
15. Are they from many different countries?

Is there a library in this building?
Yes, there is.
No, there isn't

Is your school small?
Yes, it is.
No, it isn't.

Are there any rest rooms on this floor?
Yes, there are.
No, there aren't.

Are the students friendly?
Yes, they are.
No, they aren't.

Active Grammar: Prepositions

A. Prepositions. Review the prepositions in the box. Then, complete the sentences about the school diagram.

Elevator		W	M	205 Computer Lab	207	210 Library
Stairs		202	204 Nurse	206	208	

1. The library is ________ the end of the hall.
2. The nurse's office is ________ Room 204.
3. The elevator is ________ the stairs.
4. The women's room is ________ the stairs.
5. The library is ________ the second floor.
6. The stairs are ________ the end of the hall.
7. The men's room is ________ the women's room.
8. There are a few computers ________ the library.
9. There are many computers ________ the computer lab.
10. There is a computer lab ________ the second floor.

> at the end of the hall
> in Room 201
> on the second floor
> near the stairs
> next to the stairs
> across from Room 202

B. Take a tour of your school. When you return, sit in a small group and write about the facilities in your school.

C. Pronunciation: Sentence stress. Listen and repeat.

1. The **cafeteria** is on the **first floor.**
2. The **nurse's office** is across from the **elevator.**
3. The **swimming pool** is in the **athletic center.**
4. The **bookstore** is in the **student center.**
5. There is a **copy machine** in the **library.**
6. The **rest rooms** are next to the **stairs.**

> The more important words in a sentence receive stress. We say these words a little more clearly and give them a little more emphasis.

Read the sentences in Exercise A with a partner. Pay attention to the stress.

Active Grammar: Quantifiers

A. Read these sentences. Ask about the meaning of any new words.

1. All of the students speak Spanish.

2. Most of the students speak Spanish.

3. Many of the students speak Spanish.

4. Some of the students speak Spanish.

5. A few of the students speak Spanish.

6. A couple of the students speak Spanish.

7. One of the students speaks Spanish.

8. None of the students speaks Spanish.

B. Complete these sentences about an English class. Circle the correct verb.

Present Tense: Third Person Singular

One of us	is married.
None of us	has a computer.
He	is from Colombia.
She	lives in ______________.
	walks to school.

Present Tense: Third Person Plural

All of us	
Most of us	are married.
Some of us	have a computer.
A few of us	are from Colombia.
None of us	live in ______________.
We	walk to school.
They	

1. Many of us **is / are** from Spanish-speaking countries.
2. Some of us **is / are** married.
3. None of us **is / are** under 18 years old.
4. All of us **is / are** studying English.
5. A few of us **works / work** part time.
6. She **is / are** a new student at this school.
7. He **has / have** a computer.
8. They **lives / live** in the dormitory.
9. A couple of us **likes / like** to play soccer.
10. One of us **wears / wear** glasses.

C. Sit in a group of four or five students. Every student in the group should answer each question. After each question use the information to write sentences about your group with *All of us, Many of us,* etc.

1. Are you married?
2. Are you from Japan?
3. Are you a U.S. citizen?
4. Are you a new student at this school?
5. Do you have a computer?
6. What city do you live in?
7. How do you get to school? Do you walk?
8. Do you work full time?
9. Are you a teenager?
10. Do you play a sport?

The Big Picture: Class Expectations

In my country, we can come to school a few minutes late.

We call the teacher "Teacher," not his or her name.

Only the teacher can talk. We can speak if the teacher calls our name.

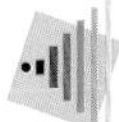

A. Listen to these statements about school in other countries. Then, make statements about schools and colleges in your country and in the United States.

B. Check (✓) the statements that are true for your class.

_____ **1.** Come to class on time.

_____ **2.** Bring your books, paper, and a pencil.

_____ **3.** It is OK to speak to your classmates when the teacher is explaining something.

_____ **4.** Do your homework every night.

_____ **5.** I can do my homework on any piece of paper.

_____ **6.** I can bring a cup of coffee to class.

_____ **7.** I can answer my cell phone during class time.

_____ **8.** If I want to ask a question, I raise my hand.

_____ **9.** Speak English in class.

_____ **10.** I can leave school early every day.

_____ **11.** If I need to use the rest room, I should ask the teacher if I may leave.

C. What are two other expectations in your class?

____

____

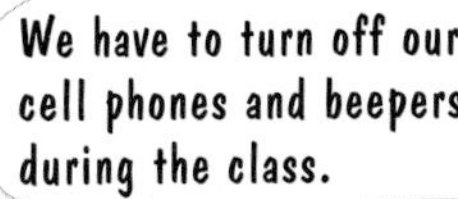

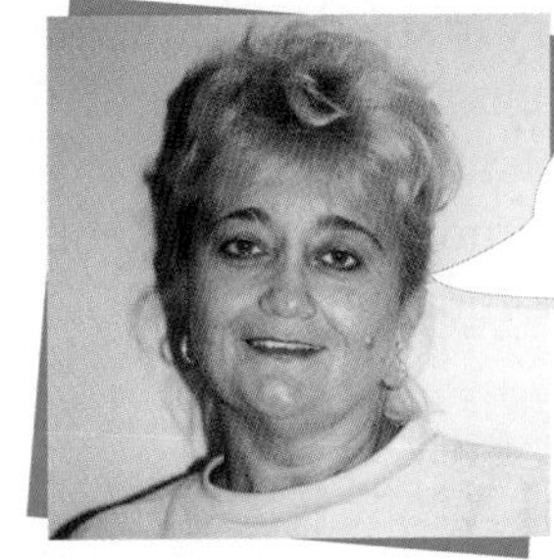

D. Ask your teacher these questions about your school and your class.

1. Where is your office?
2. Can I e-mail you? What is your e-mail address?
3. Does this school have a computer lab? Can I get a student account?
4. May I bring a tape recorder to class?
5. Is there a library in this school? How do I get a library card?
6. Do we have homework every night?
7. What should I do if I don't understand something?
8. What are we going to study in this class?
9. Do we have a break?
10. Do we have any vacation days?

Write two more questions about school and class. Then, ask your teacher your questions.

____

____

Reading: English Is Frustrating!

A. These students are studying English. Underline the problem(s) each student is having.

I work 50 hours a week as a taxi driver, so I talk to people all day. They understand me, but I know I make a lot of mistakes. No one corrects me. My vocabulary is strong. Grammar is my problem. I'm trying to change little by little. For example, I don't use the past tense. I always say, "I drive him to the office this morning" instead of "I drove him to the office this morning."

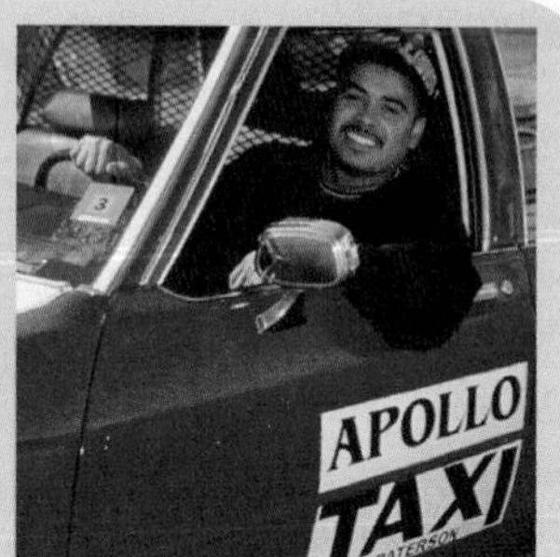

Pablo

I live in an area where everyone speaks my language. My neighbors and friends speak Spanish. I can speak Spanish in the supermarket and at the post office. I don't work, so it's really difficult to find ways to practice English.

Maria Luisa

I understand the grammar and the readings in my class and I think my writing is good, but I'm very nervous when I speak English. I don't want to make any mistakes because people will think that I'm stupid. Also, my pronunciation isn't good. When I speak, people often say, "What? Say that again."

Li-Ping

I have been in the United States for one year. I'm studying hard and I'm learning grammar, but the vocabulary is very difficult. When I listen, I don't understand many of the words. When I try to read, there are three or four new words in every sentence. I feel discouraged.

Yoshi

B. After You Read. These are some suggestions for learning English. Add one more suggestion of your own.

1. Watch one TV program in English every day.
2. Listen to songs. Sing along.
3. Try to speak English when you go out in the community.
4. Use the Internet. There are several ESL study sites.
5. Don't worry about mistakes. It's natural to make mistakes when you are learning a language.
6. Use ESL computer programs in your computer lab.
7. Find a study partner. Work together one or two days after school.
8. Make a friend from your school who doesn't speak your language. Meet once a week after class for conversation practice.
9. Read the newspaper in English.
10. Be kind to yourself. Understand that learning English takes time.
11. Keep an English journal. Write a mistake you made while speaking. Then, write the sentence correctly. Or, write new words and sentences you hear.
12. ______________________________

C. Give each student in the reading two or three suggestions from the list above. Write the numbers of the suggestions on the lines next to their names.

Pablo	____	____	____
Maria Luisa	____	____	____
Li-Ping	____	____	____
Yoshi	____	____	____

D. English can be frustrating! List two of your strengths in English. List two of your difficulties. Which suggestions can you try?

My strengths	**My difficulties**
______________________	______________________
______________________	______________________

1. I'm going to ______________________________.
2. I'm going to ______________________________.

Writing Our Stories: Yaneth

A. Read Yaneth's story.

My name is Yaneth and I am from Bogotá, Colombia. I came to the United States five years ago. My sister, Gloria, is here with me, but my mom and dad and my six brothers all live in Colombia. I miss them a lot, but I have a computer and I'm on the Internet, so we e-mail each other all the time.

I work full time at a small printing company. I can do several jobs at this company. Sometimes I do data entry; at other times, I'm a press operator.

I don't have much free time, but I enjoy music, especially rock and romantic music. On Sunday evenings, I play tennis with the tennis club at my school.

Right now, I'm studying English and I plan to major in communications and work in the TV industry. There are many dreams in my mind. Someday I would like to live in Florida and have a family.

B. Before Yaneth wrote her story, she organized a few of her ideas.

My family	My work	My interests	My future
Gloria	printing company	music	communications
six brothers	full time	tennis	TV
Mom and Dad	data entry		Florida
	press operator		family

C. Before you write your own story about yourself, organize a few of your ideas below. Then, begin your story. Introduce yourself to your teacher.

My family	My work	My interests	My future

D. Editing. Correct the mistakes in the underlined singular and plural nouns.

1. I have two ~~brother~~ brothers and three ~~sister~~ sisters.
2. I work in clothing store.
3. I'm cashier.
4. I'm student at adult school.
5. I'm taking four class.
6. I don't have computer.
7. I work part time, twenty hour a week.
8. I have two childrens.
9. I came to the United States two year ago.
10. I work at restaurant.

E. Sit in a small group of students. Share your stories with each other. You can ask each other questions about your stories.

Looking at the Internet

You can use the Internet to improve your English. Ask your teacher if he or she knows any Web sites to practice English. Do any of the students in your class know any good sites for practicing English?

Try this site: ______________________________

Try this site: ______________________________

Practicing on Your Own

have long hair
have short hair
have wavy hair
have curly hair
have blond hair
like to exercise
play tennis
play basketball
play baseball
lift weights
have a dog
(be) short
(be) tall

A. Complete the sentences about the seven sisters. Use the expressions from the box.

1. All of the girls Like Exercise ______________.
2. Some of the girls have long hair ______________.
3. Many of the girls be tall ______________.
4. One of the girls play basketball ______________.
5. A few of the girls play tennis ______________.
6. None of the girls haves a dog ______________.
7. Most of the girls ~~have blond hair~~ be tall ______________.
8. A couple of the girls lift weights ______________.

B. In your notebook, write ten sentences about Pierre.

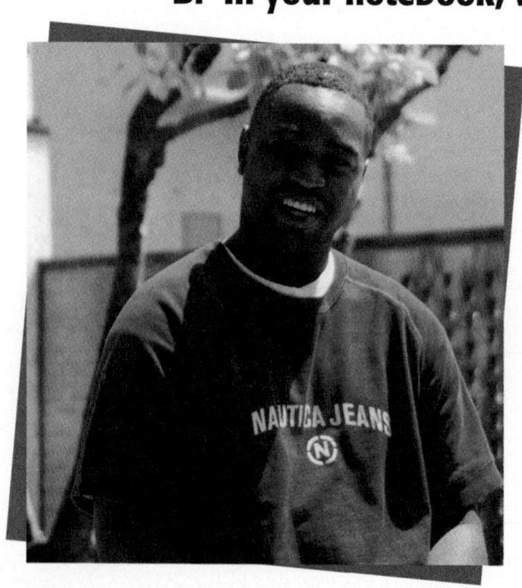

Name:	Pierre Dorval
Age:	29
Country:	Haiti
Years in U.S.:	Four
School:	Bay Adult School; intermediate level; Mondays and Wednesdays, 9 A.M. to 11:50 A.M.
Marital Status:	Married, a son
Occupation:	Waiter; West Hotel; six nights a week
Interests:	Soccer and guitar
Computer:	No
Music:	Jazz and rock

Grammar Summary

1. Present tense statements

I am from Japan.	She **is** from Japan.
I live in Texas.	He live**s** in Texas.
I work in a factory.	He work**s** in a factory.
I have a computer.	She **has** a computer.

2. *There is/There are*

There is a library in this building.		
Is there a library in this building?	Yes, there is.	No, there isn't.
There are some computers in the lab.		
Are there any computers in the lab?	Yes, there are.	No, there aren't.

3. Prepositions

Where's the nurse's office?	It's **at the end of** the hall.
	It's **in** Room 305.
	It's **on** the first floor.
	It's **next to** the elevator.
	It's **across from** the library.

4. Quantifiers

All, Most, Many, Some, A few, and *A couple* are plural.

One is singular.

None is singular or plural.

All of the students have computers.

Most of the students have computers.

A few of the students have computers.

One of the students has a computer.

None of the students has a computer.

None of the students have a computer.

2 The Average American

A. Statistics. Read each sentence about the average American. Guess the correct answer.

> The average American means the *typical* American.

1. The average American teenager listens to music **one / two / three** hour(s) a day.
2. The average American eats **one / three / seven** hamburger(s) a week.
3. The average American drinks **one / two / three or more** cups of coffee a day.
4. The average American family has **one / two / three** TVs.
5. The average American woman lives for **75 / 80 / 85** years.
6. The average American man lives for **70 / 72 / 74** years.
7. Most Americans **take a bus / take a subway / drive** to work.
8. Most American women get married at age **19 / 25 / 29**.
9. Most Americans eat **eggs / toast / cereal** for breakfast.

Source: U.S. Census Bureau / Carlsons Restaurants Worldwide, Inc.

Check your answers on page 245. If your guess was wrong, cross it out and circle the correct answer. Did any of the information surprise you?

Active Grammar: Simple Present Tense Statements

A. Complete the statements about your life.

1. I watch TV ___5___ hour(s) a day.
2. My family has ___4___ TVs.
3. I drink **one / two / three or more** cup(s) of coffee a day.
4. I sleep **six / seven / eight** hours a night.
5. I **take a bus / take a subway / drive** to work.
6. I listen to music ___12___ hour(s) a day.
7. I eat ___cereal___ for breakfast.
8. I eat ___one___ hamburger(s) a week.

Discuss your answers with your classmates. Are you similar to the average American?

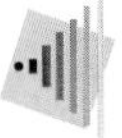

B. Charlie. Listen to Charlie describe himself and his lifestyle. Take notes. Compare Charlie to the average American male.

Charlie	The Average American Male
32—single	gets married at 26 or 27
weighs 210 pounds ~~drinks two cups of~~	is 5'10" tall
he work eight hours a day	weighs 170 pounds
he Lives in a house	likes his job
he walk or take a bus to work	works eight hours a day
lives in a horse	earns $30,132
he has a cat pepi	lives in a house
earns 60 000 dollars	drives to work
6.2 tall	has a pet, usually a cat or a dog

Source: U.S. Census Bureau

A. Circle the correct answer.

I work.	He works.	I don't work.	He doesn't work.
You work.	She works	You don't work.	She doesn't work.
We work.	It works.	We don't work.	It doesn't work.
They work.		They don't work.	

Do you wear a seat belt?

1. The average person **wears / doesn't wear** a seat belt.
2. Most people **wear / don't wear** seat belts.
3. I **wear / don't wear** a seat belt.
4. My teacher **wears / doesn't wear** a seat belt.

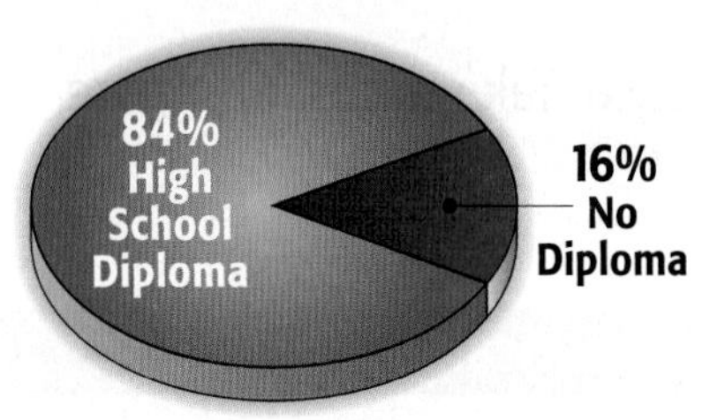

Do you have a high school diploma?

5. The average person **has / doesn't have** a high school diploma.
6. Most people **have / don't have** high school diplomas.
7. I **have / don't have** a high school diploma.

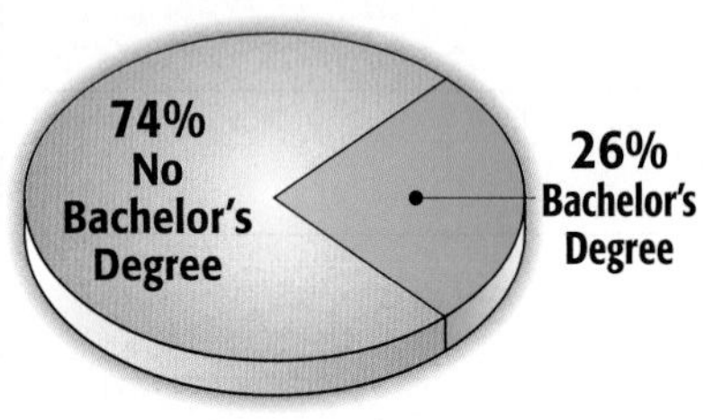

Do you have a bachelor's degree?

8. Most Americans **have / don't have** a bachelor's degree.
9. I **have / don't have** a bachelor's degree.

Culture Note
A bachelor's degree is a four-year college degree.

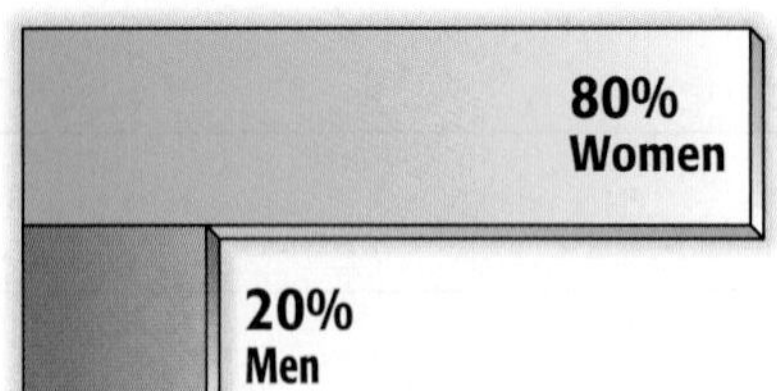

Do you send greeting cards?

10. The average American man **sends / doesn't send** greeting cards.
11. Most American women **send / don't send** greeting cards.
12. I **send / don't send** greeting cards.

B. Your teacher. Listen to your teacher talk about his or her life. Is your teacher "the average American"? Circle *Yes* or *No* for each item. Then, circle *Yes* or *No* about yourself. Make sentences about yourself. Compare your answers.

The Average American	My Teacher	Me
1. The average American lives in a house.	Yes No	Yes No
2. The average American works eight hours a day.	Yes No	Yes No
3. The average American eats cereal for breakfast.	Yes No	Yes No
4. The average American drinks 1.7 cups of coffee a day.	Yes No	Yes No
5. The average American takes 24 minutes to travel to work.	Yes No	Yes No
6. Most Americans listen to music in their cars.	Yes No	Yes No
7. Most Americans drive to work.	Yes No	Yes No
8. Most Americans go to California or Florida for vacation.	Yes No	Yes No
9. Most Americans have computers in their homes.	Yes No	Yes No
10. Most Americans have a cat or a dog.	Yes No	Yes No

C. *Yes/No* questions. With a partner, ask and answer the questions.

Do you live in a house?	Yes, I do.
Do you live in an apartment?	No, I don't. I live in a house.

1. Do you live in a house?
2. Do you drink coffee or tea?
3. Do you put sugar in your coffee or tea?
4. Do you eat breakfast every day?
5. Do you work? If "yes," do you drive to work?
6. Do you work full time?
7. Do you read the newspaper every day?
8. Do you speak English at home?
9. Do you cook for your family?
10. Do you exercise?
11. Do you have a computer at home?
12. Do you go to bed before midnight?

A. Pronunciation: Final *s*. Listen and repeat.

/s/	/z/	/əs/*
likes	owns	watches
wants	has	washes
sleeps	drives	uses
takes	earns	exercises
eats	wears	
costs	studies	
works	lives	
	goes	
	spends	* This group of verbs adds an extra syllable to the ending.

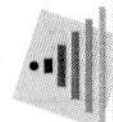

B. Which sound do you hear? Circle the correct sound.

a.	/s/	/z/	/əs/	**e.**	/s/	/z/	/əs/	**i.**	/s/	/z/	/əs/
b.	/s/	/z/	/əs/	**f.**	/s/	/z/	/əs/	**j.**	/s/	/z/	/əs/
c.	/s/	/z/	/əs/	**g.**	/s/	/z/	/əs/	**k.**	/s/	/z/	/əs/
d.	/s/	/z/	/əs/	**h.**	/s/	/z/	/əs/	**l.**	/s/	/z/	/əs/

C. Student A: Say one of the words from Exercise A.
Student B: Which sound do you hear: /s/, /z/, or /əs/ ?

D. Practice reading the sentences.
Student A: Read sentences 1–4. Pay attention to */s/, /z/,* and */əs/.*
Student B: Listen for */s/, /z/,* and */əs/.* Then, read sentences 5–8 to Student A.

1. He drives to work.
2. She walks to work.
3. He gets up at 6:00.
4. She watches TV every night.
5. She studies French.
6. He owns two computers.
7. She eats a light breakfast.
8. He uses a microwave every day.

A. Time expressions. Complete the sentences with a time expression.

every morning	once a week
every day	twice a month
every night	three times a year

once—one time
twice—two times

1. I study English twice a week.
2. I go to work every day.
3. I work overtime every morning.
4. I go to the dentist once a month.
5. I take a vacation three times a year.
6. I sleep late every night.
7. I buy new clothes once a week.

Note: Put time expressions at the **end** of a sentence.

B. Ask and answer these questions with a partner.

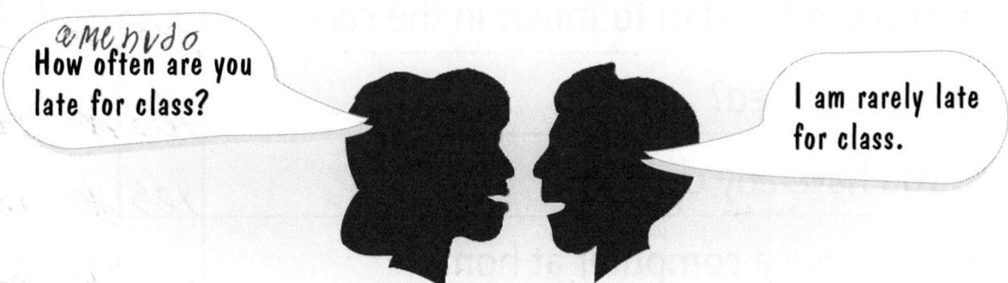

1. How often do you call your native country? always
2. How often do you exercise? usually
3. How often are you absent from class? always
4. How often do you eat out at a restaurant? some times
5. How often do you have a day off from work or school? rarely
6. How often do you go dancing? some times
7. How often do you eat breakfast? some times
8. How often are you in an emergency room? never
9. How often do you speak English outside of class? some times

Place adverbs of frequency **after** the verb *to be* and **before** all other verbs.

I am **always** on time.
I **never** arrive late.

always	100%
usually	80–90%
often frequently	70–75%
sometimes	50%
rarely seldom	5–15%
never	0%

A Class Survey

A. In the column on the left, answer each question about your life. Circle *Yes* or *No*.

- One student is the leader and will ask each question to the entire class. For example, "Do you take public transportation?"
- Raise your hand to answer, "Yes."
- Two students will be the counters. They will count everyone's answers.
- Write the totals in the columns on the right.

Your Answers		Questions	Totals			
			Yes	No	Men	Women
Yes	No	**1.** Do you take public transportation?				
Yes	No	**2.** Do you work full time?				
Yes	No	**3.** Do you have a car?				
Yes	No	**4.** Do you wear your seat belt?				
Yes	No	**5.** Do you like to listen to music in the car?				
Yes	No	**6.** Are you married?				
Yes	No	**7.** Do you have any children?				
Yes	No	**8.** Do you have a computer at home?				
Yes	No	**9.** Do you have a VCR or a DVD player?				
Yes	No	**10.** Do you go to bed between ten and midnight?				

B. Complete the sentences about your class. Some of the sentences can be negative.

1. Most students ______________________.
2. The average student ______________________.
3. Many students ______________________.
4. A few students ______________________.
5. Only one student ______________________.

6. The average man in our class are Marred.

7. The average woman in our class are children.

8. Most of the men hov a ver a DVD player.

9. Most of the women dont hav a computer.

10. None of the students Go to bed en Midnight.

C. Look at the pictures. Write a sentence about each picture. Some of the sentences are negative.

drink	eat	earn	listen to	live	send birthday cards	travel	watch

1. The average American eats one hamburger a week.
2. Most men drik 1.5 cups of coffe a day.
3. Most children watch tv 4 hours a day.
4. The average teenager listen ho music.
5. The average woman earn $26,324.
6. Most people dont send birthday.
7. Most people over 75 don't like travel.
8. The average person over 75 live in homes.

The Big Picture: The Shaw Family

A. Look at the pictures of one American family. Talk about the pictures.

1.

2.

3.

4.

5.

6.

B. Listen and complete the information on the pictures about the Shaw family.

C. Read each fact about the average American family. Is the Shaw family an average American family? Circle *Yes* if the fact is also true about the Shaw family. Circle *No* if the fact is not true about the Shaw family.

1. The average American works six to eight hours a day. Yes No
2. The average husband earns more money than his wife. Yes No
3. The average family earns $39,000 to $75,000 a year. Yes No
4. The average family has one or two cars. Yes No
5. The average commute to work is 25.5 minutes. Yes No
6. The average family is a nuclear family: a mother, a father, and one or two children. Yes No
7. The average family has one pet. Yes No
8. The average house costs $132,000. Yes No
9. The average American family eats out on Saturday night. Yes No
10. The average family takes a vacation twice a year. Yes No
11. Most families own three TVs. Yes No

D. Complete. Write the correct form of the verbs. Some of the verbs are negative.

1. Mr. Shaw (drive) ___doesn't drive___ a minivan.
2. Mr. Shaw (work) ____________ close to home.
3. Mrs. Shaw (take) ____________ public transportation to work.
4. Mr. and Mrs. Shaw (have) ____________ one child.
5. Mr. and Mrs. Shaw (live) ____________ in an apartment.
6. The parents (earn) ____________ $80,000 a year.
7. Mrs. Shaw (work) ____________ in an office.
8. The family (eat) ____________ out once a week.
9. Mark (have) ____________ a pet bird.
10. The Shaws and the grandparents (live) ____________ in the same house.

"Family" takes a **singular verb**, but sometimes people use "they" when they talk about family.

Reading: Busy Families Take a Break

A. Before You Read.

1. How many nights a week do you and your family eat meals together?
2. What activities do you and your family like to do together?
3. Do you think that you spend enough time with your family? Why or why not?

Many American families have busy schedules. Every week, the children participate in sports, music lessons, club meetings, play rehearsals, and they have many other commitments, including hours of homework. The parents are busy, too. They work, take care of their homes, cook meals, and drive their children to activities. Some families do not have time to eat meals together more than once a week. One American community decided that it was time to take a break.

After seven months of planning, the community of Ridgewood, New Jersey, took one night off. They called the night "Family Night," a night for families to spend time together. Sports teams cancelled practices, and teachers did not give homework.

On Family Night, families agreed to turn off the televisions. They also decided not to answer the telephone. Answering machines said, "Please call back tomorrow." Many families ordered take-out pizza and other take-out food so that they wouldn't spend time cooking.

Popular activities included board games and card games. These games gave families a chance to spend time together the way families did many years ago when children and parents didn't have such busy schedules and children didn't spend so much time playing video games and watching television. On Family Night, families relaxed and spent the evening together. The town hopes to have many more "Family Nights."

In Minnesota, a similar program is growing. Putting Family First is an organization of parents and community leaders who, like those in Ridgewood, feel that families are important and need to spend more time together. Putting Family First believes that there has to be a balance between family time and outside activities.

The idea for Putting Family First comes from a book written by Bill Doherty, a professor at the University of Minnesota. At a conference on family time and habits, many parents, school officials, and community leaders complained that families did not spend enough time together. In 1999, a group of parents and community leaders began making a plan. Their plan included (1) making family time and family activities the most important part of life; (2) limiting outside activities; (3) limiting time spent on television, computers, and other technological devices; and (4) finding ways to spend time together. Today, the Putting Family First movement continues to attract more families and more communities.

Source: www.usatoday.com, www.guardian.co.uk, www.puttingfamilyfirst.us

B. Circle *True* or *False*.

1.	Many American families are too busy.	True	False
2.	Children go home immediately after school.	True	False
3.	Ridgewood took one night to plan their special "Family Night."	True	False
4.	During "Family Night," families watched television together.	True	False
5.	During "Family Night," there were many soccer games for the children.	True	False
6.	During "Family Night," many families did not cook.	True	False

C. Reading for details. Find the answers to the questions in the reading. Underline and number the answers.

1. How many months did the community spend planning "Family Night"?
2. How did teachers help?
3. What did families order for dinner?
4. What kinds of activities did families do?
5. Will there be more family nights?
6. In what other state are families working to spend more time together?
7. What is the name of the organization?
8. What do the members of the organization believe?
9. Who wrote a book about family life?
10. Does the Putting Family First plan include unlimited time for television?

Writing Our Stories: The Average Portuguese

A. Read.

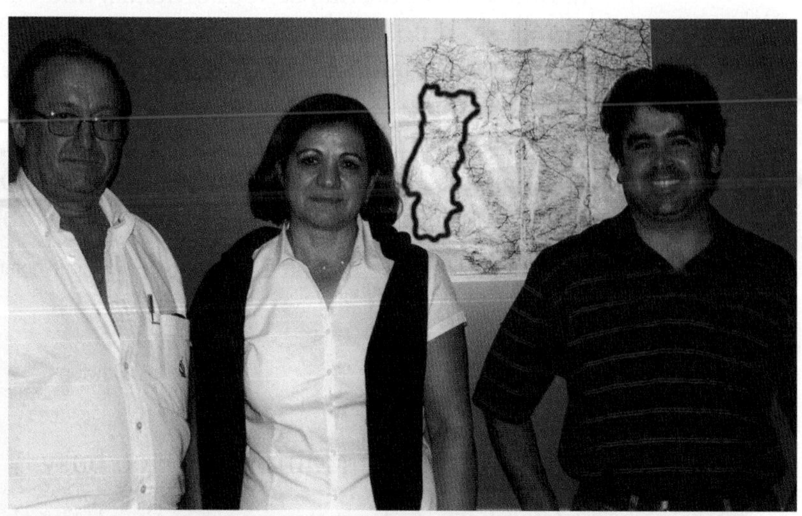

We are from Portugal. Portugal is in Europe, to the west of Spain. It is a small country. The population is ten million, and the capital is Lisbon. Over half a million people live in Lisbon, and most people live in the big cities like Porto. Portuguese people speak our native language, Portuguese, but many people understand Spanish because the languages are similar.

There are four seasons in Portugal, and the weather is usually hot in the summer and cool in the winter. Most tourists visit during the spring or the summer. Most Portuguese families like to spend time on the beautiful beaches on the north and south coasts.

Most Portuguese eat fish regularly. The average Portuguese meal consists of fish, like bacalau, or fried fish, and boiled potatoes.

The typical Portuguese worker has a job in one of our major industries: textiles, shoes, agriculture, or tourism.

There are many festivals in Portugal. Portuguese people enjoy the big celebrations before and during the Easter holiday season.

Dinis, Maria, and Manuel

B. The average ________. With a group of students from your native country, or by yourself, write a paragraph about the lives of average people from your native country. Here are some of the topics you can describe. What do people like to do in their free time? Where and when do people like to eat? How does the average person get to work? Use some of the following phrases.

The average man / woman

The average teenager

The average senior citizen

Most ________s (Mexicans, Ukrainians, Haitians, Koreans, Chinese, etc.)

Many men / women / children

C. Edit. Read each sentence. Check the underlined verbs. If there is a mistake, correct the mistake on the blank line. If the verb is correct, write "correct."

1. Most Americans <u>drives</u> to work. drive
2. Many Americans <u>take</u> public transportation. correct
3. The average American <u>go</u> to the dentist once a year. ________
4. Most American women <u>doesn't</u> <u>get</u> married before age 25. ________
5. The average American man <u>earns</u> $30,132 a year. ________
6. The average American <u>doesn't eat</u> a large breakfast. ________
7. Most American men <u>drinks</u> 1.7 cups of coffee a day. ________
8. Most American schools <u>has</u> computers. ________
9. The average American <u>drive</u> to work. ________
10. Most American families <u>has</u> one or two children. ________

Looking at the Internet

Every ten years, the United States government takes a census of the population. A census is a survey—a list of questions about family, income, work, transportation, interests, vacation, and more.

Search the U.S. census Web site: www.census.gov
Find one or two interesting facts that you can tell your classmates.

Practicing on Your Own

A. An average high school student. Read this story about one American teenager and write the present tense form of the verb in parentheses.

Max ____is____ (be) a typical high school senior. He ______________ (go) to school five days a week from September to June. Most American high school students ______________ (attend) school ten months a year. They ______________ (have) time off for a few national holidays. Max ______________ (want) to go to college after he ______________ (graduate), so he ______________ (study) English, chemistry, American history, math, and French. Many American high schools ______________ (require) physical education, or gym, three to five days a week. Max ______________ (swim) during gym because he ______________ (belong) to his school swim team. Most high schools ______________ (offer) after-school activities, such as sports or the school newspaper.

B. Looking at graphs. Write the correct form of the verbs. Some of the verbs are negative.

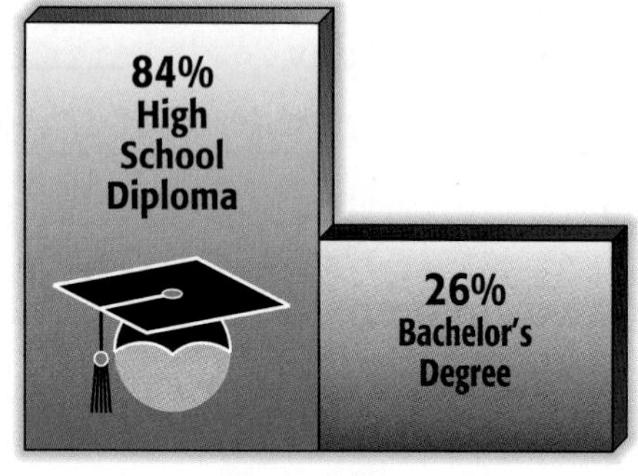

Source: U.S. Census Bureau

1. The average American ______________ a high school diploma.
2. The average American ______________ a bachelor's degree.
3. I ______________ a high school diploma.
4. I ______________ a bachelor's degree.

With sugar 63%

Black; no sugar 37%

Source: Coffee Research Institute

1. Most Americans ______________ their coffee with sugar.
2. The average American ______________ coffee without sugar.
3. I ______________ coffee.
4. I ______________ my coffee with sugar and milk.

Grammar Summary

▶ 1. Simple present tense The simple present tense describes actions that happen every day, every week, every month, etc.

I **sleep** seven hours a night.

You **don't sleep** seven hours a night.

He **drinks** one cup of coffee a day.

She **doesn't drink** coffee.

It **takes** twenty minutes for me to get to work.

We **spend** an hour on homework.

They **don't spend** an hour on homework.

▶ 2. Singular and plural expressions

Singular	**Plural**
The average woman works.	Many women work.
The average man works.	Most men work.
The average person works.	Some people work.
	Seventy percent of all women work.

▶ 3. Time expressions and *How often* questions

How often do you take a vacation?	I take a vacation **once a year.**
How often do you exercise?	I exercise **four times a week.**
How often do you go to the movies?	I go to the movies **once a month.**
How often do you go to the dentist?	I go to the dentist **twice a year.**

▶ 4. Adverbs of frequency Place adverbs of frequency **after** the verb *to be*. Place adverbs of frequency **before** all other verbs.

100%	always
80–90%	usually
70–75%	often frequently
50%	sometimes
10–15%	rarely
0%	never

1. I **always arrive** on time for class.
2. We **usually have** homework.
3. Our teacher **often plays** videos in class.
4. Our teacher **frequently gives** tests.
5. We **are sometimes** quiet in class.
6. You **are rarely** absent.
7. They **are never** absent.

3 Pets

A. Match. These are six popular breeds of dogs in the United States. Write the name of the breed under each picture.

Poodle	German shepherd	Beagle
Shih Tzu	Labrador retriever	Chihuahua

1. Labrator

2. German shepherd

3. Poodlgle

4. Beagle

5. Chihuahva

6. Shih Tzu

B. Discuss.

1. What pets are popular in your country?
2. Are dogs popular? Do they live in the house?
3. Are cats popular?
4. Are there special stores for pets and pet products?
5. Do you know anyone with an aquarium? What kind of fish do they have?
6. Do you have a pet? If so, tell the class about your pet.

Culture Note

Use *it* to talk about a breed of dog or cat.

Use *he* or *she* to talk about an individual dog or cat.

C. Looking at graphs. Answer these questions about pet ownership.

Source: U.S. Bureau of the Census, 1998

1. What percentage of Americans have dogs?
2. What percentage of Americans have cats?
3. What percentage of Americans have birds?

D. Is a dog right for you? Answer these questions. Decide if a dog is a good pet for you.

1.	Do you like dogs?	Yes, I do.	No, I don't.
2.	Are you allergic to dogs?	Yes, I am.	No, I'm not.
3.	Is your home large enough for a dog?	Yes, it is.	No, it isn't.
4.	Does your apartment allow dogs?	Yes, it does.	No, it doesn't.
5.	Do you travel a lot?	Yes, I do.	No, I don't.
6.	Do you have small children?	Yes, I do.	No, I don't.
7.	Do you want to train a dog?	Yes, I do.	No, I don't.
8.	Do you have time to walk a dog three times a day?	Yes, I do.	No, I don't.
9.	Do you have time to play with a dog?	Yes, I do.	No, I don't.
10.	Are you away from home all day?	Yes, I am.	No, I'm not.
11.	Do you need a friend?	Yes, I do.	No, I don't.

E. Check (✓) one of the statements below. Give two reasons for your decision.

☐ I think I should get a dog.
☒ I don't think I should get a dog.

First, I don't like a dogs.

Second, I don't have a time.

Active Grammar: *Yes/No* Questions

***Yes/No* Questions: Present Tense**

Do	I you we they	live	in an apartment?
Does	he she it		

Yes/No* Questions: Present Tense *Be

Am	I	friendly?
Are	you we they	
Is	he she it	

A. Complete. Write *Do, Does, Am, Is,* or *Are.*

1. Do you like animals?
2. Do you live in an apartment?
3. Is your home large?
4. Do you have a cat?
5. Are you allergic to cats?
6. are cats noisy?
7. Is a cat affectionate?
8. Is a cat playful?
9. Do cats sleep a lot?
10. are cats friendly?
11. does your teacher have a cat?
12. Do cats like birds?
13. Do cats like dogs?
14. Is a cat expensive?

B. Pronunciation: *Does he/Does she.*
Listen and repeat.

1. **a.** Does he have a dog? **b.** Does she have a dog?
2. **a.** Does he like cats? **b.** Does she like cats?
3. **a.** Does he want a pet? **b.** Does she want a pet?

Listen and complete.

1. Does she work full time?
2. Does he have any free time?
3. Does he exercise every day?
4. Does she have any children?
5. Does she live in an apartment?
6. Does she walk the dog?
7. Does he sleep well?
8. Does he understand you?
9. Does she travel a lot?
10. Does he like to walk?

Practice the sentences with a partner.

Active Grammar: *Wh*- questions

***Wh*-questions: Present Tense**

Where	do	I you we they	work? study? walk the dog?
When	does	he she it	

A. Read Buddy's schedule. Complete and answer the questions about his day.

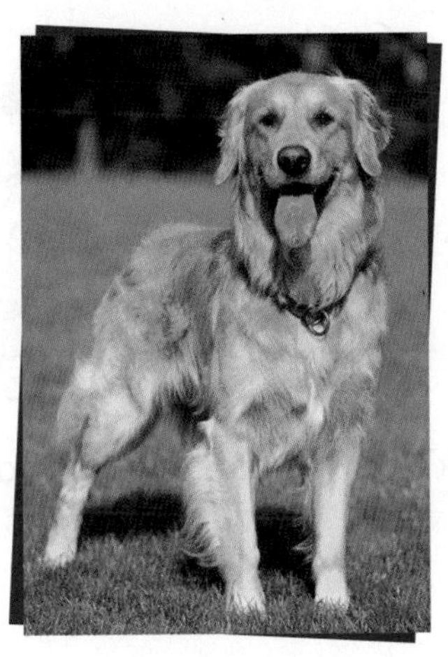

7:00	Wakes up
7:30	Short walk with Mr. Jackson
8:00	Eats breakfast
8:30 to 4:00	Guards the house
	Barks at the mailman
4:00	Takes a long walk with Mrs. Jackson
5:00	Plays with the children
6:00	Eats dinner
7:00	Watches TV with the family
9:00	Takes a short walk with Mrs. Jackson
10:00	Goes to sleep

1. What time ___does___ Buddy ___wake___ up? (wake)
2. __________ Mr. Jackson __________ him for a long walk? (take)
3. How many walks __________ he __________ a day? (take)
4. Where __________ they __________ the dog? (walk)
5. Who __________ he __________ at? (bark)
6. When __________ the children __________ with Buddy? (play)
7. How often __________ he __________ during the day? (eat)
8. __________ the children __________ Buddy? (walk)
9. What time __________ he __________ to sleep? (go)

B. Complete these questions about Buddy's schedule.

1. ______________________________? At 8:00.
2. ______________________________? He takes a long walk.
3. ______________________________? After dinner.

C. Ask a partner about his or her schedule. Use these cues.

What time do you get up?

1.

What time / get up?

2.

How / get to school?
What time / get to school?

3.

Where / work?
How many hours / work?

4.

What / be / favorite TV show?
How many hours of TV / watch?

5.

When / do your homework?
How many hours / study?

6.

What time / go to bed?
How many hours / sleep?

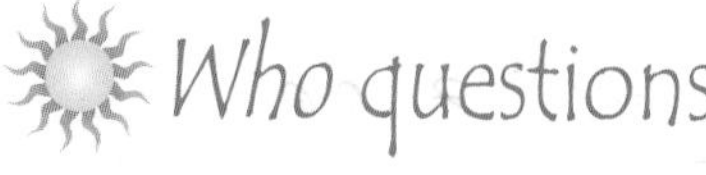

Who questions

***Who* questions: Present Tense**
***Who* as subject**

Who	works? walks the dog?

D. Sit in a group of four or five students. Ask and answer these *Who* questions. Look at the examples in the answer boxes.

1. Who has a dog?
2. Who has a cat?
3. Who gets up before 7 A.M.?
4. Who walks to school?
5. Who takes the bus to school?
6. Who works full time?
7. Who watches a lot of TV?
8. Who watches the news on TV?
9. Who studies more than an hour a day?
10. Who goes to bed at midnight?

(name) does.
No one does.

I do.
(name) and (name) do.
Two of us do.
A couple of us do.
A few of us do.
All of us do.

E. Student to student dictation.
Student A: Turn to page 240.
Student B: Read the answers below. Student A will ask you seven questions. Write each question next to the appropriate answer. When you finish, change pages.

1. how Many children you have? Two.
2. Da you have a dog? Yes, I am.
3. ______________________? A lot.
4. ______________________? Yes, I do.
5. ______________________? Brazil.
6. ______________________? Once a week.
7. ______________________? Ten miles.

F. Match the pets and their owners. Give reasons for your choices. Who doesn't have a pet?

Claudia Mehmet Billy Ohida

Doberman Poodle Chihuahua

Billy ohida Claudia

Interviews

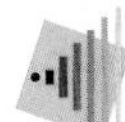

A. Interview: A dog owner. Listen. Then, answer the questions.

1. What's the dog's name?
2. Is she friendly?
3. How old is she?
4. How often does she walk Lucky?
5. How often does she feed her?
6. Is she good with children?
7. Does she comb the dog every day?
8. Is she a good watchdog?
9. Does she bark at the letter carrier?

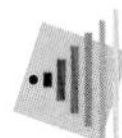

B. Listen again. What do you know about Lucky and her owner?

C. Interview: A cat owner. Listen. Then, complete the questions.

1. What's ____________________? Her name is Midnight.
2. What color ____________________? She's black.
3. How old ____________________? She's fourteen.
4. Is ____________________? No, she isn't.
5. Where ____________________? In the front window.
6. Where ____________________? In her basket.
7. Does ____________________? No, she doesn't.

Owning a Pet

A. Is a pet expensive? Sit in a group and discuss these expenses. How much does a dog cost? What expenses does a dog owner have?

a collar

a leash

Cost of a dog	Free to $500 or more
Rabies immunization (every 3 years)	Free to $75
Pet License	$10 or more
Collar	$10 to $20
Leash	$20 to $30
Food (per year)	$100 to $200
Veterinarian (once or twice a year)	$50 to $75 a visit
Grooming (six times a year)	$30 to $50 a visit

As a group, decide what expenses a cat owner has.

B. What's the law? Match these common regulations for dog owners. Are there other regulations in your city or town?

___c___	**1.** You must obtain	**a.** your dog.
______	**2.** You must curb	**b.** on a leash.
______	**3.** You must clean up	**c.** a license for your dog.
______	**4.** You must walk your dog	**d.** after your dog.
______	**5.** Your dog must not disturb	**e.** a rabies vaccination.
______	**6.** Your dog must not run	**f.** your neighbors.
______	**7.** Your dog must have	**g.** free.

The Big Picture: The Humane Society

A. Discuss the meanings of these words.

cage	stray
wag	tail
lick	housebroken

Culture Note

Many towns have a humane society. These organizations care for lost and abandoned animals and try to find good homes for them.

B. Listen and complete the information on the card on the right.

1. Where is this family?
2. Which dog do they like? Why?

Breed: ______________________
Color: ______________________
Sex: Male Female
Good with children: Yes No
Good with other animals: Yes No
Housebroken: Yes No
Reason here: ______________________
Date of arrival: ______________________
Rabies immunization: Yes No

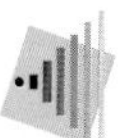

C. Listen to the conversation between the manager of the Humane Society and Mr. and Mrs. Vento. Complete the form as you listen.

HUMANE SOCIETY

Adoption Application

Name: Antonio and Rebecca Vento

Who will be primarily responsible for the pet? ☐ Self ☐ Spouse ☐ Children ☐ Other

How many children at home? ______ Ages: ______

Do you ☐ own a house? ☐ rent an apartment?

Landlord's name: ______ Landlord's phone: ______

How many hours a day will your pet be outside? ______

Do you have a yard? ☐ Yes ☐ No If yes, is your yard fenced? ☐ Yes ☐ No

Do you have other pets at home now? ______

Have you ever owned a pet before? ☐ Yes ☐ No

What kinds of pets did you own? ______

Where did you get your pets from? ______

What happened to your last pet? ______

Did you ever adopt from the Humane Society before? ☐ Yes ☐ No

If so, when? ______

D. Circle the correct form of the verb.

1. This family ______ a humane society.
   a. is visiting **b.** visited **c.** will visit **d.** visits
2. They ______ at dogs for adoption.
   a. are looking **b.** looked **c.** will look **d.** look
3. Daisy's owner ______ to an apartment.
   a. is moving **b.** moved **c.** will move **d.** moves
4. Mrs. Vento ______ responsible for Daisy during the day.
   a. is **b.** was **c.** will be **d.** were
5. This family ______ another dog before Daisy.
   a. is having **b.** had **c.** will have **d.** has
6. They ______ their last dog from Mrs. Vento's brother.
   a. are getting **b.** got **c.** will get **d.** get
7. This family ______ Daisy home tomorrow.
   a. is taking **b.** took **c.** will take **d.** takes

Reading: Seeing Eye® Dogs

A. Before You Read.

1. What does "blind" mean?
2. Have you ever seen a Seeing Eye® dog or a dog guide?

The Seeing Eye was the first dog guide school in the United States. Dorothy H. Eustis started the program in 1929. Since then, it has matched over 12,500 trained Seeing Eye® dogs with 6,000 blind men and women from across the United States and Canada. The Seeing Eye helps blind people to greater independence, dignity, and confidence through the use of Seeing Eye® dogs.

Photo courtesy of The Seeing Eye®.

1. What kind of dogs do you use?
   The Seeing Eye has its own German shepherds, Labrador retrievers, and golden retrievers. At times, we use boxers and mixed breeds.
2. How long does it take to train a dog?
   Training a Seeing Eye® dog is a long process. When the dog is about eight weeks old, it goes to the home of a volunteer, where it learns basic commands and gets lots of love. When it is about 18 months old, the dog returns to the Seeing Eye and begins a four-month training program with a sighted instructor. When the dog is ready, it is paired with a blind person. The person and the dog then train together for 27 days.
3. How does a dog know when to cross the street?
   Dogs are color-blind and can't read traffic lights. The dog's owner learns to understand the movement of traffic by its sound. When the owner feels that it is time to cross the street, he or she will say "Forward." The dog will not cross the street until it is safe.
4. How does a dog know where a blind person wants to go?
   Blind people usually know their own towns and can direct their dogs where they want to go. The basic commands are "forward," "right," and "left." In a new location, blind people will ask for directions and tell them to the dog.
5. How long does a dog work?
   Most dogs work for seven to eight years. Many Seeing Eye® dogs work until they are 12 or 13 or longer. When they retire, people keep Seeing Eye® dogs as pets or give them to a relative as a pet, or return them to the Seeing Eye.

6. How much does a Seeing Eye® dog cost?
The Seeing Eye is an organization that receives contributions from individuals and companies. Each student pays only $150. This fee includes the dog; the student's training with the dog; room and board during the 27-day training; and round-trip transportation from anywhere in the United States or Canada.

7. Are people with guide dogs allowed in public places?
The American Disabilities Act as well as laws in all 50 states and the provinces of Canada allow a Seeing Eye® dog and its owner in all public places.

8. Are all dogs that help blind people Seeing Eye® dogs?
Only dogs trained by The Seeing Eye, Inc. of Morristown, New Jersey, are officially called Seeing Eye® dogs. There are other programs and other schools. The general word for a dog that assists a blind person is "dog guide" or "guide dog."

(Information adapted courtesy of The Seeing Eye®.)

B. Vocabulary. Think about each pair of words. If the words mean the same, write *S*. If the words have a different meaning, write *D*.

____	blind person	sighted person	____	Forward!	Stay!
____	dignity	respect	____	contributions	gifts
____	training	instruction	____	allow	prohibit
____	obedience	disobedience	____	assist	help
____	paired	matched	____	public	private

C. Answer. You work at The Seeing Eye. A person calls and asks these questions. How will you answer?

1. What kind of dogs do you use?
2. How old are the dogs?
3. Who trains the dogs?
4. How long does it take to learn to use a Seeing Eye® dog?
5. Does a dog understand traffic lights?
6. What happens to the dog when it is too old to work with me?
7. How much does it cost to get a Seeing Eye® dog? Why is it so reasonable?
8. Can I take the dog with me on an airplane flight?

D. Think about it. This article answered some basic questions about Seeing Eye® dogs. What other questions do you have?

Writing Assignment

1. Read the model composition.
2. Prepare your interview questions.
3. Conduct your interview.
4. Write your story.
5. Edit your story.

A. Tamara interviewed her neighbor about her dog. Read Tamara's composition.

My neighbors, the Redmans, have a beagle named Max. They bought Max three years ago when he was eight weeks old. Max is brown and white with a black nose. He is active and friendly, and he thinks he is part of the family. He follows Mrs. Redman around the house all day. She takes him for a walk in the morning and in the afternoon. When she goes to the store or picks up the children from school, he sits next to her in the front seat. Max is very happy when the children come home because he likes to play with them. During dinner, Max sits under the table and the children pass him little pieces of food. Unfortunately, Max doesn't like to be alone. When Mrs. Redman leaves the house, he barks for hours.

B. Prepare the interview questions. Before writing, interview a neighbor, a student at your school, a teacher, or a co-worker, about a pet. When you have specific information, it is easier to write. In a group, write ten questions you could ask the pet owner. Look through this unit or develop your own questions.

1. ______________________________?
2. ______________________________?
3. ______________________________?

4. ____?

5. ____?

6. ____?

7. ____?

8. ____?

9. ____?

10. ____?

C. Edit. Find and corrrect the verb mistakes in these sentences.

1. My neighbor ~~have~~ has a cat.
2. Her cat have five years old.
3. The cat sit in the window and watch birds.
4. Where the cat sleeps?
5. The cat not like dogs.
6. What kind of cat you have?
7. Does your cat catches mice?
8. Do you allergic to cats?
9. I starts to sneeze when I am near a cat.
10. How often you take your cat to the veterinarian?

Looking at the Internet

A. Look on the Internet and find information about one breed of dog or cat.

Search words: Dogs and breeds
Cats and breeds
American Kennel Club

B. Print out a picture of one breed of dog or cat you like.

C. Show your picture to your class or your group. Describe the breed. Give three or four facts that you found on the Internet.

Practicing on Your Own

Notes: Labrador retriever (Lab)
Large dog
Short hair
Colors: Yellow, black, chocolate
Needs lots of exercise
Loves water
Great with children
Easy to train

A. Answer.

1. Do you have a Labrador retriever? ____________________
2. Is a Lab a large dog? ____________________
3. Does it have short hair? ____________________
4. Are Labs easy to train? ____________________
5. Is a Lab good with children? ____________________
6. Does a Lab like to swim? ____________________

B. Match the two parts of these questions. Then, write the correct answer from the box.

$18.	Five miles.	Near the window.
Yes, I am.	My teacher does.	Never.
✓ At 6:30.	Yes, I do.	Good, thanks.
Forty hours.		

c	1. What time	a. hours do you work?	1. At 6:30.
___	2. How many	b. do you live from school?	2. ________
___	3. How often	c. does your alarm clock ring?	3. ________
___	4. How far	d. has a pencil sharpener?	4. ________
___	5. Who	e. do you come to class late?	5. ________
___	6. How	f. does it cost?	6. ________
___	7. How much	g. you ready?	7. ________
___	8. Where	h. you have a cell phone?	8. ________
___	9. Do	i. do you feel today?	9. ________
___	10. Are	j. do you sit in class?	10. ________

Grammar Summary

▶ 1. Simple present tense: *Yes/No* questions

Do	I	work?	Yes, you do.	No, you don't.
	you		Yes, I do.	No, I don't.
	we		Yes, we do.	No, we don't.
	they		Yes, they do.	No, they don't.
Does	he		Yes, he does.	No, he doesn't.
	she		Yes, she does.	No, she doesn't.
	it		Yes, it does.	No, it doesn't.

▶ 2. *Wh-* questions

When do you leave?	At 8:00.
Where does she live?	In Springfield.
When do we arrive?	At 8:30.
When do they get there?	At 9:00.
How far do you live from work?	Fifteen miles. *or* Thirty minutes.
How does he get to school?	He takes the bus.
How long does it take?	Twenty minutes.

4 The States

A. Discuss these geography features.

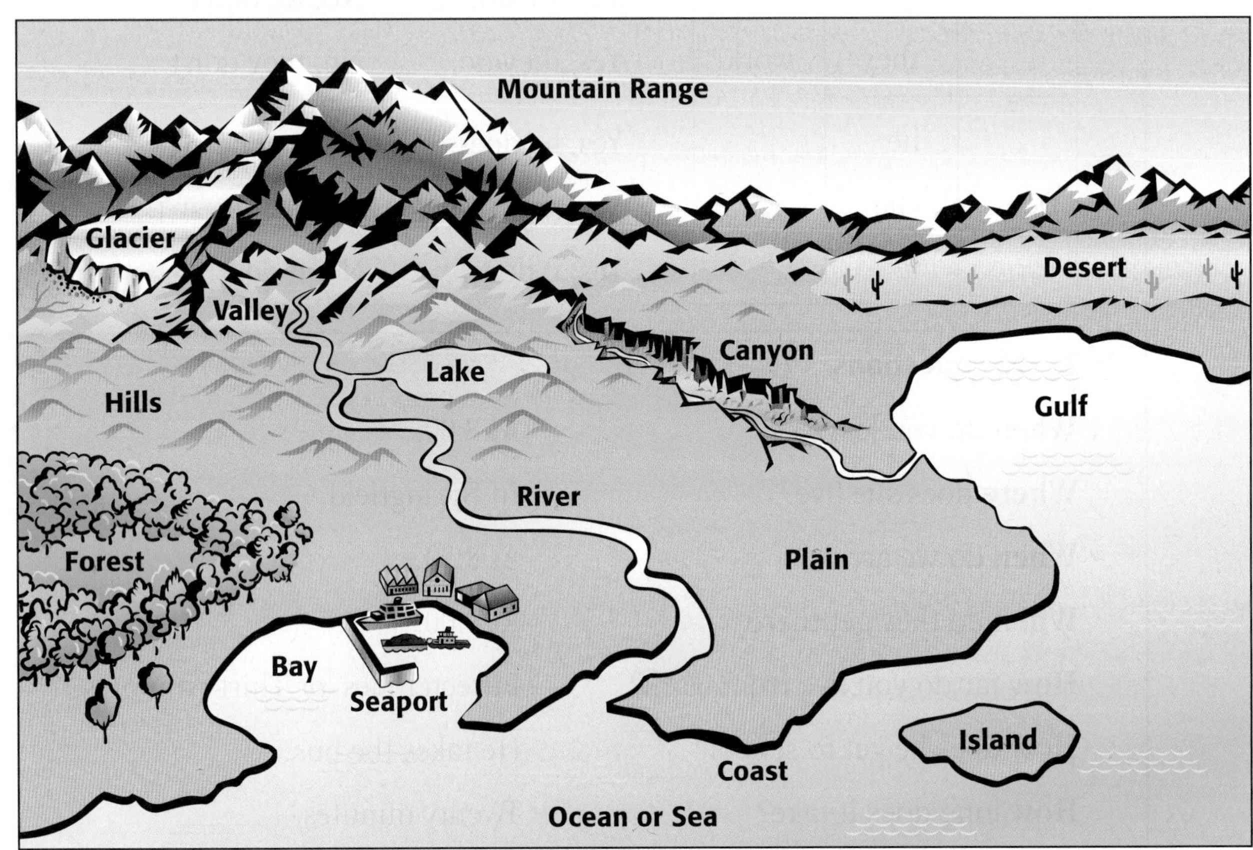

B. Read each statement. Circle *True* or *False* about your city.

1. We can see mountains from our school. True False
2. This city/town is on a river. True False
3. If I drive an hour, I can see the Atlantic or the Pacific Ocean. True False
4. This city is the capital of the state. True False
5. There is a desert near here. True False
6. This city/town is near a lake. True False
7. There are many farms near here. True False
8. This city/town is also a seaport. True False

Active Grammar: Count Nouns

A. Decide if these count nouns are singular (S) or plural (P).

Count nouns are people, places, or things that we can count individually.
Count nouns can be singular or plural.
Plural nouns usually end with *s* or *es*. Some exceptions: *men, women, children, people.*
Expressions with *one of the, every,* and *each* are singular.
Expressions with *a few of the, some of the, many of the,* etc., are plural.

S a desert	S one of the cities	P seaports
P mountains	S a mountain range	P all of the states
S a farm	P ranches	P millions of tourists
P rivers	S an ocean	S every state
P many of the people	P canyons	P several of the islands

B. Decide if the subject is singular or plural. Circle the correct form of the verb.

Simple Present Tense

A desert **is** a dry area.	A desert **has** interesting plants.
Deserts **are** dry areas.	Deserts **have** interesting plants.

1. A plain **is** / **are** a large area of flat land.
2. A range **is** / **are** a group of mountains.
3. Canyons **is** / **are** long, deep cracks in the earth's surface.
4. A city **has** / **have** a lot of traffic.
5. Cities **has** / **have** a lot of traffic.
6. A river often **begins** / **begin** in the mountains.
7. Millions of tourists **visits** / **visit** the national parks every summer.
8. A dairy farm **produces** / **produce** milk.
9. Every state **has** / **have** interesting places to visit.
10. All the states **has** / **have** interesting places to visit.
11. Farmers **grows** / **grow** many kinds of vegetables.
12. A map **shows** / **show** cities and highways.
13. A skyscraper **is** / **are** a tall building.

a skyscraper

A Map of the United States

A. Pronunciation: Syllables and stress. Listen and repeat.

At·lan·tic O·cean

Ap·pa·la·chian Moun·tains

Mis·sis·sip·pi Ri·ver

Listen and mark the stress.

Ca·na·da	Rock·y Moun·tains	Ha·wai·i
Mex·i·co	Grand Can·yon	Pa·ci·fic O·cean
The U·ni·ted States	A·las·ka	Death Val·ley

B. Mark your own location on the map. Then, listen and point to each location on the map.

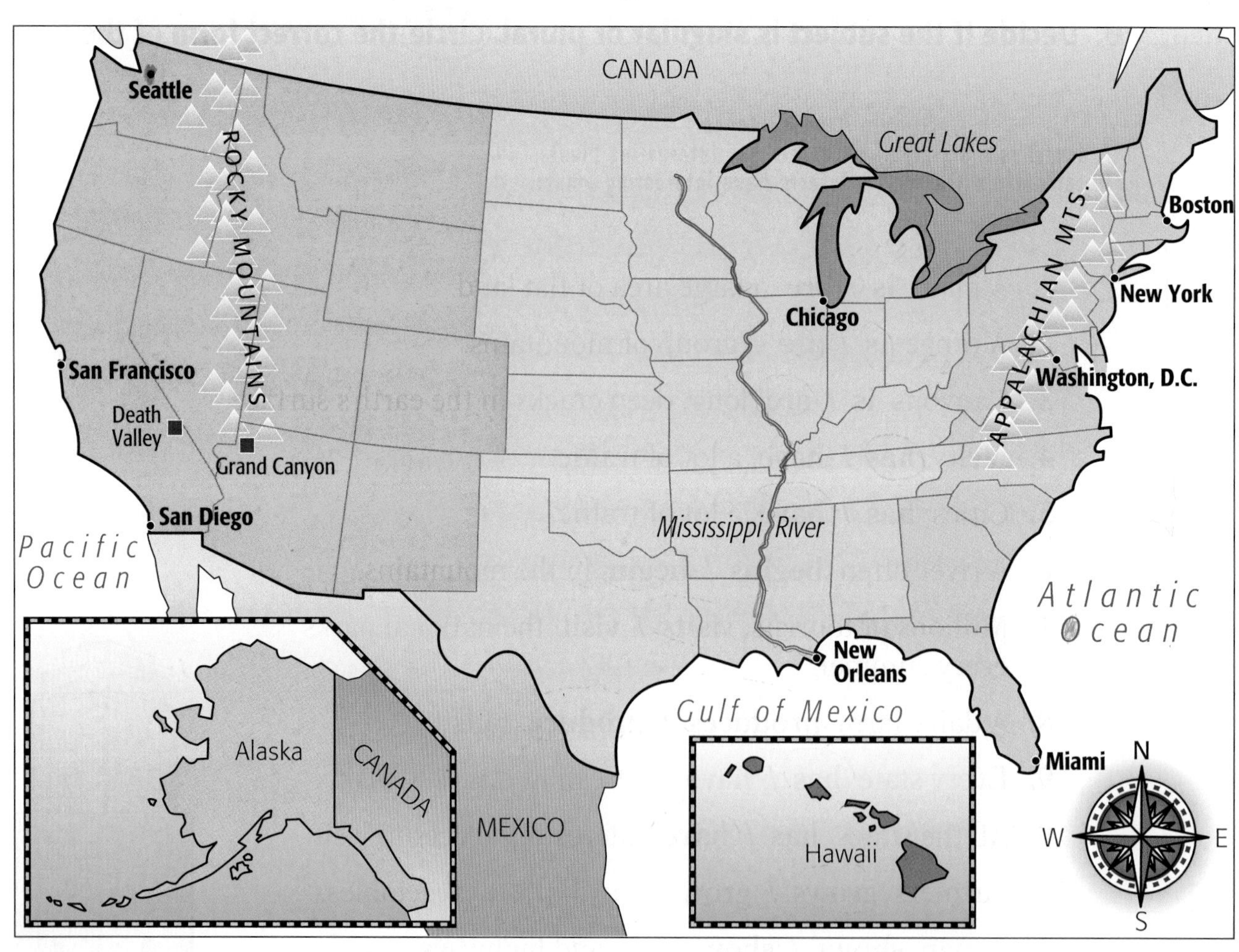

C. Form sentences about the map of the United States.

> Use **There is** for singular count nouns.
> **There is** a long mountain range in the west.

> Use **There are** for plural count nouns.
> **There are** a lot of farms in the United States.
> **There are** a few lakes in the Southwest.
> **There are** no deserts in the east.

			seaport	in the United States.
		a/an	seaports	on the coast.
	is	a lot of	fifty states	in the north.
	isn't	many	big cities	in the east.
There	are	several	farms	in the south.
	aren't	a few	mountain range	in the west.
		any	mountains	in the central part of the country.
			deserts	on the Gulf of Mexico.
			parks	______________.

D. Answer these questions about the map on page 50.

> **General questions**
> Is there a **good seaport** on the coast? — Yes, **there** is. — No, **there** isn't.
> Are there **many rivers** in the east? — Yes, **there** are. — No, **there** aren't.
>
> **Specific questions**
> Is **New Orleans** a seaport? — Yes, **it** is. — No, **it** isn't.
> Are **the Rocky Mountains** in the west? — Yes, **they** are. — No, **they** aren't.

1. Are there many mountains in the west?
2. Are the Rocky Mountains very high?
3. Are there many farms in the central part of the United States?
4. Is there a seaport on the Gulf of Mexico?
5. Is New Orleans on the Atlantic Ocean?
6. Is Hawaii in the Atlantic Ocean?
7. Are there many beaches in Hawaii?
8. Are there many large cities in the east?
9. Is New York a seaport?
10. Are the Great Lakes in the south?

Active Grammar: Count and Non-count Nouns

Count nouns are items that we can count individually (one by one): lake—lakes
Non-count nouns are only singular. They include:

1. Liquids or gases: water, oil, oxygen, rain
2. Items that are too small or too numerous to count: sand, corn, rice
3. General categories: traffic, scenery, music, tourism
4. Abstract ideas: information, beauty, work

Note: Some words can be both count and non-count: crime—crimes, industry—industries

A. Classify these words as count or non-count.

✓mountain	seaport	museum	university
✓industry	farm	snow	ranch
✓pollution	crime	skyscraper	tourism
✓tourist	river	factories	rain
✓unemployment	noise	traffic	country

Count Nouns	Non-count Nouns
mountain seaport	industry snow
industry river	pollution traffic
tourist museum	unemployment rain

B. What major city is your school in or near? Complete these sentences about that city. Use *is/isn't* or *are/aren't* in each sentence.

1. There ____________ a lot of skyscrapers.
2. There ____________ many tourists.
3. There ____________ a lot of tourism.
4. There ____________ a lot of snow in the winter.
5. There ____________ a lot of jobs.
6. There ____________ a lot of unemployment.
7. There ____________ ____________ immigrants.
8. There ____________ ____________ traffic.
9. There ____________ ____________ noise.
10. There ____________ ____________ colleges and universities.

C. My native country. Sit in a group of three or four students. If possible, each student should be from a different country.

Count Nouns: How many seaports are there in your country?
Non-count Nouns: How much snow is there in your country?

1. What country are you from?
2. Where is your country?
3. How many skyscrapers are there in your country?
4. How much tourism is there in your country?
5. How much traffic is there in your country?
6. How many immigrants are there in your country?
7. How many farms are there in your country?
8. How much snow is there in your country?
9. How many mountain ranges are there in your country?
10. How much crime is there in your country?
11. How many universities are there in your country?
12. How many deserts are there in your country?

My State

A. Where are you now? Draw a map of your state or country in this box.

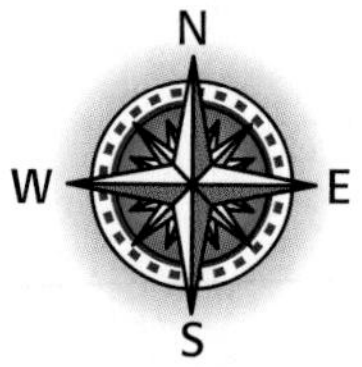

B. On your map, do the following.

1. Mark the capital.
2. Name and locate three major cities.
3. Locate and label the largest airport.
4. Show your present location on the map.
5. Write in the bordering states, countries, and oceans.
6. Draw in one major river or lake.
7. Show mountains with triangles and forests with trees.
8. Mark and name any major geographical features, such as canyons or deserts.
9. What other features do you want to include?

C. Complete these questions about your state. Use *How much* or *How many*. Then, answer the questions.

Count Nouns
How many lakes are there in (state)?
There is one.
There are a few.
There are a lot.
There are many.
There aren't any.

Non-count Nouns
How much tourism is there in (state)?
There is a lot.
There is a little.
There isn't any.

1. How ___much___ rain **is / are** there in ______________?
2. How ___________ rivers **is / are** there in ______________?
3. How ___________ snow **is / are** there in ______________?
4. How ___________ deserts **is / are** there in ______________?
5. How ___________ industry **is / are** there in ______________?
6. How ___________ tourism **is / are** there in ______________?
7. How ___________ farms **is / are** there in ______________?
8. How ___________ traffic **is / are** there in ______________?
9. How ___________ national parks **is / are** there in ______________?
10. How ___________ pollution **is / are** there in ______________?

A. Discuss this feature map of Montana.

1. What are Montana's borders?
2. What is the capital?
3. What geographical features do you see on this map?

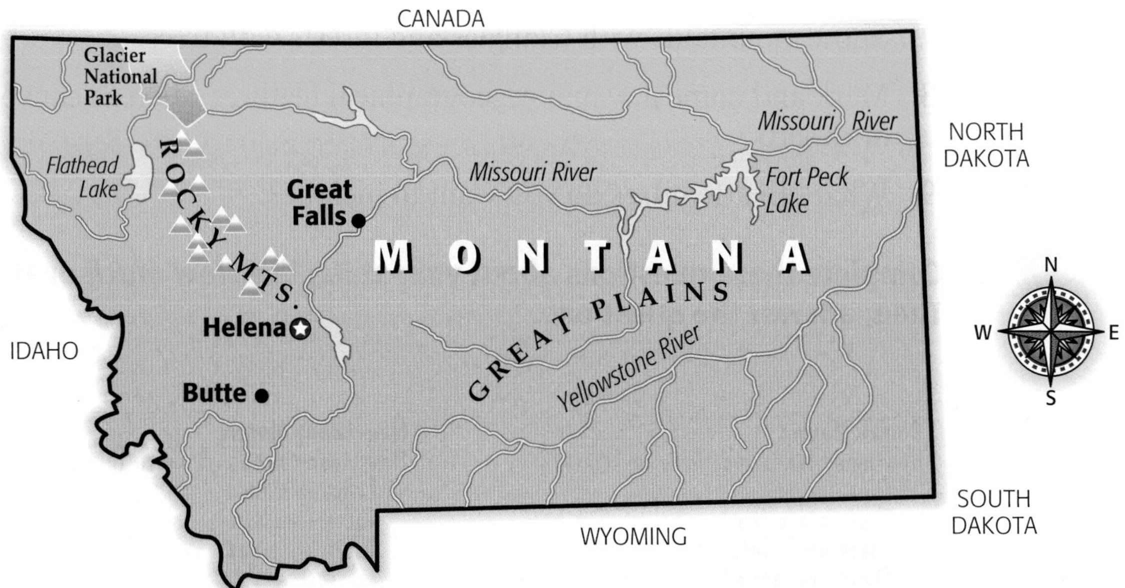

B. Look at the map and listen to the information about Montana. Then, make statements using the words.

General and Specific Statements
General statements:
There is a large national park in Montana.
Specific statements:
Glacier National Park is in Montana.
Do not say: There is Glacier National Park in Montana.

rain	the Missouri River	lakes
the Rocky Mountains	rivers	Fort Peck Lake
Indian reservations	Glacier National Park	people
Helena	national park	Canada
horse ranches	tourism	snow

C. Circle the correct answer.

1. What is the weather like in the western part of the state?

   a. It's cold and wet. b. It's cold and dry. c. It's hot and wet.

2. What is the weather like in the eastern part of the state?

   a. It's cold and wet. b. It's cold and dry. c. It's hot and dry.

3. Why is the eastern part of Montana dry?

   a. because it is so far north b. because the mountains stop the clouds

4. Where are there many horse ranches?

   a. in the eastern part of the state b. in the western part of the state

5. What is one of Montana's major industries?

   a. fishing b. manufacturing c. tourism

6. What country is to the north?

   a. Wyoming b. Canada c. Glacier National Park

D. Complete with the correct form of the verbs.

1. The Missouri River ______________ in Montana. (begin)
2. The western part of Montana ______________ a lot of snow. (receive)
3. Montana ______________ very cold winters. (have)
4. Thousands of tourists ______________ Montana. (visit)
5. The Rocky Mountains ______________ the rain clouds. (stop)
6. Many of the Native Americans ______________ on reservations. (live)
7. Snow ______________ the mountains. (cover)

E. Student to student dictation.
Student A: Turn to page 240.
Student B: Write the questions Student A dictates below. When you finish, change pages.

1. How many ____?
2. How many ____?
3. How much ____?
4. ____?
5. ____?

A. What do you know about life in the desert? Circle *True* or *False*.

1. A desert receives very little rain. True False
2. The only plants in the desert are different kinds of cactuses. True False
3. Animals cannot live in the desert. True False
4. Summer is the best time to visit the desert. True False

B. Match.

__c__	**1.** precipitation	**a.**	a show or display of art, plants, animals, etc.
_____	**2.** sea level	**b.**	to change or adjust to new conditions
_____	**3.** roots	**c.**	rainfall
_____	**4.** exhibit	**d.**	the part of the plant that grows into the earth and brings in water
_____	**5.** varieties	**e.**	to stay away from
_____	**6.** adapt	**f.**	at the same height as the sea or ocean
_____	**7.** avoid	**g.**	kinds or types

Death Valley National Park is the largest national park in the continental 48 states. This 3.3 million acre park in southern California is the lowest, hottest, and driest place in North America. The lowest point is 282 feet (86 m) below sea level. In the summer, the average temperature is 115° (46 Celsius), and the highest temperature ever recorded here was 134° (56.6 Celsius). There are some summers when Death Valley receives no rain, and the average precipitation is fewer than two inches.

The first visitors to this desert area were different tribes of Native Americans. They walked through this area but did not stay. In 1849, people heard about the discovery of gold in California. Thousands of people began the long trip to the west. This large desert area was so difficult to cross that it received the name Death Valley.

Today, tourists and nature lovers from all over the United States travel to Death Valley to enjoy its natural beauty. There are over one thousand varieties of plants in this desert, including many kinds of cactuses and flowers. Cactuses, with their interesting and unusual shapes, need very little rain. Their roots are close to the surface of the ground so they can quickly collect any rainfall. A few days after the first rain in the spring, thousands of wildflowers cover the desert.

Prickly pear cactus

There are also many animals that have learned to adapt to this hot climate. Most are active at night, sleeping during the day to avoid the hot desert sun. For example, the kangaroo rat sleeps deep underground while the sun is out. It can live its entire life without drinking any water, getting its water from the food it eats.

Kangaroo rat

If you are planning a trip to Death Valley, winter is the best time to visit. There are nine campgrounds with more than fifteen hundred campsites. The main visitor area is Furnace Creek with nature exhibits, a museum, and a bookstore. Be sure to watch the informative film on desert life. After that, you can explore the desert by car, by bike, or on foot. Park rangers offer programs on desert life, the history of Death Valley, and the desert sky at night. If you are planning a trip to Death Valley, don't forget these four essentials: a sun hat, sunblock, lots of water, and a camera.

C. Write specific information from the reading to prove each fact.

1. Death Valley is the largest park in the continental 48 states.	It is a 3.3 million acre park.
2. It is the lowest place in North America.	
3. It is the hottest place in North America.	
4. It is the driest place in North America.	

D. Match the two parts of each sentence.

c **1.** Visitors need to bring sunblock

c **2.** Native Americans didn't stay in Death Valley

a **3.** Desert animals are active at night

F **4.** Cactus roots are near the surface

b **5.** This area was named Death Valley

g **6.** This area is so dry

d **7.** After the first spring rain,

a. because it is cooler at this time.

b. because it was so difficult to cross.

c. to protect their skin from the sun.

d. millions of wildflowers cover the desert.

e. because they needed a lake or river for water.

f. to quickly collect rainwater.

g. because high mountains block the rain clouds.

Writing Our Stories: My State

A. Read this student report.

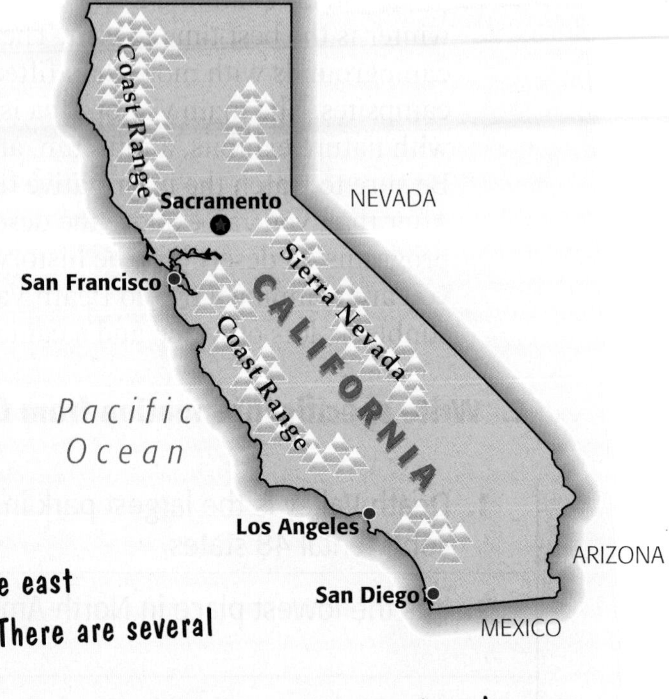

California is on the west coast of the United States and it's the third largest state. Its borders are Oregon to the north, Nevada and Arizona to the east, Mexico to the south, and the Pacific Ocean to the west. Sacramento is the capital. The population is over thirty-four million.

California is a beautiful state. The coast of California has hundreds of miles of beautiful beaches. There are two mountain ranges, the Sierra Nevada in the east and the Coast Ranges along the Pacific. There are several deserts in the southeast.

Two of the major cities are San Francisco and Los Angeles. San Francisco is on the hills over San Francisco Bay. Tourists visit Chinatown and ride up and down the hills on the cable cars. Los Angeles is in southern California. It is the home of Hollywood and the movie industry.

For most of the year, the weather along the coast is sunny and mild. In the winter, there is snow in the mountains. In the south, the weather is hot and dry.

Agriculture and tourism are two of the major industries. California grows more than half of the nations' fruits and vegetables. Many Californians also work in the tourist industry in the cities, parks, and resorts.

B. Writing a report.

1. Choose a state in the United States.
2. Draw a map of that state. Show the borders, the capital, and major geographical features.
3. Fill out the information form on the next page. Look up information on the Internet, in an almanac, or in an encyclopedia.
4. Write a short report.
5. Share your information with the class.

C. Complete this information. Write a few important words, not sentences. Then, use the information to write a report about the state. Do not copy sentences from books or from the Internet!

State	California is a largest state
Location	is on the coast
Borders	Pacific ocean oregon nevado Arisona Mexico
Capital	Sacramento
Population	is over thirty Four Millon
Geography	north oregon
Two major cities	San Francisco los Angeles
Weather	is hot and dry
Two industries	Agriculture Hollywood and movies idustry

Locations

in the north	in the northern part
in the south	in the southern part
in the east	in the eastern part
in the west	in the western part

D. Share your information with the class. Tell the class the name of the state you chose. Show a map of the state and describe the location. If you have a map of the United States, point to the state. Do not read your report to the class! Give one or two interesting facts about the state. Try to talk without looking at your report.

Practicing on Your Own

A. Circle the correct form of the verbs.

The Mississippi River **is / are** the longest river system in the United States. It **flows / flow** 2,300 miles from Minnesota to New Orleans on the Gulf of Mexico. The name *Mississippi* **comes / come** from a Native American word that means "Big Water."

The Mississippi **provides / provide** a transportation route for farm and industrial products going up and down the river. Goods **travels / travel** from the center of the nation to the Gulf of Mexico. There **is / are** many tugboats on the river. These tugboats **pushes / push** barges, which are large, flat boats, up and down the river. There **is / are** sometimes one hundred barges or more together in large convoys.

A barge on the Mississippi

The Mississippi also **serves / serve** other purposes. It **provides / provide** water for irrigation for farming. There **is / are** large refining companies along the river that **needs / need** thousands of gallons of water to process oil. People **fishes / fish** the waters, weekend boaters **speeds / speed** up and down the river, and bird lovers **watches / watch** for the hundreds of species of birds that stop at the river on their way north or south.

The Mississippi **does / do** not always **flows / flow** along peacefully. Sometimes there **is / are** heavy rain, and the river **rises / rise** many feet. Miles of towns and homes **needs / need** protection from the river. So, the government **builds / build** walls, called "levees," along the river. But the Mississippi **has / have** a mind of its own, and major floods still **occurs / occur** from time to time.

Grammar Summary

Count Nouns

1. Use

Count nouns are items that we can count individually, one by one. They can be singular or plural.

town—towns
city—cities

2. Quantifiers

For a count noun, use the exact number or use one of these quantifiers:

(number)	There are four parks in this state.
a lot of	There are a lot of farms.
many	There are many rivers.
a few	There are a few parks.
one	There is one lake.
no	There are no deserts.
any	There aren't any mountains.

3. *Yes/No* questions

For a singular noun, use *Is there a*:

Is there a desert in your state?
Yes, there is. No, there isn't.

For a plural noun, use *Are there any*:

Are there any deserts in your state?
Yes, there are. No, there aren't.

4. *How many* questions

Use *How many* for a count noun.

How many deserts are there in your state?
There is only one.
There are several.
There aren't any deserts.

Non-count Nouns

1. Use

Non-count nouns cannot be counted individually. They are only singular. They include:

1. Liquids or gases (water, oil, oxygen)
2. Items that are too small or too numerous to count (sand, corn, snow)
3. General categories (scenery, traffic)
4. Abstract ideas (information, beauty, life)

2. Quantifiers

For a non-count noun, use one of these quantifiers:

a lot of	There is a lot of traffic.
much	There is much snow.
a little	There is a little industry.
no	There is no pollution.
any	There isn't any traffic.

3. *Yes/No* questions

Use *Is there any*:

Is there any pollution in your state?
Yes, there is. No, there isn't.

4. *How much* questions

Use *How much* for a non-count noun.

How much snow is there in your state?
There is a lot of snow.
There isn't any snow.

5 Computers and the Internet

A. Label the computer.

CD-ROM	keys	mouse pad
floppy disk	monitor	speakers
keyboard	mouse	screen

B. Discuss your computer use.

1. Do you have a computer at home? at school? at work?
2. Are you connected to the Internet? What online service do you use?
3. Does your school have a computer lab? Do you have a student account?
4. Check (✓) the ways you, your family, or friends use a computer.

☐ play video games	☐ send e-mail	☐ pay bills
☐ write papers	☐ watch movies	☐ enter data
☐ shop for clothes	☐ find recipes	☐ listen to music
☐ read the news	☐ check the weather	☐ make airline reservations

5. What else can a person do with a computer?

Present Continuous

I am sending an e-mail.	I'm not sending an e-mail.
You are sending an e-mail.	You aren't sending an e-mail.
We are sending an e-mail.	We aren't sending an e-mail.
They are sending an e-mail.	They aren't sending an e-mail.
He is sending an e-mail.	He isn't sending an e-mail.
She is sending an e-mail.	She isn't sending an e-mail.
It is working well.	It isn't working well.

A. Read about how each person is using the Internet. Underline the verbs in the present continuous.

1. Li-Ping is writing an e-mail to her brother in China. She's telling him about her new job at a dot.com company.
2. Raul is taking a virtual tour of an art museum. He likes modern art, so he's looking at paintings by Picasso and Dalí.
3. Mr. and Mrs. Chan are going into the city this weekend. They are checking the reviews of several restaurants. They are making reservations for a show.

B. Explain how each person is using the Internet. Use the cues in the box.

look for / houses	fill out / an application	make / airline reservations
order / a CD	look at / job postings	check / weather
check / car prices	read / movie reviews	look at / baby names

1. Bob is going to fly to Miami next month.
   He's making airline reservations.
2. Sarah just lost her job.
3. Mr. and Mrs. Garcia are going to move to Florida.
4. Pablo loves classical music.
5. Tamara wants to go to the beach.
6. The Parks are planning to buy a new car.
7. Edgar and Marta are expecting their first baby.
8. Kevin is planning to go to college.
9. Gus wants to see a movie this weekend.

C. Student to student dictation: Computer use.
Student A: Turn to page 241.
Student B: Listen to Student A. How is each person using the computer? Write the sentence next to the correct person. Then, change pages. You will read statements 9 to 16 to Student A.

reservations	racquet	announcements	immunizations
favorite	stroller	matches	designing

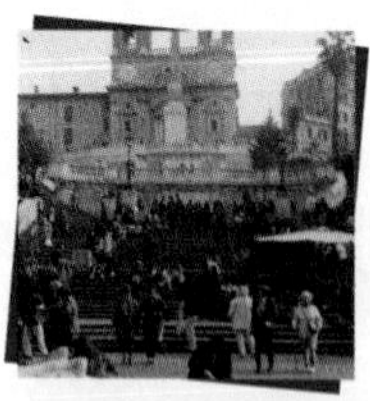

Henry is studying Italian.

____

____

Mr. and Mrs. Patel are planning a trip to San Antonio.

____

____

John loves to play tennis.

____

____

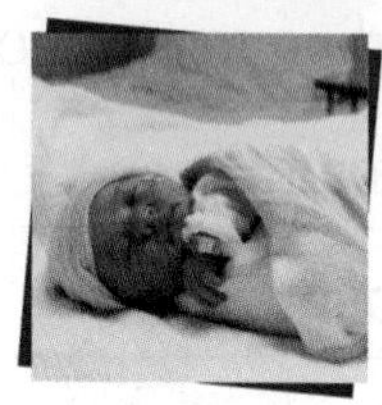

Sean and Tammy are new parents.

____

____

D. Pronunciation: *Wh-* questions. *Wh-* questions have rising/falling intonation. Listen and repeat these questions.

1. Where is he going?
2. Who are you e-mailing?
3. What is she studying?
4. Who is she calling?
5. What are you listening to?
6. What game is she playing?
7. What are you ordering?
8. What site are you looking at?

Listen. Then, practice this conversation with a partner.

A: What are you doing?
B: I'm ordering plane tickets.
A: What site are you using?
B: Wings.com.

Active Grammar: Present Continuous Questions

Am	I	
Are	you we they	playing video games?
Is	he she it	

Yes, you are.	No, you aren't.
Yes, I am.	No, I'm not.
Yes, we are.	No, we aren't.
Yes, they are.	No, they aren't.
Yes, he is.	No, he isn't.
Yes, she is.	No, she isn't.
Yes, it is.	No, it isn't.

A. Use the cues. Ask and answer questions about these computer activities.

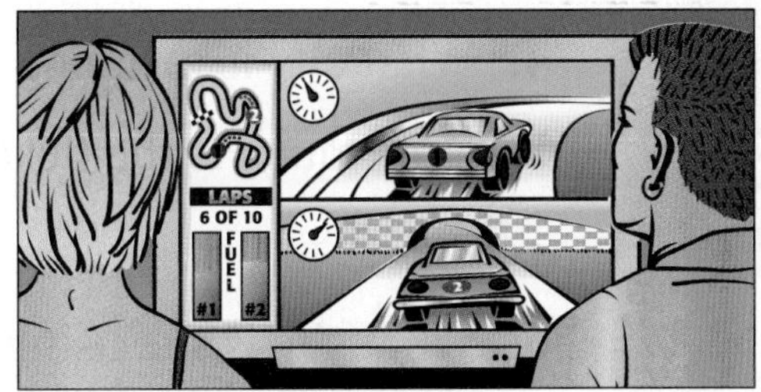

1. play video game?
2. check the prices of new cars?
3. write an e-mail to her boss?
4. write an e-mail to her friend?

5. buy airline tickets?
6. order a book?
7. get directions to Boston?
8. check weather in Boston?

B. Ask and answer questions about the students in this computer lab.

1. talk?
2. work together?
3. type?
4. listen to music?
5. sit?
6. look at the screen?
7. use headphones?

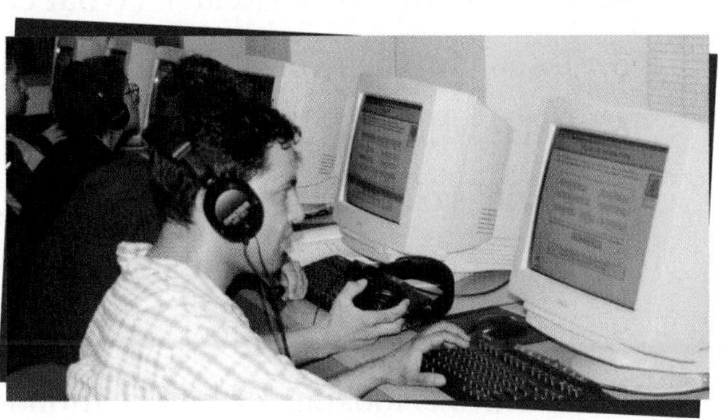

C. Look at the computer screens. Answer the questions.

What	am	I	doing? reading? sending?
	are	you we they	
	is	he she it	

1. What site is he looking at?
2. What is he buying?
3. What city is he leaving from?
4. What city is he flying to?
5. How much is the ticket?

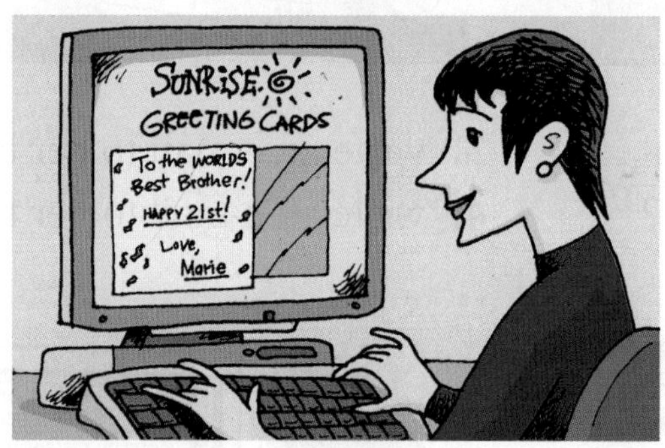

6. What site is she using?
7. What is she designing?
8. Who is she sending the card to?
9. Why is she sending him a card?
10. How old is her brother?

D. Read each statement. Then, ask and answer questions with a partner.

1. Mohammed is sending an e-mail. (Who / to?)
   Who is he sending an e-mail to? He's sending an e-mail to his boss.
2. Bob is ordering a CD. (Which CD?)
3. Rosa is applying for a loan. (Why?)
4. Irina is ordering a sweater. (What color sweater?)
5. Joseph is paying bills. (Which bills?)
6. Raj is writing a report. (What / about?)
7. Kevin is checking the weather. (What city / for?)
8. Barbara is ordering contacts. (What company / from?)
9. Philippe is buying a stock. (What stock?)
10. Gustavo is looking for information for his report. (Where?)

Active Grammar: Stative Verbs

Some verbs in English do not usually take the present continuous. They are called nonaction verbs or stative verbs.

hate	appear	agree	belong
like	feel	believe	cost
love	hear	forget	have
prefer	look (to appear)	know	need
	see	(not) mind	
	smell	remember	
	seem	think	
	sound	understand	
	taste		

I **have** a computer.	I'm **having** a good time. She **is having** a party.
I **think** he's a good teacher.	I'm **thinking** about my boyfriend.

A. Complete. Write the present or the present continuous form of the verbs.

1. I ________ (have) two computers, a desktop and a laptop.
2. Which word processing program ________ you ________ (prefer)?
3. I ________ (remember - negative) my password for this site.
4. I ________ (try) to find a good recipe for banana cake. This one ________ (sound) good.
5. They ________ (save) money to buy a computer. Their children ________ (need) one for school.
6. Hannah ________ (sit) in front of the computer. She ________ (look) confused. ________ she ________ (know) how to use a computer?
7. I ________ (like) this printer. The copies ________ (look) very clear.
8. A computer ________ (cost) from $500 to $2,000 dollars, but I ________ (think) we need to buy one.
9. My son ________ (belong) to the computer club at school. They ________ (make) a movie on the computer.

Active Grammar: Simple Present versus Present Continuous

Present Continuous	Simple Present	
now	usually	once a day
right now	never	every day
at this moment	always	every morning
at this time	sometimes	all the time

The present continuous describes actions that are taking place at the moment. The simple present describes a routine or habitual activity.

A. Complete with a time expression from the list above.

1. Linda is checking her e-mail ______________.
2. She receives about five e-mails ______________.
3. Shanta is looking at her horoscope ______________.
4. Bill ______________ makes airline reservations with a travel agent. He ______________ uses the airline Web site.
5. Sarah just finished her report for science. She is using the computer program's spell check ______________.
6. Stanley is taking a break ______________. He's playing a card game.
7. My Internet connection ______________ works very slowly.

B. Answer these questions about yourself. Then, ask your partner the questions and write the short answer.

Yes, I am. No, I'm not.	Yes, I do. No, I don't.	Yes, s/he is. No, s/he isn't.	Yes, s/he does. No, s/he doesn't.

	Me	My partner
1. Do you have a computer?	________	________
2. Are you using a computer now?	________	________
3. Do you have a cell phone with you?	________	________
4. Is your cell phone working?	________	________
5. Are you carrying a wallet?	________	________
6. Is your wallet in your pocket?	________	________
7. Do you have credit cards in your wallet?	________	________
8. Are you working with a partner now?	________	________
9. Do you often work with partners?	________	________
10. Are you writing now?	________	________

C. Listen to these conversations. Then, answer the questions.

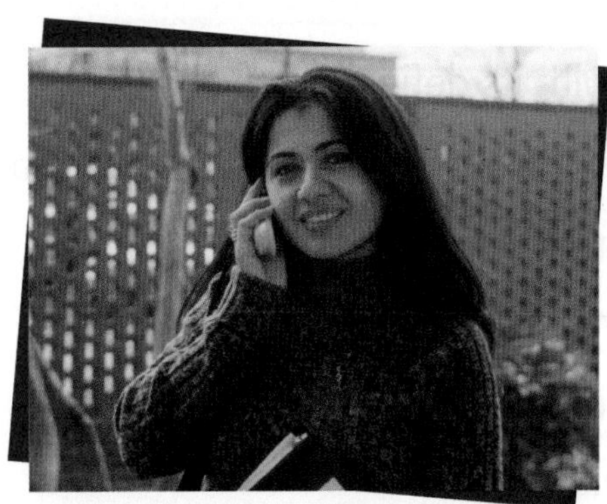

Conversation 1

1. What is Gloria doing?
2. Who is she talking to?
3. How many minutes does she get a month on her calling plan?
4. How long does she talk on the phone a day?

Conversation 2

5. What is Mary doing?
6. What is her son doing?
7. Where do her parents live?
8. How often do her children see them?

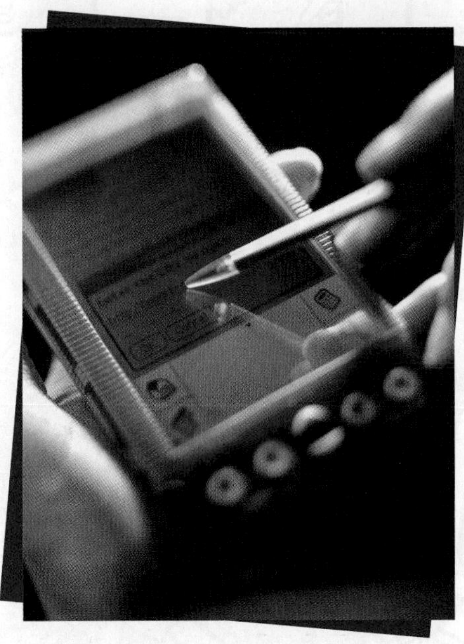

Conversation 3

9. What is a PDA?
10. Who is talking?
11. What kind of products is the woman ordering?
12. What information does Nam keep on his PDA?

D. How does it work? Do you have one of the devices listed below? Show the class the device. What do you use it for? Explain how it works.

cell phone	electronic dictionary
PDA / a hand-held	digital camera
beeper	laptop computer

The Big Picture: Cruiseaway.com

A. Vocabulary. Match each word or phrase with its definition.

__d__	**1.** site	**a.**	to fix errors in a computer program
__c__	**2.** tourist	**b.**	working well
__e__	**3.** design	**c.**	traveler
__a__	**4.** debug a program	**d.**	a location on the Web
__F__	**5.** up and running	**e.**	to plan
__F__	**6.** go down	**f.**	a travel company with ships
__h__	**7.** cruise line	**g.**	cookies, potato chips, pretzels, etc.
__g__	**8.** snacks	**h.**	stop working

B. Listen to the information about the Internet company Cruiseaway.com.

C. What is each person at Cruiseaway.com doing?

D. From the story, what information is true of small Internet companies? Circle *True* or *False*.

1. Many Internet companies are small. True False
2. All of the workers are young. True False
3. The office is informal. True False
4. The employees work long hours. True False
5. Men usually wear jackets and ties. True False
6. Most programmers are female. True False
7. It's important that the site is always working. True False

E. Read the questions. Listen to the story again. Then, answer the questions.

1. What information can travelers find at cruiseaway.com?
2. Does cruiseaway.com work with travelers directly?
3. Who do tourists call if they need more information?
4. What do most workers wear? What is Samip wearing?
5. Who is Michael talking to? Is Michael the manager?
6. What is Megan doing? What is she playing with?
7. Who is arriving? How does he get to work?
8. What hours does he work?
9. Why does one programmer always wear a beeper?
10. How many hours do most of the programmers work a day?

F. Complete. Write the simple present or the present continuous form of the verbs.

1. Megan ________________ with a stress ball now. She often ________________ with a stress ball while she works. (play)
2. At this moment, Antonio ________________ a break. He ________________ four or five breaks a day. (take)
3. Lee ________________ at work now. He ________________ at 10:00 every morning. (arrive)
4. Michael ________________ with six or seven cruise lines a day. He ________________ with a cruise line now. (talk)
5. Samip ________________ jeans today. He always ________________ jeans. (wear)

Do you use e-mail?
What program do you use?
Who do you e-mail?

A. Before You Read. Which icon do you need to click?

1. You want a paper copy of an e-mail. __________
2. You want to look up someone's e-mail address. __________
3. You want to answer an e-mail. __________
4. You want to write an e-mail to a friend. __________
5. You want to send an e-mail you received to another person. __________
6. You want to erase an e-mail you received. __________

For most of the twentieth century, people communicated by telephone or by mail. This is now changing, and e-mail (electronic mail) is becoming the preferred method of communication. It's faster than regular mail. It's cheaper than a postage stamp or a phone call. And for those who are concerned with the environment, it saves trees because it uses no paper.

There are several different e-mail programs, but most work the same way. When you click *New Mail*, a form appears on the screen. It asks you to type your e-mail address, the e-mail address of the person you are writing to, and the subject of your message. As you write, remember that there are several unwritten rules of e-mail communication.

Be polite and friendly. Start your message with a greeting. If you are writing to a friend, you can begin *Hi Sandra*. If you are writing your boss or your teacher, begin your message with *Dear Mr. Alonso*. You need a closing at the end of your e-mail. Many people just type their names. Others say *Bye*, *Cheers*, or use abbreviations like *BFN* ("bye for now"). If you are writing a business memo, you can use a more formal closing, such as *Sincerely* or *Thank you*. Remember that e-mail messages can be saved or forwarded to another person. Don't say anything that you will regret later. If you write to your friend and say, *I think Maria's new hairstyle makes her look ten years older*, she can save that message and then forward it to Maria when she's mad at you.

Look good. When someone receives an e-mail message from you, they might not know anything about you. They don't know your age, your race, your finances, your height, or your weight. They will judge you from your e-mail message, so make yourself look good. Type your message, then read it again aloud. Sometimes sentences seem clear when you write them, but don't make sense when you read them back. When typing a message, break it into paragraphs, and put a space between each paragraph. This makes your message easier to read. Use regular punctuation with small and capital letters. Some people use all capital letters to show that something is important. A message with all capital letters is called "flaming." It looks like you are angry or shouting. Before you send your message, click the spell check button on your e-mail to check your spelling and typing.

Organize your e-mail. If you start to use your e-mail several times a week, your message box will soon fill with mail. After a few weeks, you can have a list of 60 or 70 messages! It is easy to delete the messages you don't want anymore. If your messages are important, you can save them in folders. If you aren't sure how to save or organize your e-mail, ask a friend. It only takes about five minutes to learn. After you become comfortable with e-mail, you will seldom use snail mail (i.e., regular mail) again.

B. Vocabulary. Match each word with its meaning.

______ **1.** folders	**a.** the opening of a letter
______ **2.** e-mail	**b.** files for messages
______ **3.** snail mail	**c.** a short form of a word or phrase
______ **4.** greeting	**d.** feel sorry about
______ **5.** closing	**e.** a message with all capital letters
______ **6.** flaming	**f.** electronic mail
______ **7.** regret	**g.** the end of a letter
______ **8.** abbreviation	**h.** regular mail

C. Read each statement. Then, write *T* for true or *F* for false.

______ **1.** E-mail is more expensive than regular mail.

______ **2.** You should open your e-mail message with a greeting.

______ **3.** People might judge you on the looks of your e-mail.

______ **4.** If you want to show that information is important, use capital letters.

______ **5.** If you don't want a message anymore, you can save it in a folder.

______ **6.** If you are mad at your sister, it is a good idea to wait a day or two before you e-mail her.

Writing Our Stories: E-mail Messages

A. Read.

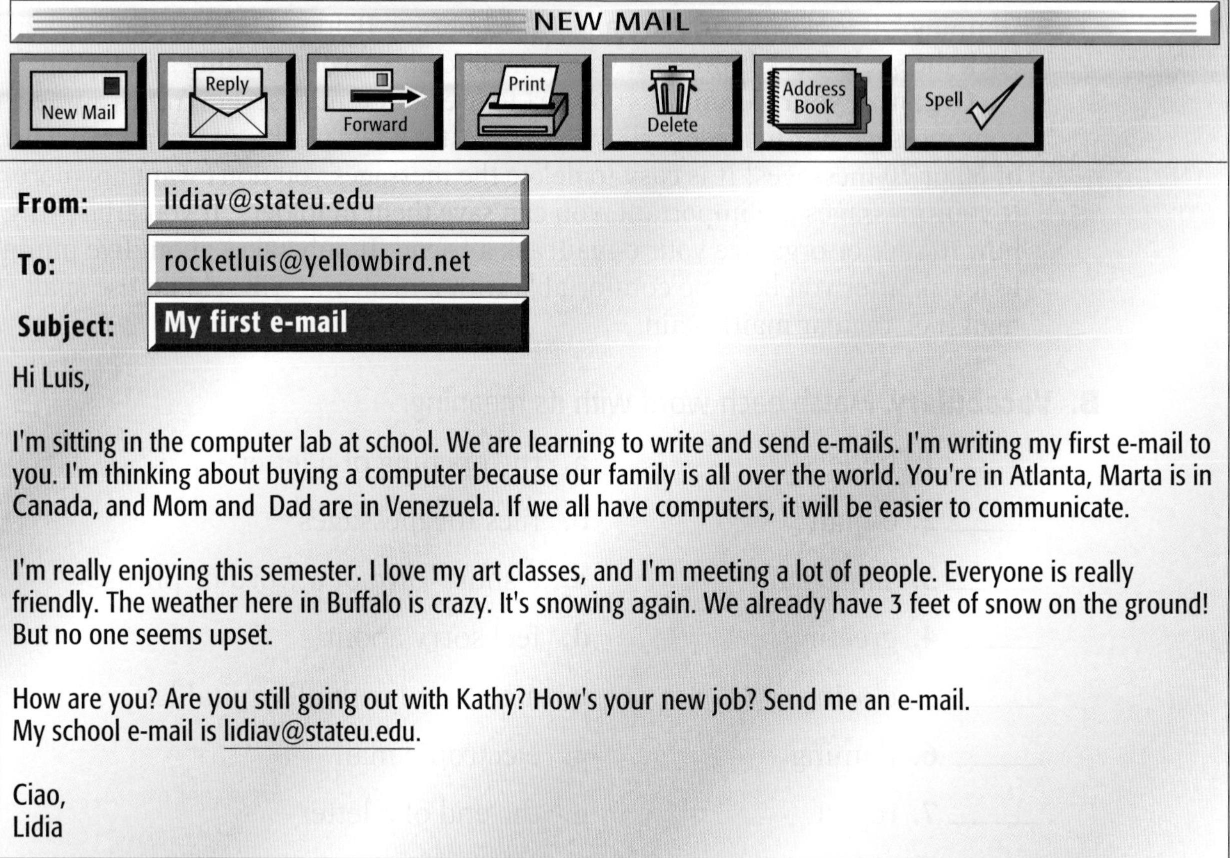

NEW MAIL

New Mail | Reply | Forward | Print | Delete | Address Book | Spell

From: lidiav@stateu.edu

To: rocketluis@yellowbird.net

Subject: **My first e-mail**

Hi Luis,

I'm sitting in the computer lab at school. We are learning to write and send e-mails. I'm writing my first e-mail to you. I'm thinking about buying a computer because our family is all over the world. You're in Atlanta, Marta is in Canada, and Mom and Dad are in Venezuela. If we all have computers, it will be easier to communicate.

I'm really enjoying this semester. I love my art classes, and I'm meeting a lot of people. Everyone is really friendly. The weather here in Buffalo is crazy. It's snowing again. We already have 3 feet of snow on the ground! But no one seems upset.

How are you? Are you still going out with Kathy? How's your new job? Send me an e-mail.
My school e-mail is lidiav@stateu.edu.

Ciao,
Lidia

B. Answer.

1. Who is writing this e-mail?
2. Who is she writing to?
3. Is she using her own computer? Where is the computer she is using?
4. Does she have a student account? Can other students read her e-mail?

C. Edit. Find and correct the mistakes in these sentences.

1. She is ~~send~~ sending an e-mail.
2. She learning how to use a computer.
3. The school have a computer lab.
4. She sits in the lab right now.
5. You writing an e-mail to your brother?

6. How everything with you?
7. What classes she is taking?
8. Does she has a computer?
9. She is meet a lot of people.
10. You are still going out with Kathy?

D. Write an e-mail to a friend or classmate in this message box.

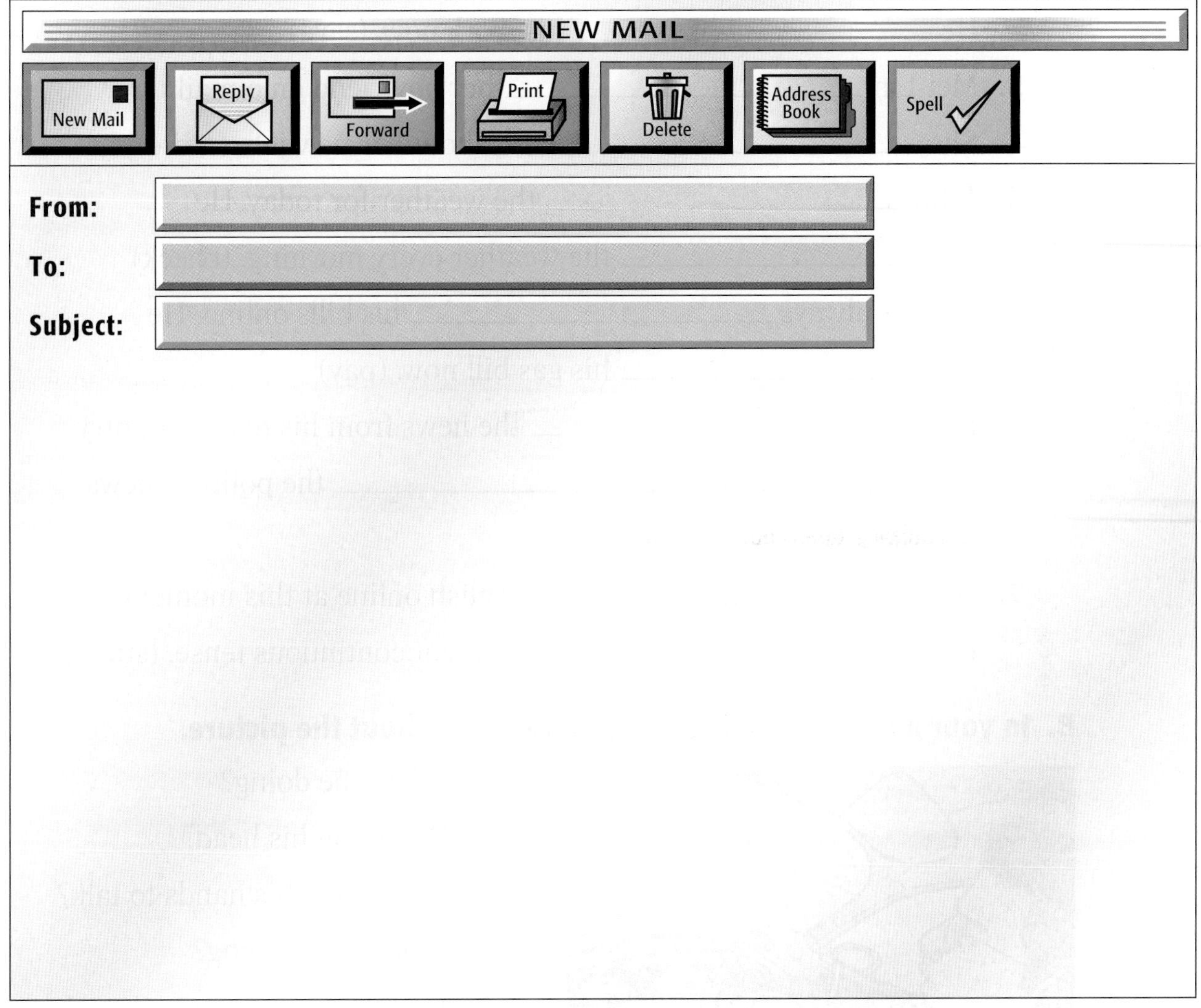

Looking at the Internet

Spend some time on the Internet. If you don't have access to a computer, visit your public library or school library. Find a Web site you enjoy. Print the home page. Tell your classmates about the site. What is the address? What is on the site?

Practice on Your Own

A. Complete. Write the verbs in the correct tense—simple present or present continuous.

1. Gina usually ______________________ on her desktop computer, but today she ______________________ on her laptop computer. (work)
2. Simon ______________________ his work every ten minutes. He ______________________ his work now. (save)
3. Mei-Lin ______________________ her boyfriend an e-mail now. She ______________________ him about her new job. (write)
4. John ______________________ the weather for today. He ______________________ the weather every morning. (check)
5. Charles always ______________________ his bills online. He ______________________ his gas bill now. (pay)
6. Pierre ______________________ the news from his native country every day. He always ______________________ the political news and the sports page. (read)
7. Hans ______________________ English online at this moment. He ______________________ the present continuous tense. (study)

B. In your notebook, answer these questions about the picture.

1. What's he doing?
2. What's on his head?
3. Is he using his hands to talk?
4. Where is he going?
5. Does he know the way?
6. How is he getting directions?
7. What is he drinking?
8. Is he paying attention to the road?
9. Is he wearing his seat belt?
10. What's the weather like?

Grammar Summary

▶ 1. Present continuous tense

In the present continuous tense, we talk about an action that is happening now.

He**'s using** his computer.
She**'s checking** her e-mail.

Some common time expressions are: *now, right now, at this moment, at the present time.*

▶ 2. Statements

I	**am** **am not**	**working.**
He She It	**is** **isn't**	
We You They	**are** **aren't**	

▶ 3. *Yes/No* questions

		Short answers	
Am I **paying** bills?	Yes, you are.	No, you aren't.	No, you're not.
Are you **buying** a ticket?	Yes, I am.		No, I'm not.
Is he **reading** the news?	Yes, he is.	No, he isn't.	No, he's not.
Is it **working**?	Yes, it is.	No, it isn't.	No, it's not.
Are we **doing** this right?	Yes, you are.	No, you aren't.	No, you're not.
Are you **watching** a movie?	Yes, we are.	No, we aren't.	No, we're not.
Are they **playing** a game?	Yes, they are.	No, they aren't.	No, they're not.

▶ 4. *Wh-* questions

What **are** you **writing?**	A report.
Who **is** he **sending** an e-mail to?	His brother.
What **are** they **doing?**	Playing card games.
What **is** she **ordering?**	Airline tickets.
Where **are** we **going?**	To the computer store.

▶ 5. Spelling

1. Most verbs → add ***-ing***: walk**ing**, talk**ing**
2. Verbs that end with ***e*** → drop the ***e*** and add ***-ing***: writ**ing**, mak**ing**
3. One-syllable words that end with a consonant, vowel, consonant → double the final consonant (except ***x, y,*** or ***z***): sit**ting**, shop**ping**, pay**ing**

6 A Healthy Lifestyle

A. Staying healthy. Discuss each picture. Where is each person? What is happening? What else happens during a physical or an examination at the doctor's?

have a physical	take an X ray	write a prescription
eye chart	fill a cavity	give a urine specimen
check cholesterol	examine	take a blood sample
immunization	listen to heart	check blood pressure

1

2
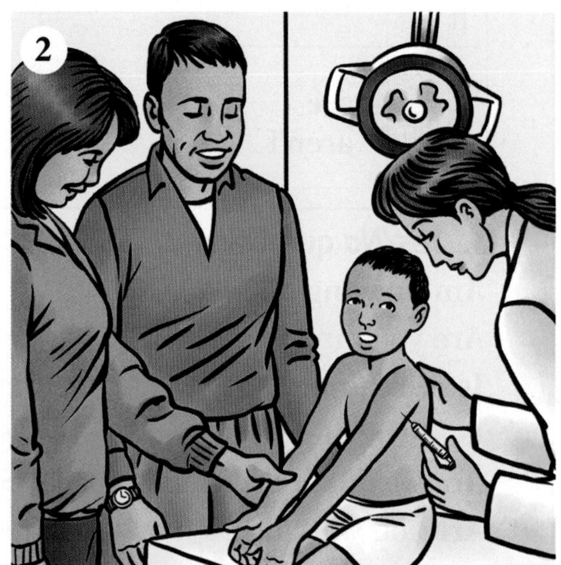

3
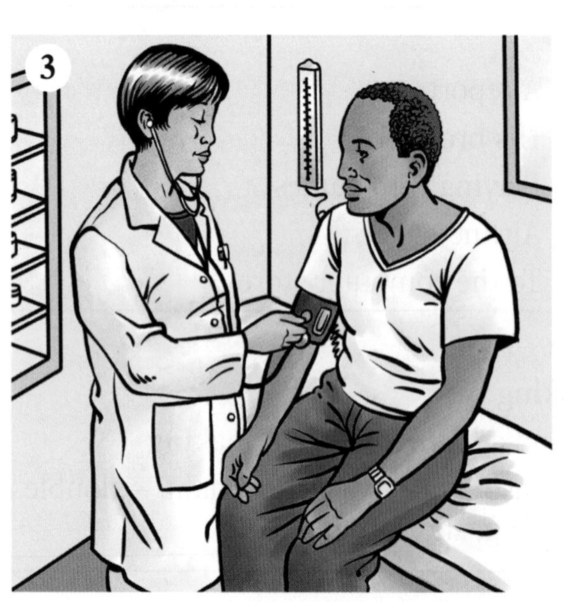

4

Active Grammar: Future—*Going to*

Future: *be* + *going to* + verb

I	am	going to	see a cardiologist.
He She It	is		call a cardiologist.
We You They	are		need a cardiologist.

A. Listen to the names of these doctors. Mark the stressed syllable.

súr·geon	pe·di·a·tri·cian	ob·ste·tri·cian	gy·ne·col·o·gist
car·di·ól·o·gist	fam·i·ly doc·tor	gen·er·al prac·ti·tion·er	al·ler·gist
oph·thal·mol·o·gist	in·ter·nist	der·ma·tol·o·gist	psy·chi·a·trist

Listen again. Repeat the name of each doctor.

B. What kind of doctor is each person going to see?

1. Roy has a bad rash on his face. *He's going to see a dermatologist.*
2. Phil has high blood pressure.
3. Henry is feeling very depressed.
4. Paola thinks that she is pregnant.
5. Nancy and José have a new baby.
6. Linn has a new job and she needs a physical.
7. Pierre is having trouble reading the words on the board.
8. Jack's son coughs a lot. Sometimes he is short of breath after playing outside.
9. Tim has the flu.

Culture Note

If a person needs a specialist, his family doctor will suggest one. People also find the name of a specialist by asking their friends or co-workers.

C. Ayumi has the flu. Use the cues and talk about her day. What is she going to do? What isn't she going to do?

- go to work
- stay in bed
- take aspirin
- use a heating pad
- drink a lot of fluids
- watch TV
- do her homework
- take a shower
- take a walk
- do the food shopping

D. What are your plans for today? Sit with a partner. Ask these questions. Write your partner's response and your response.

1. What are you going to do after school?

_______________ is going to _______________________________

(your partner's name)

I am going to _______________________________________

2. What are you going to do this evening?

____

____

3. Are you going to exercise? If yes, what are you going to do?

____

____

4. When are you going to do your homework?

____

____

5. What time are you going to go to bed?

____

____

Questions

Yes/No Questions		
Are you going to see the doctor?	Yes, I am.	No, I'm not.
Is she going to make an appointment?	Yes, she is.	No, she isn't.
Is it going to hurt?	Yes, it is.	No, it isn't.
Are they going to visit me?	Yes, they are.	No, they aren't.

A. George sprained his ankle while he was playing basketball. Read the doctor's orders. Then, answer the questions.

Elevate your leg.

Put an ice pack on your ankle several times a day for two or three days.

In a few days, after the swelling goes down, use a heating pad.

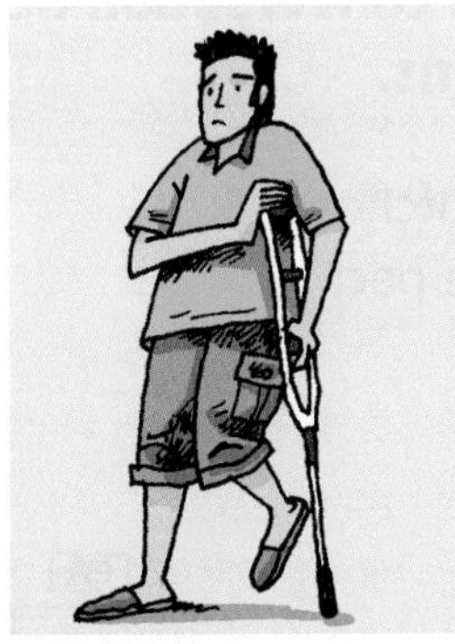

Use crutches this week.

During the day, use an elastic bandage.

Take aspirin or ibuprofen for pain.

1. Does George have a bad sprain? Yes he does
2. Does he have a broken ankle? No he dosn't
3. Is he going to use an ice pack today? no he isen't
4. Is he going to elevate his leg? Yes he is
5. Is he going to use a heating pad today? no he isen't
6. Is he going to need crutches this week? Yes he is
7. Does he need an elastic bandage? Yes he does
8. Is he going to take aspirin for the pain? yes he is
9. Can he walk on his ankle? no he can
10. Is George going to go to work today? no he isent

B. Find someone who. . . . Stand up, walk around the room, and ask your classmates these questions about their plans for the year. Try to find someone who answers *Yes* for each question. Write that student's name on the line.

Are you going to join a health club?	No, I'm not. (Continue to ask other students.)
Are you going to join a health club?	Yes, I am. (Write that student's name.)

1. join a health club? ________________
2. change jobs? ________________
3. visit your native country? ________________
4. buy a house? ________________
5. move? ________________
6. get married? ________________
7. get a driver's license? ________________
8. buy a computer? ________________

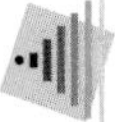

C. Discuss the new vocabulary. Then, listen to the conversation between Mr. West and the doctor. Answer these questions.

broken leg	swollen	tetanus	crutches
cast	swelling	painkiller	ice pack

1. What's the matter with Jimmy?
2. Is the doctor looking at the X rays?
3. What is the nurse putting on Jimmy's leg? Why?
4. How long is Jimmy going to stay in the hospital?
5. When is the doctor going to put a cast on his leg?
6. How long is Jimmy going to be in a cast?
7. What kind of shot is the doctor going to give him?
8. What are they going to give him for pain?
9. When can he go to school?
10. Is he going to need crutches?

Wh-questions

When	am	I	going to	come?
Where	is	he she it		operate?
Why	are	we you they		exercise?

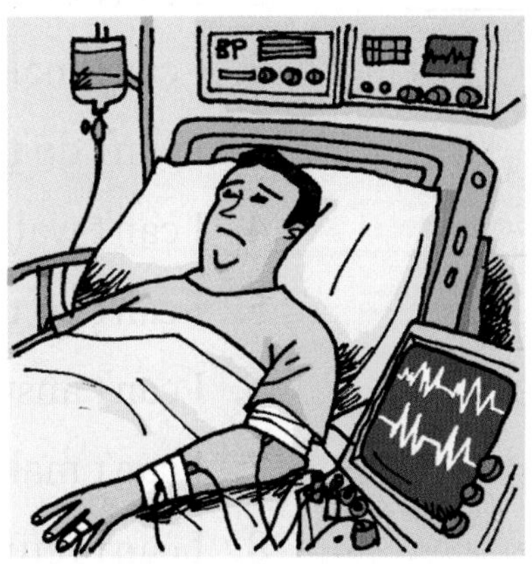

D. Student to student dictation: A hospital visit.
Student A: Turn to page 241.
Student B: Listen to Student A and write the questions. When you finish, change pages. You will read five new questions to Student A.

1. How Are You Feeling ______?
2. Are you going to need an operation ______?
3. How long Are You going to [illegible] ______?
4. ______?
5. ______?

Look at the picture to ask and answer the questions above. Use your imagination!

Active Grammar: Future—*Will*

Use *will* to talk about actions and plans in the future.
Use *will* to express a promise or an offer to help.
Use *will* to make predictions.
Use *will* to talk about possibility or uncertain future.

She **will** see the doctor tomorrow.	She**'ll** see the doctor tomorrow.
I **will** answer the phone.	I**'ll** answer the phone.

A. Pronunciation: *I'll.* Listen and repeat.

1. I'll help you.
2. I'll call her.
3. I'll drive you.
4. I'll make dinner.
5. I'll visit you.
6. I'll take you to the doctor.
7. I'll pick up your prescription.
8. I'll see you tomorrow.

Practice the sentences with a partner.

B. Your sister has a broken leg and needs help for a few weeks. Offer to help her. Pay attention to the pronunciation of *I'll*.

1. I can't drive the children to school.
2. I can't make dinner.
3. I can't do the laundry.
4. I can't walk the dog.
5. I can't do the food shopping.
6. I can't answer the phone.
7. I can't make the beds.
8. I can't return those library books.
9. I can't mail these letters.
10. I can't wash my hair.
11. I can't deposit my paycheck.
12. I can't change that light bulb.

> Use *it, them, him,* or *her* for the underlined words.
>
> I can't drive the children to school.
> I'll drive **them** to school.
>
> I can't make dinner.
> I'll make **it**.

C. Sit with a small group and read these predictions about the future. Decide if you agree or disagree with each one. Give your reasons.

Prediction	I agree	I disagree
1. Most people will live to be 100.		
2. There will be a cure for cancer.		
3. Health care will be free.		
4. People will decide the sex of their children.		
5. Most cars will run on electricity.		
6. Most homes will have big screen TVs.		

How will life be different twenty years from now? With your group, write one future prediction about each topic.

Computers: ______________________

Jobs: ______________________

Health: ______________________

Immigration: ______________________

D. George went to the doctor with chest pains. He didn't have a heart attack, but the doctor is concerned about his lifestyle. Read the doctor's advice. Will George listen to his recommendations?

Statements that show possibility or uncertainty:
I think he will change his diet.
He will *probably* change his diet.
He might change his diet.
He may change his diet.

Change your diet.
Stop smoking.
Get more sleep.
Start to exercise.
Use less salt.
Lower your cholesterol.
Cut down on sweets.
Get a pet.
Walk to work.
Lose weight.

E. Read each situation. What will happen? Use *I think, probably,* or *may/might* in your answers.

1. Trudy has two children, Anna and Gregory. Anna just came home from school with red spots on her face and neck.

2. Cindy was walking home from work a few minutes ago. She passed a man who was walking his dog. The dog jumped at Cindy and bit her leg.

The Big Picture: The Accident

A. Discuss the vocabulary.

witness	blood pressure	blanket
pressure bandage	IV	windshield
bleeding	stretcher	concussion

B. Listen to the story. Then, complete the sentences with the new vocabulary.

1. Luis is ____________________ heavily, so the emergency worker is applying a ____________________ to his arm.
2. The emergency worker is taking Luis's ____________________.
3. The woman is lying on a ____________________.
4. She might have a ____________________.
5. The ____________________ of her car is broken.

C. Answer these questions about the story.

1. Describe Luis's injuries.
2. What are the emergency medical workers doing?
3. Why are they going to start an IV?
4. What is going to happen to him at the hospital?
5. Describe the woman's injuries.
6. What is going to happen to her at the hospital?
7. Whose injuries are more serious?

D. Complete. Write the future or the present continuous form of the verbs.

1. Luis ________________ (lie) by the side of the road.
2. An emergency worker ________________ (apply) a pressure bandage.
3. The workers ________________ (start) an IV.
4. They ________________ (take) him to the hospital.
5. The workers ________________ (put) a woman in the ambulance.
6. A doctor ________________ (examine) her carefully.
7. A police officer ________________ (direct) traffic.
8. He ________________ (file) an accident report.
9. When Luis gets to the hospital, he ________________ (need) thirty stitches.
10. The doctor ________________ (keep) him in the hospital overnight.

E. Listen and circle the correct answer.

1.	a. Yes, he is.	b. No, he isn't.	c. Yes, he does.	d. No, he doesn't.
2.	a. Yes, he is.	b. No, he isn't.	c. Yes, he does.	d. No, he doesn't.
3.	a. Yes, she is.	b. No, she isn't.	c. Yes, she does.	d. No, she doesn't.
4.	a. Yes, she is.	b. No, she isn't.	c. Yes, she does.	d. No, she doesn't.
5.	a. Yes, she is.	b. No, she isn't.	c. Yes, she does.	d. No, she doesn't.
6.	a. Yes, she is.	b. No, she isn't.	c. Yes, she does.	d. No, she doesn't.
7.	a. Yes, he is.	b. No, he isn't.	c. Yes, he does.	d. No, he doesn't.

Reading: Asthma

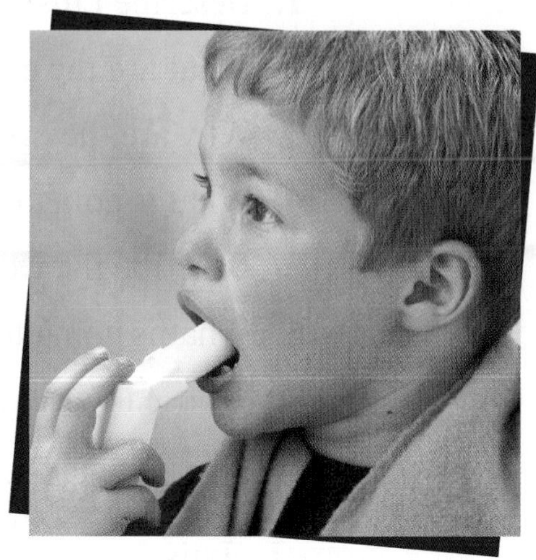

A. Before You Read.

1. What do you know about asthma?
2. Does anyone in your family have asthma? What treatment is this person receiving?

Ricky Garcia is going to play outside with his friends. He is taking out his inhaler and taking two puffs. Five minutes later, he's on the field with his friends, running after a soccer ball. Ricky has asthma, but he knows how to control it.

Asthma is a lung disease. The airways of the lungs become swollen and **inflamed,** making it difficult to breathe normally. A person with asthma may have wheezing, coughing, a tight feeling in the chest, or shortness of breath. Serious breathing problems are called **asthma attacks.** They may be mild or very serious, requiring immediate medical attention.

Asthma can begin at any age. Childhood asthma, often beginning when a child is younger than 10 years old, is one of the most common childhood diseases. Doctors report that the number of young people with asthma is increasing, with over four million children affected by the disease. It is the number one cause of absence from school. Asthma is often **genetic.** If a parent has asthma, the children are more likely to develop the disease. Children in homes where an adult smokes are more **at risk** for asthma. Children with asthma need to be under a doctor's care. They and their parents can learn to understand this condition and learn how to handle the symptoms.

It is important to find out the "**triggers**" for asthma. In other words, what starts the attack? The most common triggers are exercise, viral infections, stress, and **irritants** like dust, pollen, or animals. Once a child learns the triggers, he can help prevent future attacks.

There are two kinds of asthma medications—control drugs and quick-relief drugs. Children take control drugs once or twice a day to help prevent asthma attacks. If a child begins to have an asthma attack, a quick-relief drug is necessary. This is often an inhaler. School-aged children usually carry their inhalers with them. This medication works quickly and children begin to breathe more easily in a few minutes. If a child has a serious asthma attack, he may need emergency care at a hospital or a doctor's office.

About half of all children **outgrow** asthma and their asthma attacks stop when they are teenagers. However, many people live with the disease into adulthood.

B. Vocabulary: Definitions in context. These words are in **bold print** in the article. Find the definition of each word in the same sentence or in an adjoining sentence.

1. inflamed ______swollen______
2. asthma attacks ____________
3. genetic ____________
4. at risk ____________
5. triggers ____________
6. irritants ____________
7. outgrow ____________

C. What do you understand about asthma? Circle *T* for True; or *F* for False.

1. Asthma can begin when a child is three years old. T F
2. If a parent smokes, a child is more likely to develop asthma. T F
3. Allergies trigger all asthma attacks. T F
4. An inhaler can help if a child begins to have an asthma attack. T F
5. A parent must take the child to the hospital for every asthma attack. T F
6. Many children with asthma need to take daily medication. T F
7. A child with asthma has breathing problems. T F
8. There is no way to control asthma. T F

D. Read these suggestions for protecting the child with asthma. What other suggestions can you think of?

Protecting the Child with Asthma

- Take your child to the doctor. Develop a plan together to handle the condition.
- Use an air conditioner at home and in your car.
- Don't use feather pillows.
- Clean when your child is not home.
- Do not use products with strong smells or fragrances.
- When it's very cold, you may need to limit the time your child can play outdoors.
- Decide if your child can tolerate a pet in the house.

Writing Our Stories: My Health

A. Take this health survey about your lifestyle.

Questions	
1. Do you smoke?	Yes No
2. Do you drive everywhere?	Yes No
3. Do you exercise three or more times a week?	Yes No
4. Do you play a sport regularly?	Yes No
5. Do you eat fresh fruit and vegetables every day?	Yes No
6. Do you eat much fried food?	Yes No
7. Do you always put salt on your food?	Yes No
8. Do you take vitamins?	Yes No
9. Do you drink a lot of caffeine?	Yes No
10. Do you eat a lot of sweets?	Yes No
11. Do you sleep at least six or seven hours a night?	Yes No
12. Do you drink six to eight glasses of water a day?	Yes No

B. Read this student's story about her lifestyle.

My diet is very healthy. In the morning, I eat a good breakfast. I always have fruit and then I have cereal or yogurt. There's a small cafeteria at work and I order soup or a salad for lunch. For dinner, I usually stir-fry some vegetables and meat and eat that with rice. But, my diet isn't perfect. First, I use too much salt. I love to put soy sauce on my food, but from now on I'm going to buy light soy sauce. Also, I drink three or four cups of coffee every day. I need a cup of real coffee in the morning. I'm going to try to drink decaf in the afternoon and evening.

Unfortunately, I don't exercise enough. I work and I go to school, so it's hard to find the time. There's a park near my house. I will try to walk there for 30 minutes on Saturdays and Sundays. At school, my classroom is on the third floor. I usually take the elevator, but from now on I'm going to take the stairs.

C. Infinitives. Complete each sentence with an infinitive after the verb.

> Many verbs take the infinitive form. Use an infinitive after *try, need, plan, like,* and *love.*
>
> An infinitive is *to* + the simple form of the verb.
> I will try **to walk** in the park.
> I love **to put** salt on my food.

1. I will try ______________________ (exercise) more.
2. I plan ______________________ (walk) to work.
3. I like ______________________ (eat) sweets, especially chocolate.
4. I need ______________________ (lose) twenty pounds.
5. I will try ______________________ (go) to bed earlier.

D. Write about your lifestyle. Talk about the things you do that are healthy. Then, explain one or two things you would like to change.

E. Edit. Find and correct the mistakes in these sentences.

1. I ~~not~~ don't smoke.
2. I need to drinking more water.
3. I going to walk to school.
4. I will going to take vitamins.
5. I am going use less salt.
6. I might to join a health club.
7. I go to eat more fruit and vegetables.

Looking at the Internet

There are many excellent health sites on the Internet. Find one site that talks about health.

Name of Internet site: ______________________________

URL: ______________________________

This site includes information about the following (circle all that apply):

Diseases and conditions	Drugs
Prescription medicines	Diet and nutrition
Fitness	Pregnancy
First aid	Mental health
Alternative medicine	

A. Complete these conversations. Use the simple present, present continuous, or future tense form of the verbs.

1. **A:** My sister is in the hospital. The doctor thinks she ______________ kidney stones. (have)

   B: ________ she ______________ an operation? (need)

   A: The doctor ______________ (negative—know). They ______________ some tests now. (do)

   B: When ________ they ______________ the results? (know)

   A: Tomorrow.

2. **A:** My brother is in the hospital. He ______________ (need) bypass surgery.

   B: When ________ they ______________? (operate)

   A: Tomorrow.

   B: When ________ you ______________ him? (visit)

   A: Tonight.

3. **A:** How's your leg?

   B: Much better. I ______________ happy when the cast comes off. (be)

   A: When ________ the doctor ______________ the cast? (remove)

   B: Tomorrow!

   A: When ________ you ______________ to work? (return)

   B: Next week.

B. How is each person going to change his or her lifestyle? Write two or three sentences about each picture. Use your imagination!

Example: Susan only drinks one or two glasses of water a day. She's going to keep a glass of water on her desk and try to drink six or seven glasses a day.

Grammar Summary

▶ 1. Future: *be + going to*

Be + going to talks about actions and plans in the future.

I'm going to walk in the park later.

He**'s going** to see an allergist next week.

▶ 2. Future time expressions

tomorrow	next week	soon
the day after tomorrow	next month	in the future
in a few minutes	next year	someday
in a little while		

▶ 3. *Yes/No* questions

Are you **going to call** the doctor?	Yes, I am.	No, I'm not.
Is he **going to make** an appointment?	Yes, he is.	No, he isn't.
Are they **going to join** a health club?	Yes, they are.	No, they aren't.

▶ 4. *Wh-* questions

What **are** you **going to buy?**

When **is** the doctor **going to operate?**

Where **are** you **going to walk?**

▶ 5. Future: *will*

Will expresses a promise or an offer to help.	**I'll drive** you.
Will is used to make predictions.	They **will find** a cure.
Will talks about possibility or uncertain future.	He **will** probably **operate** tomorrow.
Will talks about actions and plans in the future.	I **will visit** my sister tomorrow.

▶ 6. *Yes/No* questions

Will you **make** dinner tonight?	Yes, I will.	No, I won't.
Will she **stay** home from work?	Yes, she will.	No, she won't.
Will they **visit** John?	Yes, they will.	No, they won't.

▶ 7. *Wh-* questions

When **will** you **call** me?

How **will** he **change** his diet?

Where **will** they **meet** you?

7 People and Places

A. Sandra and Patricia. Sandra and Patricia are twin sisters from Colombia. Sandra is on the left, and Patricia is on the right. They are the same in many ways, but they are also different. Read Sandra and Patricia's conversation. What's the same? What's different?

Sandra: When we were young, about fifteen years old, we liked to wear the same clothes.

Patricia: But now, Sandra likes to wear **younger clothes than** I do. I like to wear **more mature** clothes.

Sandra: Patricia is **healthier than** I am. I get more colds. Patricia is **luckier than** I am.

Patricia: We don't live together now, but we talk almost every day; sometimes we talk a few times a day.

Sandra: I like to travel **more often than** Patricia does, but we both like to dance.

Active Grammar: Comparative Adjectives

A. Write each adjective in the correct column.

short	tall	healthy	talkative	beautiful
shy	friendly	handsome	interesting	serious
small	thin	heavy	quiet	hardworking
lazy	athletic	big	pretty	long

Irregular Comparative Forms
good—better than
bad—worse than
little—less than

One-syllable adjectives	Two-syllable adjectives, ending with *-y*	Two or more syllables, not ending with *-y*
short	lazy	athletic
shy	lazy	helthy
big	pretty	talkativ
twin	heavy	beautiful
tall	athletic	interesting
long	friendly	hardworking

B. Write the comparative form of each adjective in the chart below.

One-syllable adjectives	Two-syllable adjectives, ending with *-y*	Two or more syllables, not ending with *-y*
shorter than	lazier than	more athletic than
lazy than	youngerclothes than	more beautiful than
More Mature	healthier than	more interestingthan
shier than	more often than	more heavy than
smaler than	Fridlier than	more ethletic than
taller than	healther than	more talkative than
Bigger than	heavier than	more Friendly than
longer than	prettier than	more serius than

C. Pronunciation. Listen and repeat the comparative adjectives in the chart above.

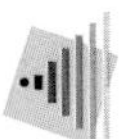

D. Two brothers. Listen and complete the sentences about Jack and Julian.

1. Jack is ___more serious than___ Julian.
2. Jack is ___more short ah___ Julian.
3. Jack is ___more lazy ah___ Julian.
4. Jack is ________________ Julian.
5. Julian is ________________ Jack.
6. Julian is ________________ Jack.
7. Julian is ________________ Jack.
8. Julian is ________________ Jack.

E. Two Sisters. Look at the picture and compare Lilia and Louisa.

1. Lilia is ___thinner than___ Louisa.
2. Lilia is ___More healthy___ Louisa.
3. Louisa is ________________ Lilia.
4. Louisa is ________________ Lilia.
5. Louisa is ________________ Lilia.
6. Louisa is ________________ Lilia.
7. Louisa's hair is ________________ Lilia's hair.
8. Lilia's hair is ________________ Louisa's hair.

healthy
thin
heavy
attractive
long
short
lazy
athletic

F. Use the adjectives in the box to compare the two famous people in the photos.

Who is more famous?
__________ is more famous than __________.

famous	beautiful	popular	intelligent	attractive	funny	talented

as . . . as, not as . . . as

My son is **as tall as** I am.
Meaning: I am 5'11" tall. My son is also 5'11" tall.

My son is **not as athletic as** I am.
Meaning: I run or exercise five days a week.
My son exercises five days a month.

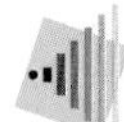

A. Like father, like son. Listen and complete the sentences.

1. Roger is ___as___ ___tall___ ___as___ Charles.
2. Roger is __________ __________ __________ __________ his father.
3. Charles is not __________ __________ __________ Roger.
4. Charles is __________ __________ __________ Roger.
5. Charles is __________ __________ __________ __________ Roger.
6. Roger is __________ __________ __________ Charles.

B. Student to student dictation.
Student A: Turn to page 242.
Student B: Write the sentences Student A dictates. When you finish, change pages.

1. ______________________________
______________________________.
2. ______________________________
______________________________.
3. ______________________________
______________________________.
4. ______________________________
______________________________.
5. ______________________________
______________________________.

C. What's your opinion? With a group of students, take turns asking and giving your opinion? Use *as . . . as.*

1. Chinese food / Italian food / tasty
2. Books / newspapers / interesting
3. People in the city / people in the country / friendly
4. Movies / TV / enjoyable
5. Home-cooked food / fast food / delicious
6. English / Mandarin Chinese / difficult

Comparing Lives

A. Answer the questions about your daily schedule and habits.

Questions	You	Your Partner
1. What time do you get up?		
2. What do you eat for breakfast?		
3. How many hours a week do you work?		
4. Is your job stressful?		
5. How many people are there in your family?		
6. How many hours a day do you watch TV?		
7. How many hours a night do you sleep?		

B. Ask your partner the same questions. Write the answers.

C. Circle the best answer to complete the sentences.

1. I get up **as early as / earlier than / later than** my partner.
2. I eat **as much as / more than / less than** my partner.
3. I work **as much as / more than / less than** my partner.
4. My job is **as stressful as / more stressful than / less stressful than** my partner's.
5. My family is **as large as / not as large as / larger than** my partner's.
6. I watch TV **as often as / more often than / less often than** my partner.
7. I sleep **as many hours as / more hours than / fewer hours than** my partner.

Comparing Places: My Neighborhood

A. Look at the picture above. Compare the neighborhood where you live now with the neighborhood in the picture. Use the adjectives from the list. You can use *as . . . as* , *not as . . . as* , ____*er than,* or *more* ____ *than.*

> My neighborhood is busier than this neighborhood.
> My neighborhood is not as convenient as this neighborhood.

convenient	crowded	noisy	safe
busy	quiet	clean	modern
old	dangerous	expensive	

A. Look at the picture on page 102. Complete each statement with *is* or *are* and *less, fewer,* or *more,* comparing your neighborhood with the picture.

> **less**—non-count nouns
> There is **less traffic** in my neighborhood
>
> **fewer**—count nouns
> There are **fewer apartment buildings** in my neighborhood.

1. There _______ __________ traffic in my neighborhood.
2. There _______ __________ restaurants in my neighborhood.
3. There _______ __________ movie theaters in my neighborhood.
4. There _______ __________ parking in my neighborhood.
5. There _______ __________ places for children in my neighborhood.
6. There _______ __________ entertainment in my neighborhood.
7. There _______ __________ laundromats in my neighborhood.
8. There _______ __________ coffee shops in my neighborhood.
9. There _______ __________ shopping in my neighborhood.

Write two more sentences, comparing your neighborhood and the one in the picture. Then, read your sentences to a partner.

____

____

B. Neighborhood improvements. What does your neighborhood need? Complete the sentences about your neighborhood.

1. My neighborhood needs more ______________________.
2. My neighborhood needs more ______________________.
3. My neighborhood needs fewer ______________________.
4. My neighborhood needs fewer ______________________.
5. My neighborhood needs less ______________________.

Read your sentences to a partner.

The Big Picture: Two Cities

Austin

Boston

A. Listen and complete the information about two cities—Austin, Texas, and Boston, Massachusetts.

	Austin	Boston
Population		
Unemployment Rate		
State Tax		
Income (per capita)		
Universities & Colleges		
Hospitals		
Art Museums/Galleries		
Symphony Orchestras		
Professional Sports Teams		

Source: Bureau of Labor Statistics; *Places Rated Almanac*

B. Listen and circle the correct city.

1. Austin Boston
2. Austin Boston
3. Austin Boston
4. Austin Boston
5. Austin Boston
6. Austin Boston
7. Austin Boston
8. Austin Boston

C. Complete the sentences with an appropriate adjective.

large	small	high	low	more	few	less

1. Austin's population is ___larger than___ Boston's.
2. Boston's population is ______________ Austin's.
3. People who live in Austin pay ______________ taxes ______________ people who live in Boston.
4. The average income for people in Austin is ______________ the average income for people in Boston.
5. There are ______________ hospitals in Austin ______________ in Boston.
6. There are ______________ colleges in Boston ______________ in Austin.

In your notebook, write five more sentences comparing Austin and Boston.

D. Read the information about the weather in Austin and in Boston. Use *as . . . as* or *not as . . . as* to compare the two cities.

	Austin	Boston
Clear days	119	100
Summer: # of days over 90°F	107	12
Winter: # of days under 32°F	21	99
Average humidity %	67%	65%

clear	hot	cold	humid

1. Boston's weather is ______________ Austin's.
2. Summers in Boston are ______________ summers in Austin.
3. Winters in Austin are ______________ winters in Boston.
4. Boston is almost ______________ Austin.

Which city would you like to live in, Austin or Boston? Why?

E. Look at the information about Austin and Boston. In your notebook, write six sentences comparing your native city to Austin or Boston.

Reading: Two Zoos

A. Before You Read.

1. Is there a zoo in your native city or country? If so, describe it.
2. What kinds of animals are there at the zoo?
3. Which zoos have you visited in North America?

endangered species(type of animal)—If an animal is endangered, there are very few of this species remaining in the wild; an example is the California condor.

threatened species—If a species is threatened, it needs special attention or protection; an example is the African elephant.

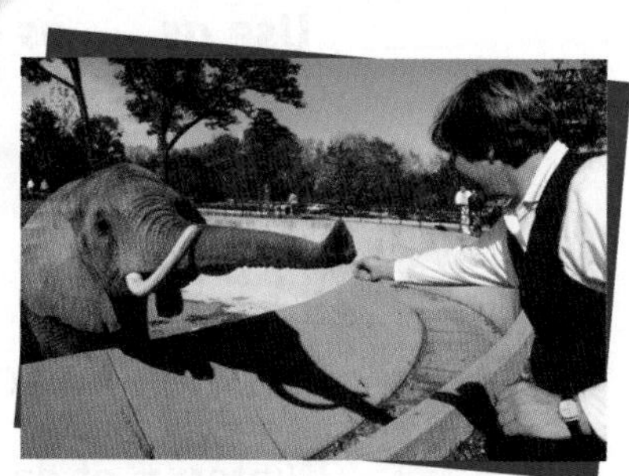

A popular destination for families is a zoological park, or zoo. There are many zoos located all over the world. Here is a look at two popular zoos in the United States—the San Diego Zoo and the National Zoo.

The San Diego Zoo is located in Balboa Park in San Diego, California. The zoo first opened in1916 with a small number of animals. Today, there are more than 4,000 animals, including 800 different species.

The San Diego Zoo is open every day, and the hours of admission change according to the season. The zoo is open from 9:00 A.M. to 4:00 P.M., but the grounds close at 6:00 P.M. An average of three million people visits the zoo every year. The price for general admission is $19.50. The zoo charges $11.75 for children, ages three to eleven. There are also deluxe admission packages, which include guided bus tours and admission to the Wild Animal Park. The San Diego Zoo is a 100-acre park, and it offers many services for its visitors. There are guided bus tours so that visitors can get an introduction to the zoo by an expert. There are also express buses that allow visitors to get around the zoo more quickly. In addition, there are tours available in Spanish and French. When visitors get hungry, they can eat at five different restaurants or at the food carts and stands, which are all over the zoo. There are seven gift shops, where visitors can buy T-shirts, film, guidebooks, hats, and other merchandise.

The National Zoo is located in Washington, D.C., on 163 acres. The United States Congress established the zoo in 1889. The zoo has more than 3,600 animals, and almost 130 of the species of the zoo's animals are **endangered** or **threatened**. An average of three million people visit the zoo every year. The zoo is open every day except Christmas Day, December 25.

Because the National Zoo is part of the group of national museums called the Smithsonian, admission is free. In the spring and summer, the grounds are open from 6:00 A.M. to 8:00 P.M. to visitors. The zoo buildings are open from 10:00 A.M. to 6:00 P.M. In the fall and winter, the grounds close earlier.

There are many facilities for visitors at the National Zoo. For hungry visitors, there are four restaurants plus many food stands. Education and community are very important to the zoo, and it offers a number of special programs for children and adults. There is a summer camp for children ages nine to twelve. There is a day camp with 52 different classes, including a bilingual Spanish-English class. The zoo also has special events for the community such as African-American Family Celebration and the Young Professional Events Series. One of the Young Professionals Events was Swinging with the Primates, an evening of music and dance instruction for young professionals and other adults.

B. Reading for details. Scan the reading and complete the chart.

Name of Zoo	Year opened	Size	Hours	# of visitors	Admission Fee		# of Animals
					Adult	Child	
The San Diego Zoo							
The National Zoo							

C. Answer the questions about the two zoos.

1. Which zoo is bigger?
2. Which zoo has longer hours?
3. Which zoo is older?
4. Which zoo has more expensive admission fees?
5. Does the San Diego Zoo have as many visitors as the National Zoo?
6. Is the National Zoo as expensive as the San Diego Zoo?
7. Which zoo has more animals?
8. Which zoo do you think is more interesting?

D. Discuss your answers in Exercise C. Which zoo would you like to visit? Why?

Writing Our Stories: Differences

A. Read.

I grew up in Istanbul, but now I live in a small modern city in the United States. My city, Istanbul, is both European and Asian. It is older and larger than the city where I live now. Transportation is better in Istanbul. We have buses, trams, ferries, taxis, and a new metro. Traffic is much heavier in Istanbul. My life is different here in the United States. In Istanbul, I lived with seven of my family members. Here, I live with just two family members—my brother and my uncle. The economy is stronger in the United States, so I work hard. I am more tired because I have to work a lot. In Istanbul, it is more difficult to find a job. Life is faster here in the United States. In Turkey, life is more relaxed and I had more free time when I lived there.

Recep, Turkey

B. In your notebook, describe the difference between the city or town where you live now and your native city or town. You may use the adjectives in the box or other adjectives.

The city or town	The people
busy	short
convenient	tall
quiet	shy
noisy	friendly
crowded	talkative
dangerous	quiet
safe	serious
expensive	hardworking
modern	polite
old	

C. *But/however.* Read each sentence. Pay attention to the punctuation and fill in *but* or *however.*

> *But* and *however* introduce contrasts. The punctuation is different.
> Put a comma **before** *but.*
>
> Put a **semicolon (;) before** *however,* and put a **comma after** it.
> The National Zoo is bigger than the San Diego Zoo, **but** the San Diego Zoo also has a wild animal park.
>
> Boston has more cultural activities than Austin; **however,** it is cheaper to live in Austin.

1. The San Diego Zoo opened in 1916, ______________ the National Zoo opened more than twenty years earlier.
2. The National Zoo is free; ______________, most other zoos charge admission.
3. The San Diego Zoo has a wild animal park, ______________ the National Zoo doesn't.
4. Visitors can go and walk on the National Zoo's grounds at six o'clock in the morning, ______________ the buildings don't open until ten o'clock.
5. There are many restaurants in both zoos; ______________, many visitors like to buy food at the food stands because they are more convenient.

D. Editing. In each sentence, there is one underlined mistake. Correct each mistake.

1. The market in my neighborhood is small than the new market.
2. The new market has more international products then my market.
3. The market in my neighborhood is not as bigger as the new market.
4. There are not as many employees than at the new market.
5. My new neighborhood is much more convenienter than my old neighborhood.

Looking at the Internet

Many zoos today have Internet sites for possible visitors. Search **zoos** or **zoological parks.** To make your search more specific, pick a city, and you will find information about zoos in that particular city. For example, type: ***zoos and New York.***

Practicing on Your Own

A. State facts. Write the comparative form of the adjective in parentheses.

1. Rhode Island is ______________________________ (small) any other state.
2. New Jersey is ______________________________ (crowded) any other state.
3. Maryland is ______________________________ (narrow) any other state.
4. Oklahoma has a ______________________________ (large) number of Native Americans than any other state.
5. Alaska is ______________________________ (large) any other state.
6. Colorado is ______________________________ (high) Florida.
7. Arizona is growing ______________________________ (fast) New York.
8. Louisiana is ______________________________ (humid) Arizona.
9. Florida is ______________________________ (sunny) Washington state.

B. Look at the pictures. Complete the sentences using *as . . . as* or *not as . . . as.*

1. Anne is ______________________________ Robin.
(tall)
2. Anne is ______________________________ Robin.
(thin)
3. Anne is ______________________________ Robin.
(old)
4. Robin is ______________________________ Anne.
(athletic)
5. Anne is ______________________________ Robin.
(fashionable)
6. Robin is ______________________________ Anne.
(smart)

Grammar Summary

▶ 1. Comparative adjectives

Use the comparative form of the adjective to compare two people, places or things.

Sandra's clothes look **younger than** Patricia's clothes.

Boston, Massachusetts is **more populated than** Austin, Texas.

▶ 2. Form

a. One-syllable adjectives — Add **-er** + **than**

old	→	old**er than**
safe	→	saf**er than**
big	→	big**ger than**

b. Two-syllable adjectives that end with ***y*** — Change the ***y*** to ***i*** + **er** + **than**

noisy	→	nois**ier than**
sunny	→	sunn**ier than**
friendly	→	friendl**ier than**

c. Adjectives with two or more syllables — Add **more** + the adjective + **than**

expensive	→	**more** expensive **than**
populated	→	**more** populated **than**
delicious	→	**more** delicious **than**

d. Irregular forms

good	**better than**
bad	**worse than**
far	**farther than**
more	**more than**
less	**less than**

▶ 3. *as . . . as / not as . . . as*

Use ***as* ... *as*** to show that two people, places or things are the same.

Sandra is ***as tall as*** Patricia.

Use ***not as* ... *as*** to show that two people, places, or things are not the same.

Sandra is ***not as lucky as*** Patricia.

8 Moving

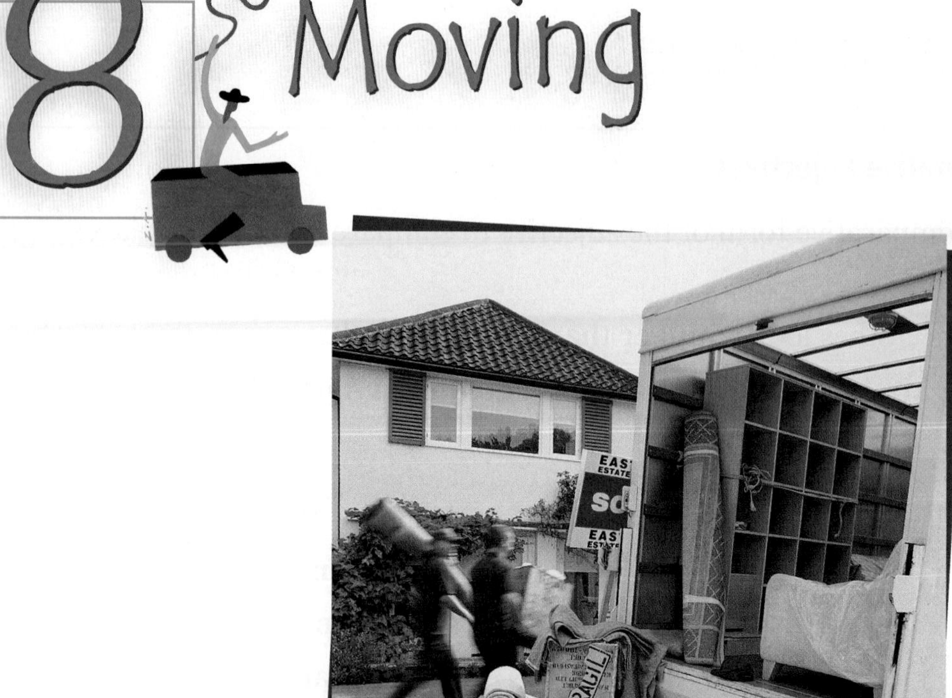

A. Read and complete. The typical American moves 11 times during his or her life. What is your experience in moving?

1. In my country, I

   a. never moved. **b.** moved once. **c.** moved _____ times.

2. I came to the United States in __________.
3. I **had / didn't have** family in the United States.
4. I came to the United States because ________________.
5. Since I came to the United States, I have

   a. never moved. **b.** moved once. **c.** moved _____ times.

6. In the United States, I have lived in ____________ (city) and ______________ (city).
7. I moved because ____________________.
8. In my first year in the United States, my biggest problem was

   ________________.

Active Grammar: Past Tense of Regular Verbs

A. Miguel and Ana's move. Read the story and underline the verbs in the past tense.

Miguel and Ana were unhappy in their last apartment. The apartment had only one bedroom and the kitchen was very small. They wanted an apartment with two bedrooms and a large kitchen. They looked in the newspaper and talked to friends. Finally, they found an apartment they liked. They signed a lease and paid a security deposit. Miguel and Ana packed their clothes, books, and kitchen items into boxes. Miguel rented a small truck. On moving day, several of their friends helped them move. They carried furniture and boxes out of the old apartment and into their new home.

Past Tense
Regular past tense verbs end with *-d* or *-ed.*
live—lived help—helped

B. Why did you move? Complete these answers using a verb in the past tense.

commute	live	want	need	like	retire	change	transfer

1. My company ____________________ me from Cleveland to St. Louis.
2. I ____________________ too far from work. I ____________________ 70 miles each way, 140 miles a day.
3. I ____________________ to be closer to my family.
4. I ____________________ when I was 65 years old. My children ____________________ in Florida and I ____________________ to be near them.
5. We have three children. We ____________________ a larger house.
6. I ____________________ jobs.
7. We ____________________ the schools in this area much better than the area we used to live in.

A. Pronunciation: Final *-ed*. Listen to these past tense verbs. Write the number of syllables you hear in each verb. Then, repeat the verbs.

After most consonants, ***-ed*** is pronounced as /t/ or /d/.
After /d/ and /t/, ***-ed*** is pronounced /əd/. This adds a syllable to the verb.

1. changed 1	6. wanted ____	11. signed ____
2. rented 2	7. helped ____	12. waited ____
3. looked ____	8. called ____	13. asked ____
4. needed ____	9. lived ____	14. cleaned ____
5. liked ____	10. painted ____	15. packed ____

B. Linking. Listen and repeat. These sentences link the final *t* or *d* sound with the first vowel in the next word.

1. He lived‿in a small apartment.
2. He looked‿at many apartments.
3. He filled‿out a rental application.
4. He signed‿a lease.
5. He packed‿all his things.
6. He borrowed‿a van.

C. My last move. When did you move into your current house or apartment? Check (✓) all the sentences that describe your move. Read them to a partner, paying careful attention to your pronunciation of the past tense of the verb.

- ☐ 1. I packed all my things.
- ☐ 2. I painted one or more of the rooms.
- ☐ 3. I filled out a change of address form at the post office.
- ☐ 4. I called the phone company.
- ☐ 5. I waited for the phone company to install a new phone line.
- ☐ 6. I cleaned the apartment/house.
- ☐ 7. I rented a truck.
- ☐ 8. I borrowed a van.
- ☐ 9. I signed a lease.
- ☐ 10. My friends and family helped me.

Active Grammar: Past Tense of Irregular Verbs

A. Listen and repeat.

Simple form	Past	Simple form	Past	Simple form	Past
be	was / were	fly	flew	say	said
become	became	forget	forgot	see	saw
begin	began	get	got	sell	sold
bite	bit	give	gave	send	sent
break	broke	go	went	sit	sat
bring	brought	have	had	sleep	slept
buy	bought	hear	heard	speak	spoke
come	came	know	knew	spend	spent
cost	cost	leave	left	steal	stole
do	did	lose	lost	take	took
drink	drank	make	made	teach	taught
drive	drove	meet	met	tell	told
eat	ate	pay	paid	think	thought
fall	fell	put	put	understand	understood
feel	felt	read	read	wake	woke
fight	fought	ring	rang	wear	wore
find	found	run	ran	write	wrote

B. Answer these questions. Use a verb from the list above.

1. When did you come to the United States?
2. How did you come?
3. How much did you pay for your ticket?
4. How many suitcases did you bring?
5. What did you bring with you?
6. What did you wear?
7. Who met you at the airport?
8. How did you feel?
9. Who did you know in the United States?
10. Where did you go when you left the airport?
11. What did you see?
12. What did you buy your first week in the United States?
13. When did you find your first job?
14. When did you begin to study English?

C. Write the irregular past tense form of these verbs.

1. speak ______________
2. ring ______________
3. tell ______________
4. break ______________
5. get ______________
6. put ______________
7. be ______________
8. drive ______________
9. pay ______________
10. see ______________
11. steal ______________

D. Finding an apartment. Put your pencil down and listen twice to Miguel and Ana s story about finding their new apartment. Then, complete the story with the verbs from Exercise A.

We ______________ lucky in finding our current apartment. Before this, we lived in a different town, but we ______________ happy there. The area ______________ safe, and last month someone ______________ into our apartment and ______________ our TV and stereo. We talked to friends and looked in the paper, but we didn't find anything. Then one day we ______________ in the car and ______________ around in a neighborhood we both liked. We ______________ on a quiet street a few blocks from town when we ______________ a two-family house with a sign in the window, "Apartment for Rent, Inquire Within." We ______________ the doorbell. The owner ______________ home and he showed us around the apartment. It ______________ sunny and clean with lots of room. We signed a lease that day and ______________ him one month's rent and a security deposit. We were very lucky! The owner ______________ us, "I just ______________ the sign in the window this morning!"

E. How did you find your apartment? Check the sentence that describes how you found your current house or apartment.

_____ A friend told me about the apartment.

_____ I read an ad in the newspaper.

_____ I saw a sign on a building.

_____ I went to a real estate agent.

Active Grammar: Negatives

Past Tense Negatives
Use ***didn't*** and the simple form of the verb.
helped—didn't help
looked—didn't look
drove—didn't drive
found—didn't find

A. Memories. Think of your home before you came to this country. Circle the information that is true for you.

1. I **lived / didn't live** in the city.
2. I **lived / didn't live** on a farm.
3. I **lived / didn't live** in a house.
4. I **lived / didn't live** in an apartment.
5. When I was a child, I **walked / didn't walk** to school.
6. I **had / didn't have** my own bedroom.
7. My family **had / didn't have** a garden.
8. We **grew / didn't grow** our own vegetables.
9. We **knew / didn't know** our neighbors.
10. We **felt / didn't feel** safe.
11. We **locked / didn't lock** our doors.
12. We **had / didn't have** a patio.

What other memories do you have of your home in your native country?

B. Then and now. How is your life now different from life in your native country? Compare the two. Use these phrases to help you.

1. watch TV
2. need a warm coat
3. study English
4. have a computer
5. drive
6. eat __________ food
7. go to the market every day
8. work
9. know my neighbors
10. eat at fast-food restaurants

Write three differences in the chart.

Then	Now
I didn't eat at fast-food restaurants.	I eat at a fast-food restaurant about once a week.
I didn't wear a warm coat in the winter.	I wear a coat in the fall and the winter.

C. The first year. Talk about your first year in the United States.

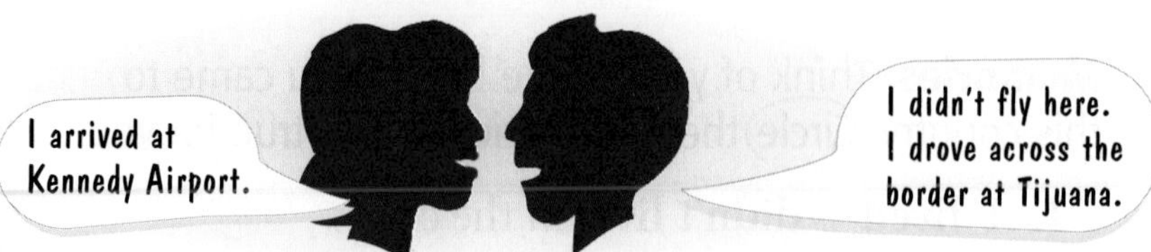

1. arrive at an airport
2. live with a relative
3. begin to study English
4. like the weather
5. like the food
6. miss your family
7. visit relatives
8. come to the United States with my family
9. find a job
10. call my family a lot
11. meet new friends
12. get a driver's license
13. travel
14. go to high school here

Active Grammar: Past Tense—*Be*

A. I'm glad I moved! Compare Boris s new apartment and old apartment.

Past Tense—*Be*	
I **was** lonely.	I **wasn't** lonely.
My apartment **was** small.	My apartment **wasn't** small.
The neighbors **were** friendly.	My neighbors **weren't** friendly.

1. The street is quiet. *The street was busy.*
2. The appliances are new. *The appliances were old.*
3. There is an elevator. *There was no elevator.*
4. The neighbors are friendly.
5. The rent is reasonable.
6. There are no cockroaches.
7. The apartment is sunny.
8. There is a laundry room.
9. The area is safe.
10. The neighborhood is clean.
11. The neighbors are quiet.
12. The apartment is large.

B. Conversation. Complete this conversation and practice with a partner.

A: Why did you move?

B: I ______________ my old apartment!

A: Why not? What was the problem?

B: ____

A: How about your neighbors?

B: ____

A: How much was the rent?

B: ____

A: How do you like your new apartment?

B: I love it! ____________________________________

C. My childhood home. Answer these questions about your childhood home.

Yes, I did.	No, I didn't.
Yes, we did.	No, we didn't.
Yes, they did.	No, they didn't.

Yes, it was.	No, it wasn't.
Yes, they were.	No, they weren't.

1. Did you live in the city? ______________
2. Did you live in the country? ______________
3. Did your family own a house? ______________
4. Was your home large? ______________
5. Did your grandparents live with you? ______________
6. Did you have a yard? ______________
7. Did you have a garden? ______________
8. Did you raise any animals? ______________
9. Did you live near town? ______________
10. Were your neighbors friendly? ______________
11. Was your neighborhood safe? ______________
12. Did you lock your doors at night? ______________

The Big Picture: Jiang

A. Listen to this conversation between Jiang and a friend from business class. As you listen, add more information to the timeline.

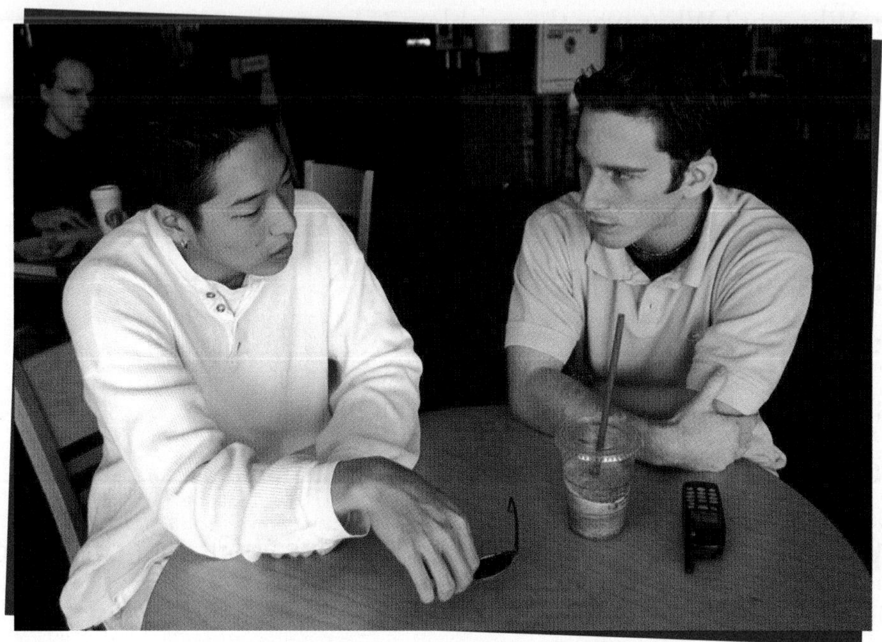

1999	2000	2001	2002
United States uncle shoe factory	studio apartment		

B. Complete these sentences about Jiang using the past tense. Some of the sentences are negative.

1. Jiang ______________ to the United States alone.
2. His uncle ______________ his family letters about the United States.
3. He ______________ any English.
4. He ______________ any friends here.
5. His uncle ______________ him a job at a shoe factory.
6. Jiang ______________ the job.
7. Everyone at the factory ______________ Chinese.
8. Jiang ______________ the job after one year.
9. He ______________ to study English.
10. He ______________ a wonderful young woman at school.

find
like
have
meet
speak
leave
begin
send
come

C. Match the questions and answers.

	Questions	Answers
______	**1.** Is Jiang from China?	**a.** No, he doesn't.
______	**2.** Is he studying computer programming?	**b.** No, he isn't.
______	**3.** Does he work at an appliance store?	**c.** No, he didn't.
______	**4.** Does he live with his uncle?	**d.** Yes, he is.
______	**5.** Did he like his first job?	**e.** Yes, he does.
______	**6.** Did his family come to the U.S. with him?	**f.** Yes, it was.
______	**7.** Did Jiang study English?	**g.** Yes, they are.
______	**8.** Was Jiang's first year in the U.S. difficult?	**h.** No, they didn't.
______	**9.** Was his wife a student at the same college?	**i.** Yes, she was.
______	**10.** Are Jiang and his wife still attending college?	**j.** Yes, he did.

D. Student to student dictation.

Student A: Turn to page 242.

Student B: Listen to Student A and circle the correct answer. When you finish, change pages. Student B will ask ten new questions.

1.	**a.** Jiang	**b.** Jiang's uncle	**c.** Jiang's family
2.	**a.** for one year	**b.** for two years	**c.** in 1998
3.	**a.** at a shoe factory	**b.** at an appliance store	**c.** at an adult school
4.	**a.** at a college	**b.** at a business school	**c.** at an adult school
5.	**a.** the owner of the store	**b.** a friend	**c.** his uncle
6.	**a.** at college	**b.** at the appliance store	**c.** at his uncle's
7.	**a.** two	**b.** three	**c.** four
8.	**a.** at a shoe factory	**b.** at the appliance store	**c.** start his own business
9.	**a.** in 2000	**b.** in 2001	**c.** in 2002
10.	**a.** with his uncle	**b.** in a studio apartment	**c.** near the college

A. Before You Read. Discuss this vocabulary used in home buying.

mortgage	real estate agent	lawyer
interest rate	approve / approval	title
down payment	closing	house insurance
inspector	pest inspection	survey

B. Complete these sentences with a vocabulary word from Exercise A.

1. A ________________ helps people buy and sell houses.
2. A new buyer needs an ________________ to check for termites, ants, or other insects.
3. A ________________ is a map of a property.
4. Some years, the ________________ is low, around 6%. At other times, it can be over 10%.
5. A ________________ is a loan to buy a house.
6. At the ________________, the buyers sign the mortgage documents and pay all required costs.
7. A ________________ is a document that proves a person owns a property.
8. The ________________ is the amount the buyers pay in cash, usually between 5% and 20% of the total price of the house.
9. A ________________ helps new buyers with the legal process.

Pierre and Marie Lucien lived in Florida in a small two-bedroom apartment. Their monthly rent was $650. Pierre was a computer programmer and Marie was a homemaker. They dreamed about having their own home, but Marie wanted to stay home with the children when they were small. When their son entered first grade, Marie got a job as a school bus driver. They were finally able to save money and in two years, they had $12,000 in the bank.

The location of their home was the most important consideration for the Luciens. They wanted a home in a town with good schools for their children and one that was close to their jobs. They spoke to a real estate agent and she suggested that their first step was to apply for a mortgage. By doing this, they would know how much they could afford to spend on a house. So, they spoke to six banks and lenders about mortgages and interest rates. They chose the bank with the best interest rate and mortgage plan. The bank checked their jobs and salaries and their credit history and two weeks later approved them for a mortgage of up to $125,000.

The real estate agent showed the Luciens over thirty houses. They finally found a home that they liked and they could afford. It was $120,000. They offered the sellers $115,000, and they agreed on $117,000. The house was in a small town with good schools. The commute was about twenty minutes to Marie's job and forty minutes to Pierre's job. The house had three bedrooms, two bathrooms, and a large living room. It didn't have a dining room, but it had a large eat-in kitchen. There were a few problems, too. It was on a busy street and it didn't have a garage. They hired an inspector to look at the house. He told them that the house was in good condition, but the roof was old and they would need a new one in three or four years. Pierre also contacted a lawyer who helped them. The lawyer ordered a survey of the land and he arranged for a title search and title insurance. Pierre and Marie also filled out an application for house insurance.

The Luciens used $7,000 for a down payment. They decided on a 30-year mortgage on the $110,000. With taxes and house insurance, their monthly payment was $1150. At the closing, they also needed $3,000 for closing costs, such as title insurance, lawyer's fees, and inspections.

On the day of the closing Pierre and Marie were very nervous. The lawyer and the real estate agent and the owners of the house were all present. The closing only took an hour. When they were finished, Pierre and Marie shook hands with everyone. Then, they walked out of the door with the keys to their new home.

C. Put these events in order.

______ They looked at houses with a real estate agent.

__1__ Pierre and Marie saved $12,000.

______ They had an inspector check the house.

______ They contacted a lawyer.

______ They applied for a mortgage.

______ The lawyer took care of the title and title insurance.

______ Pierre and Marie closed on the house.

______ They found a house they liked.

D. Looking at numbers. Complete with the correct amount.

1. Amount that Pierre and Marie saved: __________
2. Price of the house: __________
3. Amount of mortgage: __________
4. Amount of down payment: __________
5. Extra closing costs: __________
6. Monthly payment: __________

Culture Note

How is the process of buying a house the same or different in your area? What are interest rates now?

Writing Our Stories: My First Year in the United States

A. Read Arismara's story about her first year in the United States.

My arrival in the United States was a family affair. My mother and father and four brothers and I came to the United States from Peru together. My two older brothers met us at the airport. They had been here for many years and they were finally able to sponsor us.

We arrived in October, not able to speak any English. By January, I was studying English at the local adult school.

One of my brothers helped me find a job in a nail polish factory. I didn't like it at all because the salary was very low and new workers came and went every few weeks. After a year, I was able to attend beauty school and get a manicurist license. When I finished, I got a job at a nail salon. Many of my customers were American, so I was able to become more confident speaking English.

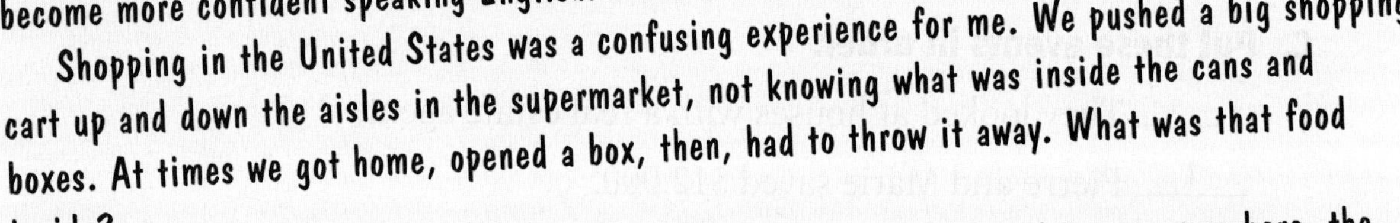

Shopping in the United States was a confusing experience for me. We pushed a big shopping cart up and down the aisles in the supermarket, not knowing what was inside the cans and boxes. At times we got home, opened a box, then, had to throw it away. What was that food inside?

I am still not used to the weather in the United States. The first winter we were here, the weather was terrible. Every week, there was a snow or ice storm. It was difficult to get to work and to school. I fell twice.

The first summer we were here, my brother taught me how to drive. I passed my driving test on my first try! At first, I only drove near my house, but now I can go a little farther.

I think the first year in this country is difficult and a little scary, but it's also exciting. It really helps if your family is together and you can help each other.

Arismara

B. Check the information that is true for you. Complete the sentences.

- ☐ **1.** I came to the United States alone.
- ☐ **2.** I came to the United States with my family.
- ☐ **3.** I found a job.
- ☐ **4.** I didn't find a job.
- ☐ **5.** I began to study English.
- ☐ **6.** I waited before I began to study English.
- ☐ **7.** I got my driver's license.
- ☐ **8.** I liked the ________________.
- ☐ **9.** I didn't like the ________________.
- ☐ **10.** I was surprised at the ____________.

C. ***So.*** Match the two parts of each sentence.

______	**1.** I didn't like my job,	**a.** so I went to live with him.
______	**2.** My brother already lived here,	**b.** so I quit.
______	**3.** I couldn't speak English,	**c.** so I registered for English class.
______	**4.** English was very difficult,	**d.** so I rented one with a friend.
______	**5.** Apartments were very expensive,	**e.** so I studied very hard.

Complete these sentences.

I didn't have a car, so ____.

My neighborhood wasn't safe, so ______________________________________.

D. **My first year in the United States.** Write about your first year in the United States. Use the information from the checklist in Exercise B to give you some ideas. Try to include one or two sentences with *so* in your story.

E. **Edit.** Find and correct the mistakes in these sentences.

1. I came to United States in 2001.
2. I not have any family in this country.
3. I live with some friends for a month.
4. I found a job, but I no like it.
5. In my country I have a better job.
6. At first, I am very lonely.
7. I miss my family a lot, so I called them every week.
8. It very expensive to call them.
9. My first year was difficult because I don't speak English.
10. I begin to study English at an adult school.

Looking at the Internet

Click "Search."
In the *Search* box, type **Real Estate** and the name of your state. You should see the names of many real estate agencies, banks, and lenders. Many real estate sites have pictures of houses for sale and their prices. Bring in pictures of one or two houses for sale. How much are the owners asking?

Practicing on Your Own

A. My first apartment. Mia is writing about her first apartment. Complete these sentences with the correct form of the past tense verb.

1. Mia ______________ (like—negative) her first apartment.
2. She ______________ (live) on the fourth floor.
3. The apartment ______________ (have—negative) an elevator.
   She ______________ (have) to carry everything up four floors.
4. One day the hall light ______________ (go) out.
   She ______________ (call) the landlord several times.
5. He ______________ (return—negative) any of her phone calls.
6. The neighbors on her left ______________ (play) loud music.
7. The neighbors on her right ______________ (have) a baby. He ______________ (cry) all night long.
8. The neighbors upstairs ______________ (fight) all the time.
9. The air conditioner ______________ (work—negative).
10. Mia ______________ (move) to a new apartment as soon as her lease was up.

B. Preposition review. Complete with in, on, or at.

in
year: **in 1998**
month: **in July**

on
day: **on Monday**
date: **on July 4**
on July 4, 2000

at
time: **at 1:00**
at noon

1. She moved _______ Saturday.
2. They closed on their house _______ May 16.
3. The meeting was _______ 5:00.
4. We always visit my sister _______ August.
5. She called the landlord _______ Monday and Tuesday. He returned her call _______ Wednesday.
6. His job interview is _______ September 10 _______ 3:00.
7. I don't like the weather _______ January.
8. He arrived in the United States _______ February 12, 2002.

Grammar Summary

1. Past tense

In the simple past tense, we talk about events in the past (yesterday, last week, etc.).
Regular past tense verbs end with ***-ed.***
Many past tense verbs are irregular. A list of irregular past tense verbs in on page 115.

2. Past time expressions

yesterday	last week	a few minutes ago	in 1975
the day before yesterday	last month	an hour ago	in 1995
	last year	a week ago	in 2000
		a year ago	

3. Statements

I We You They He She It	liked painted rented	the house.

4. Negatives

I We You They He She It	didn't did not	like paint rent	the house.

5. *Yes/No* questions

Did I **pay** the rent?	Yes, you did.	No, you didn't.
Did you **sign** the lease?	Yes, I did.	No, I didn't.
Did he **move** yesterday?	Yes, he did.	No, he didn't.
Did it **start?**	Yes, it did.	No, it didn't.
Did we **change** the locks?	Yes, you did.	No, you didn't.
Did you **buy** a table?	Yes, we did.	No, we didn't.
Did they **paint** the kitchen?	Yes, they did.	No, they didn't.

6. Spelling

a. Add ***-ed*** to most verbs.
open—open**ed**, work—work**ed**, rent—rent**ed**

b. Add ***d*** to verbs that end with ***e***.
smile—smile**d**, arrive—arrive**d**

c. If a verbs ends with a consonant-vowel-consonant, double the final consonant.
stop—sto**pp**ed, rob—ro**bb**ed
Do not double a final ***w***, ***x***, or ***y***.
fix—fix**ed**, play—play**ed**,

d. If a verb ends with a consonant and ***y***, change the ***y*** to ***i*** and add ***-ed***.
study—stud**ied**, try—tr**ied**

9 Natural Disasters

A. Match each picture with the natural disaster or event.

hurricane	heat wave	forest fire / wildfire
flood	drought	blizzard / snowstorm
earthquake	volcanic eruption	tornado / twister

a. 

b. ____________________

c. 

d. ____________________

e. ____________________

f. ____________________

g. ____________________

h. ____________________

i. ____________________

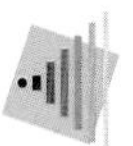

B. Before you listen, match each question to the event on page 128. Then, listen and write the answers to the questions.

temperature	mph	100°	funnel cloud	Richter scale

1. __c__ How deep was the water? ______________
2. ______ How strong was the wind? ______________
3. ______ How high was the temperature? ______________
4. ______ How much snow was there? ______________
5. ______ Was there any rain? ______________
6. ______ How high were the flames? ______________
7. ______ How strong was the earthquake? ______________
8. ______ Was there a lot of fire and lava? ______________
9. ______ How many tornados were there? ______________

C. Read each description. Write the letter of the event next to its description.

__d__ **1.** We saw a large black cloud in the sky and we ran into the basement.

______ **2.** Weather forecasters tracked the storm for days. The wind was terrible. It knocked down thousands of trees in our area. We lost part of our roof.

______ **3.** We could see the flames and the smoke for fifty miles.

______ **4.** The house shook. I quickly got under the table. Some of our pictures fell off the walls.

______ **5.** The water kept rising and rising. We had to evacuate our house.

______ **6.** For days before, the mountain was making loud noises and smoke was coming out of the top. Then one day, there was a terrible explosion and rocks shot up in the air. The lava started to flow down the mountain and into our village. Everyone ran.

______ **7.** It was so hot for days and days. The city issued a warning that people should not exercise. They asked everyone to check on their elderly neighbors to be sure that their air conditioning was working.

______ **8.** It snowed for three days. We had four feet of snow. School closed for four days. It took us two days to shovel our driveway.

______ **9.** There was no rain all summer. The state finally declared water restrictions. We couldn't water the lawn or wash our cars.

Natural Disasters

A. Discuss. This map shows the locations and dates of several natural disasters in the United States.

1. Did any of these disasters occur in your state?
2. What areas in the United States are more likely to have hurricanes? snowstorms? earthquakes? tornadoes?
3. Which of these events or disasters sometimes occur in your country?
4. Does your country experience other kinds of natural disasters? Explain them.
5. Did you ever experience a natural disaster? Tell the class about the event.

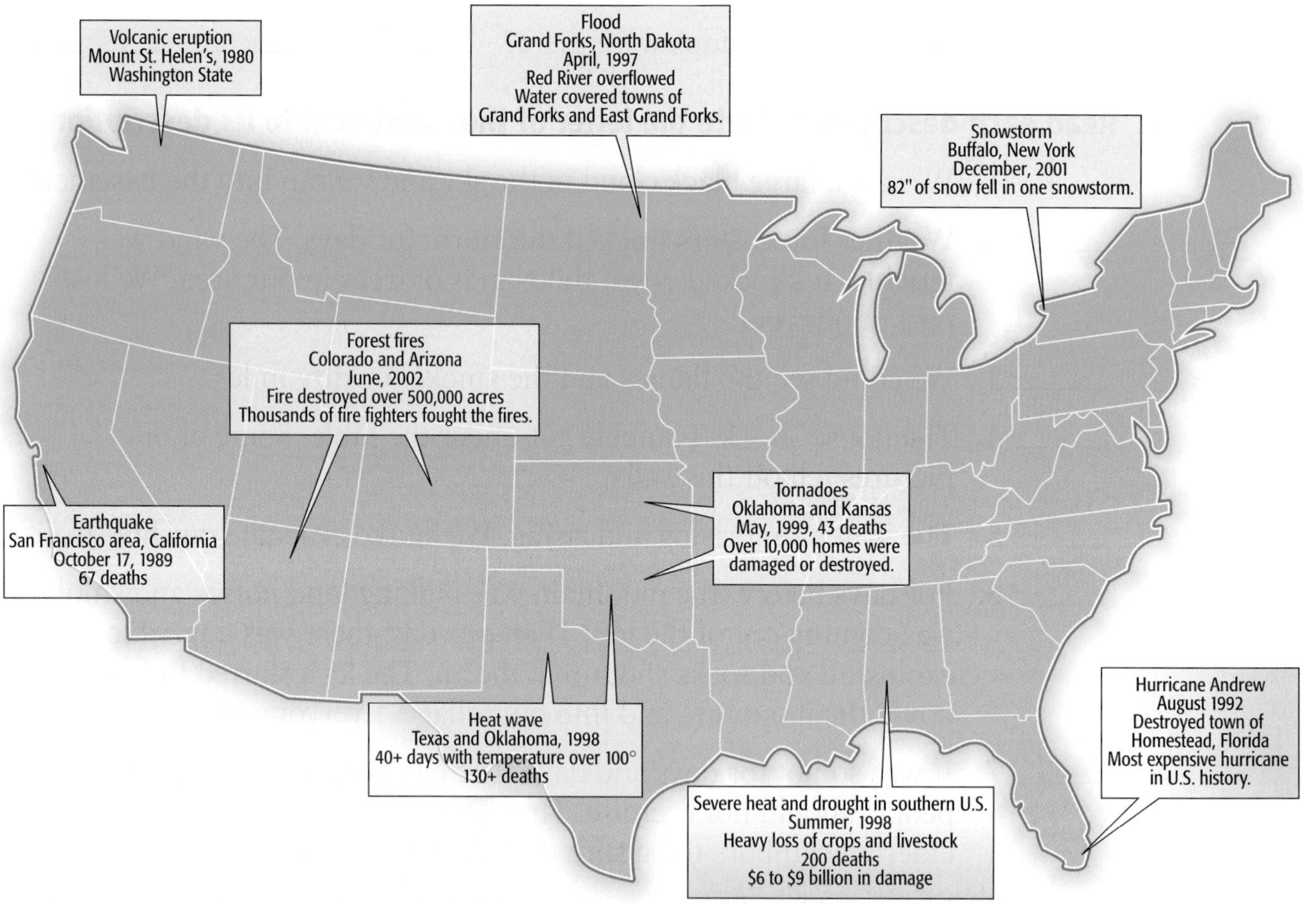

Volcanic eruption
Mount St. Helen's, 1980
Washington State

Flood
Grand Forks, North Dakota
April, 1997
Red River overflowed
Water covered towns of
Grand Forks and East Grand Forks.

Snowstorm
Buffalo, New York
December, 2001
82" of snow fell in one snowstorm.

Forest fires
Colorado and Arizona
June, 2002
Fire destroyed over 500,000 acres
Thousands of fire fighters fought the fires.

Earthquake
San Francisco area, California
October 17, 1989
67 deaths

Tornadoes
Oklahoma and Kansas
May, 1999, 43 deaths
Over 10,000 homes were
damaged or destroyed.

Hurricane Andrew
August 1992
Destroyed town of
Homestead, Florida
Most expensive hurricane
in U.S. history.

Heat wave
Texas and Oklahoma, 1998
40+ days with temperature over 100°
130+ deaths

Severe heat and drought in southern U.S.
Summer, 1998
Heavy loss of crops and livestock
200 deaths
$6 to $9 billion in damage

Active Grammar: Questions

A. Complete these questions about the events on page 130. Use *was, were,* or *did*. Then, match the questions and answers.

***Did* questions**	
Did you **evacuate** your home?	No, we didn't.
Did you **feel** the earthquake?	Yes, I did.

***Was* questions**	
Was the temperature above 100°?	Yes, it was.
Were you scared?	Yes, I was.
Was there a lot of damage?	Yes, there was.
Were there many tornadoes?	Yes, there were.

Hurricane Andrew

1. __Was__ there a hurricane in October, 1992?	**a.** Yes, they were.
2. ______ many people die?	**b.** Yes, it did.
3. ______ many people homeless after the hurricane?	**c.** Yes, there was.
4. ______ many people lose their homes?	**d.** No, they didn't.
5. ______ the hurricane destroy Homestead, Florida?	**e.** Yes, they did.

Oklahoma and Kansas Tornado

1. ______ you see the tornado?	**a.** No, it didn't.
2. ______ the tornado touch down in this area?	**b.** Yes, I was.
3. ______ the tornado hit your house?	**c.** Yes, it did.
4. ______ you scared?	**d.** Yes, I did.
5. ______ you run into a safety shelter?	**e.** Yes, I did.

Grand Forks Flood

1. ______ the Red River flood?	**a.** Yes, they did.
2. ______ the water 26 feet over flood level?	**b.** Yes, it did.
3. ______ many people evacuate their homes?	**c.** Yes, there was.
4. ______ you lose your home?	**d.** Yes, it was.
5. ______ there a lot of damage?	**e.** Yes, I did.

Where was the earthquake? It was in San Francisco.	When did the earthquake happen? It happened at 6:00 P.M.
Where were you? I was at home.	What did you do? I got under the table.

B. The earthquake. Complete the conversation.

A: I just heard about the earthquake you had last week. Are you OK?

B: Yes, yes. Just a little shaken.

A: Where ________________? (be)

B: I was in the kitchen.

A: __________ you __________ the earth shake? (feel)

B: Yes, I __________. The ground shook for about a minute.

A: What __________ you __________? (do)

B: I got under the table—fast!

A: __________ you __________ any damage? (have)

B: Nothing much. A few pictures fell.

A: __________ you __________ to work? (go)

B: No, the governor declared a state of emergency. Everything was closed.

C. Student to student dictation: The heat wave.
Student A: Turn to page 243.
Student B: Listen to Student A ask you six questions. Circle the correct answer. When you finish, change pages. You will ask Student A six new questions.

1. **a.** Yes, I was. **b.** Yes, I did.
2. **a.** Yes, I was. **b.** Yes, it was.
3. **a.** It was over 100° every day. **b.** It lasted for more than 40 days.
4. **a.** Over 130 people died. **b.** Many were elderly and they didn't have air conditioning.
5. **a.** Yes, I did. **b.** Yes, it was.
6. **a.** No, we stayed at home. **b.** We took cool showers twice a day.

D. The forest fire. Read this article about a recent forest fire. Then, complete the questions.

A forest fire that burned 15,000 acres was finally brought under control on Wednesday morning. The fire started Sunday in Black Bear State Park and quickly spread to surrounding areas.

On Monday, police evacuated the small town of Lawson and ordered more than 500 residents to leave their homes. The fire destroyed 20 homes in the area and caused heavy damage to 40 others. There were no injuries. Officials estimated the damage to homes and cars at between $1 million and $2 million. The governor declared the town a disaster area.

The fire spread quickly in the hot, dry conditions. Fire fighting was difficult because of the strong winds. Fire fighters from 55 fire departments in the state joined the National Fire Service to battle the fires. Some were on the scene for 24 hours. Fire trucks hosed houses and stores. Helicopters dropped thousands of gallons of water onto the fire. In order to contain the fire, fire fighters used bulldozers to clear a path around the fire.

Police closed Route 40 to traffic on Tuesday because of heavy smoke conditions. Thousands of travelers had to drive an hour north to Route 28 to pass the fire area.

Some residents did not follow the evacuation order. Paul Grayson sent his wife and two children to safety, but he stayed to hose down his roof with water. As flames came within 50 feet of his house, he started thinking, "Am I crazy? Did I stay here too long, just for a house?"

1. How many acres __________ the forest fire __________?

   It burned 15,000 acres.

2. When __________ the fire __________?

   It started on Sunday.

3. How many homes ______________________________?

   It destroyed 20 homes.

4. Why ______________________________?

   Fire fighting was difficult because of the strong winds.

5. How many people ______________________________?

   The police evacuated more than 500 residents.

6. Which road ______________________________?

   The police closed Route 40.

7. How much damage ______________________________?

   There was about $1.5 million damage.

8. Why ______________________________?

   He stayed because he wanted to hose down his roof.

Active Grammar: *Could/Couldn't; Had to*

Had to shows necessity or obligation.
People **had to** boil water for drinking.
Couldn't shows that an action was not possible.
The children **couldn't** go to school.

A. Natural disasters. Complete these sentences using *before, during,* or *after* in each sentence. Refer to the vocabulary on page 128.

Before the snowstorm, we had to buy extra food.
During the snowstorm, we couldn't drive.
After the snowstorm, we had to shovel our driveway.

1. During the flood __________, we had to evacuate our house.
2. ____________________, we couldn't wash the car.
3. ____________________, we had to file an insurance claim.
4. ____________________, we had to use the air conditioner all day.
5. ____________________, we had to clean up our yard.
6. ____________________, we couldn't do heavy exercise.
7. ____________________, we couldn't watch TV.
8. ____________________, children couldn't go to school.
9. ____________________, we had to wait for emergency instructions.
10. ____________________, we had to buy extra food.

B. Pronunciation: *Couldn't.* Listen and repeat.

1. We couldn't wash the car.
2. I couldn't get to work.
3. They couldn't drive.
4. They couldn't drink the water.
5. We couldn't leave the house.
6. He couldn't do heavy exercise.

Listen to this conversation. Then, practice it with a partner.

A: Could you go to work after the snowstorm?
B: No, we couldn't get out of the driveway. The city couldn't clear all the streets for three days.
A: How long were the kids home?
B: They couldn't go to school for a week. They had to make up the days during spring vacation.

C. The ice storm. Read about the ice storm. Then, use the cues to talk about the disaster. Use *had to* or *couldn't* in each sentence.

In January, 1998, a severe ice storm hit northeastern United States and Canada. Heavy ice covered roads, trees, and utility lines. Over 30,000 utility poles fell or snapped in half. The storm destroyed millions of trees. In towns and cities, power was out for ten days. In rural areas, people waited two to three weeks for their electricity to come back on again.

We **had to** boil the water for drinking.
The children **couldn't** go to school.

1. boil water for drinking
2. go to school
3. flush the toilets
4. find flashlights
5. cook on the stove
6. drive on the roadways
7. sleep in shelters
8. wear heavy clothes
9. take showers
10. use computers
11. use fireplaces for heat
12. watch TV
13. use generators for power
14. make telephone calls

D. Evacuation notice! Imagine that you live near a river. It has been raining for three days and the water is rising quickly. The police are driving up and down the streets with loudspeakers. You have 30 minutes to pack your car and evacuate your home. Sit in a small group of students. List ten items that you would take with you.

I would take ____________________.

You don't need a ____________________.

What about ____________________?

1. ____________________
2. ____________________
3. ____________________
4. ____________________
5. ____________________
6. ____________________
7. ____________________
8. ____________________
9. ____________________
10. ____________________

The Big Picture: The Hurricane

A. This family is preparing for a hurricane. Explain what they are doing and why.

B. Listen to the conversation. Then, use these cues to describe what this couple did before the hurricane, during the hurricane, and after the hurricane.

1. stay in the house *They stayed in the house during the hurricane.*
2. cut up their tree
3. watch the weather forecast on TV
4. put their lawn furniture in the garage
5. buy batteries
6. clean up their yard
7. stay in the bathroom
8. use candles
9. help their neighbor
10. fill up the bathtub with water

C. Complete these questions with *Did* or *Was*. Then, answer the questions.

1. Did ______ they listen to the weather forecast? Yes, they did. ______
2. ______ there enough warning? ______
3. ______ they buy water? ______
4. ______ the wind strong? ______
5. ______ they evacuate their home? ______
6. ______ this woman scared? ______
7. ______ she stay in the bathroom? ______
8. ______ her husband relaxed? ______
9. ______ the rain heavy? ______
10. ______ a tree fall on their house? ______

D. Complete this conversation.

A: How much warning did you have ______?

B: We had warnings for about a week.

A: Where ______?

B: We put everything in the garage.

A: What ______?

B: We bought extra food, batteries, and a power saw.

A: ______?

B: No, we didn't evacuate. We stayed in the house.

A: How strong ______?

B: It was 80 miles per hour.

A: ______?

B: Yes, we lost electricity for two days.

A: ______?

B: No, we had very little damage.

A: ______?

B: I was so scared! I stayed in the bathroom most of the time.

Reading: Tornadoes

A. Before You Read. Circle the statements about tornadoes that you think are true. Then, read the article and check your answers.

1. Tornadoes can be weak or strong.
2. There are more tornadoes in the United States than in any other country.
3. Tornadoes form over the water.
4. Tornadoes only last a few minutes.

A tornado, also called a twister, is a **violent**, spinning cloud that reaches from the ground up to storm clouds in the sky. Most tornadoes are weak, lasting only a few minutes, and have winds of less than 110 mph. But, the strongest tornadoes can last more than an hour and have wind speeds of 200 mph or more. They can destroy houses in seconds, overturn cars, and can pull people, trees, and household furniture into the air.

The United States has more tornadoes than any other country in the world. In a typical year there are 800 to 1,000 tornadoes. Most **occur** in the middle part of the country. Tornadoes **form** when warm and cool air meet. In the Midwest, the warm air from the Gulf of Mexico often meets the cold air from Canada.

Tornadoes can occur at any time of year, but the usual tornado season is March through May. Tornadoes form most often in the afternoon and early evening. There is often no **warning** of a tornado. People who live in the Midwest know the signs of tornado activity. The sky becomes dark, often a greenish color. Dark clouds appear in the sky and there is often large hail. Suddenly, there is a loud sound, like a train or a jet plane. Sometimes, tornadoes occur in groups. Two, three, five, or ten or more tornadoes can form over a large area.

This type of tornado activity hit Oklahoma and Kansas in May 1999. The day was stormy, with violent thunderstorms in the afternoon. As the wind and rain continued, tornadoes began to form. Dozens of tornadoes hit towns and neighborhoods in Oklahoma, then in Kansas. Some stayed on the **ground** for several hours, destroying everything they touched. The tornadoes killed 43 people and injured 600 others. They destroyed thousands of homes and businesses. In some areas, not one home stood. In other areas, the tornadoes destroyed every home on the left side of the street, but didn't touch any homes on the right side. Tornadoes **lifted** people and cars into the air and then threw them back down to earth. One family explained that they were all in the living room, on the sofa and chairs. The storm lifted up the house around them, but left them all **unharmed**, still sitting in the living room.

The safest place to be during a tornado is in a safety shelter. People build these small rooms under the ground to protect their families. Other people go into their basements or into their first floor bathroom, which is often the strongest room in the house.

B. The first word in each line is from the reading. Circle the other word in the line with a similar meaning.

1. lift	(pick up)	destroy
2. form	active	develop
3. warning	typical	sign
4. occur	happen	area
5. unharmed	injured	safe
6. ground	underground	surface
7. violent	strong	overturn

Complete with one of the words in the first column above.

1. A weak tornado will not do much damage, but a ____________ tornado can cause loss of life and property.
2. The tornado destroyed our house, but we were all ____________.
3. Weather forecasters can predict a hurricane a week or two in advance, but there is often no ____________ of a tornado.
4. Tornadoes can ____________ any time of year.
5. The tornado was so strong that it ____________ the car off the ground.

C. Looking at True/False statements.

In a True / False statement, be careful of words like *all, every, always,* and *never.* These statements are often false.
Sentences with words like *many, some, sometimes,* and *often* are usually more accurate.
Look at the difference:

All tornadoes cause damage.	False
Many tornadoes cause damage.	True

Decide if these sentences are true or false. Circle *T* or *F*.

1. All tornadoes can destroy homes. T F
2. Some tornadoes cause millions of dollars of damage. T F
3. Tornadoes always occur in the afternoon or early evening. T F
4. Tornadoes never occur at night. T F
5. Most of the tornado activity in the world occurs in the United States. T F
6. All families in the Midwest have safety shelters. T F
7. People always know when a tornado is going to occur. T F
8. Tornadoes can come in groups of two, three, or more. T F

Writing Our Stories: Writing a short report

A. Taking notes. When you are preparing to write a report, look at several sources of information: books, encyclopedias, almanacs, newspapers, and the Internet. Take notes on the information you read, but do not copy sentences. In a report, it is important to use your own words. Look at these notes about Hurricane Mitch. Then, read the report.

Notes:

October 29, 1998
Hurricane Mitch: 180 mph (290 km)
Central America: Honduras, Belize, Nicaragua, and Mexico
First—hurricane; Next—tropical storm with heavy rain for five days
Some places—25" (65 cm) in one day; terrible floods
Completely destroyed many towns and villages
Deaths: 10,000
Homeless—2 million people

Hurricane Mitch

One of the strongest hurricanes of the century, Hurricane Mitch, hit Central America on October 29, 1998. Powerful winds of 180 miles per hour (290 km) tore through Honduras, Belize, Nicaragua, and Mexico. The hurricane then became a tropical storm and brought five days of heavy rain. Some areas received 25 inches (65 cm) of rain in one day. Rivers flooded and many towns and villages were completely under water. In some towns, the wind and water destroyed every home and building. In all, over 10,000 people died. The storm left over two million people homeless.

B. Write a report. Use these notes to write a short report about the earthquake that hit Kobe, Japan, in 1995. Choose the facts you would like to include.

Notes:

January 17, 1995 5:46 A.M. lasted for 20 seconds
Earthquake—7.2 on the Richter scale
Strongest quake to hit Japan in last 50 years
Terrible damage—bridges and roadways collapsed, 75,000 buildings and homes destroyed, power went out, fires broke out all over the city
Deaths: 5,500 people
Injured: 37,000 people
Damage: $100 billion dollars

C. Edit. Find and correct the mistakes in these sentences.

1. There were a lot of rain.
2. There was several tornadoes in Nebraska.
3. Before the hurricane, we listen to the radio.
4. People had to left their homes.
5. We couldn't to leave the house.
6. The children couldn't went to school.
7. Did you saw the fire?
8. How much damage was it?
9. How long the children were home from school?
10. Where you stayed during the hurricane?

Looking at the Internet

Click on **Search.** Type **FEMA.** This site has information on current and past disasters in the United States, how to prepare for disasters, and how to obtain assistance for the victims of a disaster.

Click on **Prevention.** What suggestions does FEMA give for different disasters?

Click on **Photos** and look at some of the pictures of past damage caused by hurricanes, snowstorms, floods, and other violent weather.

Culture Note

FEMA, the Federal Emergency Management Agency, is an independent government agency. Its purpose is to help people prepare for disasters, coordinate emergency efforts during a disaster, and help people and cities recover after a disaster.

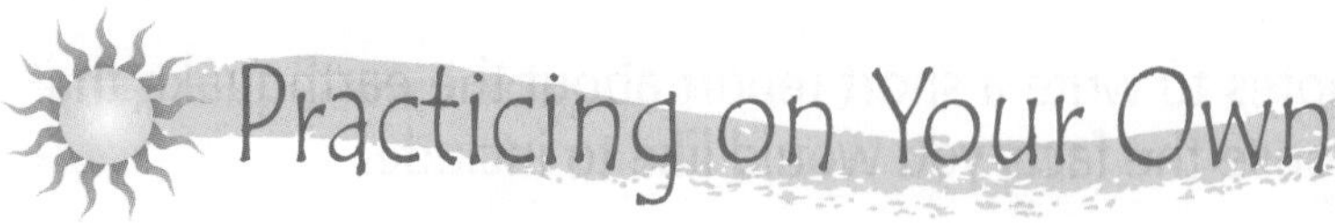

A. A flood. Complete this conversation.

A: When ________________________ to rain?

B: It started to rain on a Monday.

A: How long ______________________ ________________________?

B: It rained for six days.

A: How much rain ________________ ____________________________?

B: We got over 20 inches of rain. And it kept raining.

A: How deep ____?

B: The water was at flood level. And it kept rising.

A: ____?

B: Yes, I was very scared. It was exciting, too.

A: ____?

B: Yes, we evacuated on Sunday.

A: ____ with you?

B: We took everything we could put in our cars—photos, important papers, the computer, the TV, cameras, clothes.

A: Where ____?

B: We went to my aunt and uncle's house.

A: How long ____ there?

B: We stayed for six months. We had to rebuild our house.

Grammar Summary: Past Tense

▶ 1. *Be:* Statements

The water **was** three feet deep.
The flames **were** 100 feet high.

Yes/No questions

Was the tornado strong?	Yes, it was.	No, it wasn't.
Were the tornadoes strong?	Yes, they were.	No, they weren't.

Wh- questions

Where **was** the earthquake?	It was in Taiwan.
How strong **was** the earthquake?	It was 7.6 on the Richter scale.
Where **were** the tornadoes?	They were in Oklahoma.

▶ 2. Regular and irregular verbs: Statements

We **saw** a funnel cloud in the sky.
The tornado **destroyed** many homes.
We **ran** into the basement.

Yes/No questions

Did you **see** the tornado?	Yes, I did.	No, I didn't.
Did the flood **destroy** many homes?	Yes, it did.	No, it didn't.
Did the tornadoes **cause** a lot of damage?	Yes, they did.	No, they didn't.

Wh-questions

When **did** the hurricane **hit**?	It hit on September 5, 2001.
Where **did** you **stay**?	We stayed in a shelter.
What **did** you **take** with you?	We took our important papers.

▶ 3. *Had to*

Had to shows necessity or obligation.
People **had to** evacuate their homes.

▶ 4. *Couldn't*

Couldn't shows that an action was not possible.
The children **couldn't** go to school.

10 Wedding Plans

A. Dictionary. Look at each picture. What is each event? What is happening in each picture?

the bachelor party	the bridal shower	the ceremony	the proposal

B. Write the number next to the correct vocabulary word.

_____ bride
_____ groom
_____ best man
_____ maid of honor
_____ flower girl
_____ ring bearer
_____ bouquet
_____ wedding gown
_____ tuxedo
_____ clergyman
_____ bridesmaids
_____ groomsmen

C. Write the number next to the correct vocabulary word.

______ wedding cake	______ photographer	______ videographer
______ band	______ buffet	

D. Answer the questions about the wedding reception.

1. What are the members of the wedding party wearing?
2. What are the guests wearing?
3. What season is it?
4. Who else is sitting at the head table?
5. Who's looking at the wedding cake?
6. What are the bride and groom going to do?
7. Do you think there is going to be dancing at this wedding?
8. Is the reception almost over?

Active Grammar: Modals—*Have to/Has to*

A. What's your opinion? Discuss each statement. Then, complete with *the bride, the groom,* or *the couple.*

Have to is a modal verb. It shows **necessity** or **obligation.**

I You We They	**have to**	order the invitations. tell family and friends. buy a gown.
She He	**has to**	

1. The bride has to select a wedding gown.
2. ______________ has to rent or buy a tuxedo.
3. ______________ has to reserve a place for the ceremony.
4. ______________ has to reserve a place for the reception.
5. ______________ has to select the rings.
6. ______________ has to ask friends to be her bridesmaids.
7. ______________ has to ask someone to be his best man.
8. ______________ has to select a bouquet and decorative flowers.

B. Jennifer and Brian have just become engaged. It s November, and they plan to get married in late August. Listen to the timetable for some of their plans. Match the month and the task.

e	1. November	a. Reserve ceremony and reception sites.
____	2. Early December	b. Start planning the honeymoon.
____	3. Late December	c. Plan the guest list.
____	4. January	d. Order the invitations.
____	5. February	e. Announce their engagement.
____	6. March	f. Order dresses for the bridesmaids.
____	7. April	g. Go to the dressmaker. Hire a florist.
____	8. May	h. Apply for a marriage license.
____	9. June	i. Mail the invitations.
____	10. July	j. Book (reserve) a band.

C. Wedding plans. Sit with a partner. Talk about Jennifer s and Brian s wedding plans. What other things do couples have to do before their wedding?

Active Grammar: *Don't have to/Doesn't have to*

A. Wedding preparations. Jennifer and Brian have many things to do to prepare for their wedding. Their families are going to help them save money and time. What are some of the things that Jennifer and Brian *don't have to* do or worry about? Use the phrases below to talk about their plans.

> ***Do not (Don't)/Does not (Doesn't) have to***
> *The negative form shows that an action is not necessary.*
> I **don't have to rent** a tuxedo.
> He **doesn't have to buy** a new pair of shoes.

rent a tuxedo	contact guests who did not respond
pay for a wedding cake	change her driver s license
hire a photographer	pay a minister
worry about the weather	move to a new apartment

1. Brian owns a tuxedo. *He doesn't have to rent a tuxedo.*
2. Jennifer's sister works at a bakery. She'll take care of the cake.
3. They're going to live in Brian's apartment.
4. They're going to have the reception indoors at a wedding hall.
5. Brian's cousin is a professional photographer.
6. Everyone responded to the wedding invitations.
7. Jennifer isn't going to take her husband's last name.
8. Brian's grandfather is a minister. He's going to perform the ceremony.

B. With a partner, talk about the things that you *have to do* or *don't have to do* in your English class.

Active Grammar: *Yes/No Questions*

A. Ask your teacher questions about his or her job.

Do	I you they	have to	go? work?
Does	he she it		

1. Do you have to work in the summer?
2. Do you have to work overtime?
3. Do you have to go to many meetings?
4. Do you have to bring your lunch or dinner to school?
5. Do all the teachers have to start work at the same time?
6. Does your boss have to observe your classes?
7. Does the school have to stay open in the summer?
8. Do the teachers have to punch a time clock?

Culture Note

In schools and colleges in the United States, supervisors and other teachers sometimes observe, or watch, another teacher's class.

In your notebook, write two more questions to ask your teacher.

B. Pronunciation: *Have to/has to.* Listen and circle the correct modal.

1. (have to) has to
2. have to has to
3. have to has to
4. have to has to
5. have to has to
6. have to has to
7. have to has to
8. have to has to

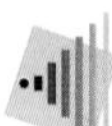

C. Listen and repeat.

1. We **have to** get married in the summer.
2. They **have to** reserve a hall.
3. The bride **has** to find a gown.
4. The groom **has to** buy the rings.
5. Do you **have to** rent a limousine?
6. Do they **have to** go on a honeymoon?
7. Does she **have to** wear white?
8. Does he **have to** pay for the reception?

Practice reading these statements and questions to a partner.

Active Grammar: *Had to/Didn't have to*

A. Read each statement about life in your native country. Circle the correct verb.

1. In my country, I **had to / didn't have to** speak English.
2. In my country, I **had to / didn't have to** work forty or more hours a week.
3. In my county, I **had to / didn't have to** buy winter clothes.
4. In my county, I **had to / didn't have to** look for a job.
5. In my country, I **had to / didn't have to** take public transportation.
6. In my country, students **had to / didn't have to** pay for their books.

In your notebook, write two more sentences about life in your country. Use *had to* or *didn't have to.*

B. Last Weekend. Ask and answer the questions with a partner.

Did	I you we they he she it	have to	work last weekend? go to school? do homework?

Yes, I did. No, I didn't.

Did you have to get up early last weekend?

No, I didn't.

go to the grocery store

get up early on Sunday

speak English

go to work

do laundry

clean your home

do homework

go to a doctor

go to a wedding

Active Grammar: *Should/Shouldn't*

A. Decisions, decisions. Leslie and Mitch are getting married. They have many decisions to make about their wedding and reception. Listen to their conversation and circle the correct answer. Discuss the couple s decisions.

Should
Should expresses advice or an opinion.
You **should have** a small wedding.
You **shouldn't have** a big wedding.

1. Who thinks that they should have a small wedding? Leslie (Mitch)
2. What are they going to do? Why?
3. Who thinks that they should get married in the summer? Leslie Mitch
4. What are they going to do? Why?
5. Who thinks that they should get married inside? Leslie Mitch
6. What are they going to do? Why?
7. Who thinks that they should have the ceremony and the reception in the same place? Leslie Mitch
8. What are they going to do? Why?

B. Student to student dictation.
Student A: Turn to page 243.
Student B: Read statements 1 4 to Student A. Listen and check (✓) Student A s opinion. Then, listen to Student A read statements 5 8. Give your opinion. Say I agree or I disagree. Discuss your opinions.

Statement	Agree	Disagree
1. The bride should take the groom s name.		
2. The bride should always wear white.		
3. The bride s family should pay for the wedding.		
4. The wedding ceremony should be in a church or other house of worship.		

A. Advice column. You write a newspaper column about weddings. With a group of three or four students, read the letters from people who are getting married. Give them advice. Use *should, shouldn't, have to,* or *don't have to.*

Culture Note

In the United States, many engaged couples hire wedding planners or coordinators to assist them with many of the wedding details.

1.

Dear Wedding Planner,

My fiancé and I want to have a small wedding with our families and closest friends. We can't afford a big wedding. Do we have to invite our bosses from work?

– A Tight Budget

2.

Dear Wedding Planner,

I'm getting married in six months. My mother wants me to wear the same wedding dress that she wore, but I don't want to wear it. I want to buy my own dress, but I don't want to hurt my mother's feelings.

– A Modern Girl

3.

DEAR WEDDING PLANNER,

IN FOUR MONTHS, I'M GOING TO GET MARRIED FOR THE SECOND TIME. MY FIRST HUSBAND AND I DIVORCED, BUT WE ARE STILL FRIENDS. HE'S A GOOD FATHER TO OUR TWO CHILDREN. SHOULD I INVITE HIM TO THE WEDDING?

- SECOND TIME AROUND

4.

Dear Wedding Planner,

I'm excited about my wedding and the reception. There will be live music at the wedding, and I love to dance. Unfortunately, my fiancé doesn't like to dance. In fact, I've never danced with him. What are we going to do at our wedding reception when they play a special song for us?

– Gotta Dance

The Big Picture: Where's My Dress?

A. Describe the picture. What are the people wearing? Where is the ceremony taking place? What season do you think it is?

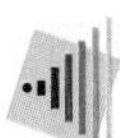

B. Listen to the interview. Circle *True* or *False*.

1. Freddy and Louise got married in the summer.	True	False
2. They got married in Freddy's home.	True	False
3. They had a small wedding.	True	False
4. Louise has many brothers and sisters.	True	False
5. Many of their relatives were in the wedding party.	True	False
6. Freddy's best man was one of his brothers.	True	False
7. Louise wore her mother's wedding dress.	True	False
8. Louise had to buy a second wedding dress.	True	False

C. Listening for details. Listen again. Complete the sentences.

1. Freddy and Louise got married on ______________________________.
2. The ceremony was at ______________________________.
3. There were ______________ attendants in the wedding party.
4. There were about ______________ people at the church ceremony.
5. Louise's father has ______________ brothers and sisters.
6. Freddy and Louise have been married for ______________ years.

D. Ask and answer the questions with a partner.

1. What happened to the first dressmaker?
2. What happened to the dresses?
3. When did she find out that she didn't have a wedding gown?
4. Did Louise have to hire another dressmaker?
5. Did she have to pay for the bridesmaids' dresses, too?
6. Did Louise contact the police?
7. How did Freddy feel about the second dress?

E. Freddy and Louise had a problem getting the wedding dress. Give advice to another couple getting married. Use *should* and *have to*.

1. Should they have a big wedding or a small wedding?
2. Should they get married inside or outside?
3. Should they invite all of their relatives?
4. When do they have to reserve places for the ceremony and reception?
5. What color dress should the bride wear?
6. Should they go on a honeymoon?

What are two more things that a couple has to remember to do?

____

____

Reading: Wedding Guest Etiquette

etiquette—rules of social behavior

A. Before You Read.

1. Describe the last wedding that you attended.
2. How early did you arrive for the ceremony?
3. Did you take a gift? What was it?
4. What did you wear to the wedding?

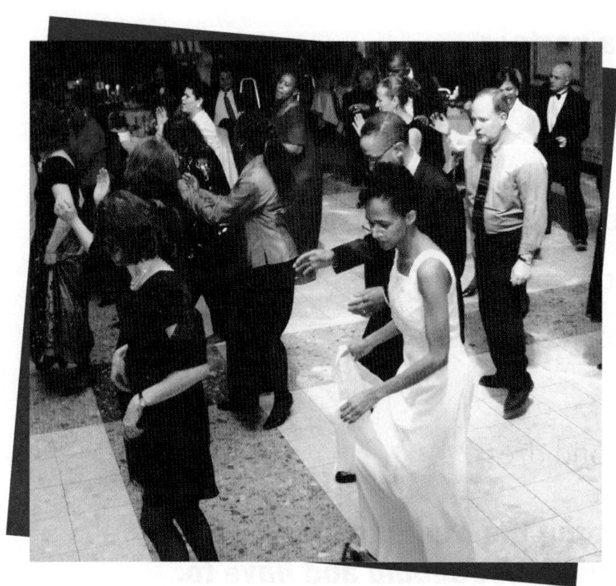

You open your mail and you find a wedding invitation. One of your friends is getting married, and you are excited about the wedding because it is your first American wedding. Weddings are different from culture to culture. What are the rules of etiquette for American wedding guests?

First of all, **respond** to the invitation as soon as possible. The bride and groom have to pay for each guest, so it is important to notify them that you will attend. If you cannot attend, it is **polite** to telephone the couple if you are close friends. If not, you could send a personal **note**.

When you read the invitation, read carefully. Can you take a guest? Maybe your invitation says, "Marianna Lopez and Guest." That means that you can bring one guest. Only one. You must not bring more than one guest, and that includes your children.

What should you wear to the wedding? Check the wedding invitation for special instructions. Maybe the invitation says "black tie" or "**casual attire**." Pay attention to the time of the wedding.

Remember, female guests should not wear white. The guests should be looking at the bride—not at the other guests.

Time and Type of Wedding	Women	Men
Morning or afternoon	nice dress; skirt; suit	suit; sports coat and slacks
Evening	elegant clothes; jewelry; evening bag	suit
Black tie	formal dress; long gown	tuxedo
Casual	casual dress or skirt; suit	business suit; tie optional; nice slacks; no jeans or sneakers

What rules should you follow at the wedding ceremony? The most important rule is to be on time. You should arrive about fifteen minutes before the wedding begins. If you're late, you should enter quietly and find a seat. If something happens during the ceremony that you do not understand, ask the person next to you to explain.

What kind of gift should you buy? Most guests at American weddings do not have to worry about choosing a gift. Many American couples use a wedding gift **registry**. The couple goes to a department store, another type of store, or even the Internet in order to register for their gifts. The bride and groom select the items that they need. When guests are ready to buy the gifts, they go to the store and look at the registry list. They can find out which items are still available. Then, the store delivers the gift. It is not necessary to bring the gift to the ceremony. In fact, it is more convenient for both you and the wedding couple if you mail the gift.

Wedding couples also **appreciate** gifts of money. In fact, money is the most popular gift that couples hope to receive. Place the cash or check in a gift card that is specially made for money. Or, put the money in an envelope, and put it in a greeting card.

Have fun at the wedding!

B. Scanning for details. Read each statement and circle the correct verb.

1. Guests **have to** / **don't have to** respond to the wedding invitation.
2. Guests **have to** / **don't have to** call the couple about the invitation.
3. Guests **should** / **shouldn't** take as many friends as they want.
4. Female guests **should** / **shouldn't** wear white.
5. All guests **have to** / **don't have to** arrive on time.
6. A guest **should** / **shouldn't** find out if the couple registered for gifts.
7. A guest **has to** / **doesn't have to** give money as a gift.

C. Vocabulary. Match each word to its definition. All of the words are in the reading.

b	**1.** respond	**a.** a list of gifts
____	**2.** polite	**b.** to answer
____	**3.** note	**c.** to like
____	**4.** casual attire	**d.** nice; kind
____	**5.** registry	**e.** informal clothes
____	**6.** appreciate	**f.** a short letter

D. Discuss the following questions with a partner.

1. Discuss the chart about clothes on page 154. Are the rules for wedding attire in the United States the same as in your native country?
2. What are common wedding gifts in your native country?
3. What gifts do most wedding couples in your country appreciate the most?

Writing Our Stories: My Wedding

A. Read.

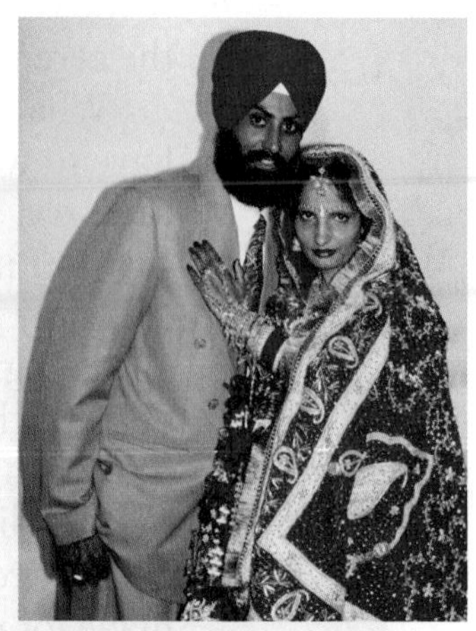

I am from India, and my family arranged my marriage. I was living in the United States when my uncle found a husband for me. My uncle told my father about a man named Justin, who would be a good husband for me. My family and I went back to India for a meeting with the man and his family. We stayed for about a month. At the end of the visit, I decided to marry Justin. We got married a year and a half later.

The prewedding activities, the ceremony, and the reception lasted about a week. On the first day, my family and Justin's family exchanged gifts. During the week, we had to participate in separate religious services. Some services were at my home, and others were at Justin's home. According to custom, the services were only for our families.

The day before the wedding ceremony, my family had to put up a large tent in our yard. About 100 guests attended our wedding. The guests gave us many gifts, including gifts of gold jewelry. We ate sweets, and took many pictures with our family and guests. The guests also gave me and Justin gifts of money, which his sister attached to his clothes.

On the day of the wedding, a priest married us. The ceremony and the reception lasted about seven hours. After the reception, Justin and I left in a car that his family had decorated with a lot of flowers.

Nisha, India

B. Write a story about your wedding or a wedding that you attended. Include the following information:

- When did the wedding take place?
- Who got married?
- Where was the ceremony?
- Was it a big wedding or a small wedding? How many guests were there?
- Was there a reception? Where was it?
- Describe the reception. Where did it take place? Was there music? What kind of music? Was there a disc jockey or a live band? What did everyone eat?
- Did you enjoy the event?

C. *Because, so, in order to*
Read the following statements.

Writing Note

Add a comma (,) before *so*.
Do not add a comma before *because*.

Because

1. The bride had to go back to the dressmaker **because** she lost weight.
2. The groom didn't have to rent a tuxedo **because** he decided to buy a new suit.

So

3. The bride lost weight **, so** she had to go back to the dressmaker.
4. The groom decided to buy a new suit **, so** he didn't have to rent a tuxedo.

In order to

5. The bride went back to the dressmaker **in order to** have her dress fixed.
6. The couple went to a department store **in order to** register for their gifts.

D. Complete. Write *because, so,* or *in order to.*

1. The bride's sister works at a bakery, ______________ they don't have to buy a cake.
2. The bride should plan a visit to a spa ______________ help her relax before the wedding.
3. The bride and groom are taking dance classes ______________ they aren't good dancers.
4. The bride and groom are saving money ______________ they want to go to Europe on their honeymoon.
5. The bride can't find a dress that she likes, ______________ she's going to go to a dressmaker for something special.
6. The bride and groom are going to two receptions today ______________ listen to two different bands.

Looking at the Internet

There are many Internet sites that can help wedding couples organize their wedding plans. There are also many gift registries on the Internet. To search an exact phrase, use " ".

Search any of the following terms:

"wedding gifts"	"bridal gowns"	"wedding planners"
"wedding gowns"	"wedding gift registry"	"wedding coordinators"
"reception halls"	"wedding halls"	"tuxedos"

Practicing on Your Own

A. *Should.* Use *should* to give your opinion about each situation.

1. Jennifer wants to have the wedding on Saturday. Brian wants to have the wedding on Sunday.
   They should have the wedding on Saturday because it's going to be an evening wedding.
2. Jennifer and Brian received three toaster ovens as gifts.
   ____
3. Jennifer wants to hire someone to take a video of the wedding. Brian thinks that this is unnecessary.
   ____
4. Five guests did not respond to the invitations.
   ____

B. Modal contrast. Complete each sentence with one of the modals from the box. More than one answer is possible.

should	has to	doesn t have to
shouldn t	have to	don t have to
	had to	didn t have to

Mrs. Sullivan is 45 years old. Two years ago, her husband died, leaving her to raise her two sons alone. Now her sons are seventeen and ten.

1. Mrs. Sullivan ______________ get married again.
2. Before her husband died, she ______________ work outside the home. She stayed home and took care of her home and family.
3. Now, she ______________ work full time in order to support her family.
4. Her company offers good medical benefits, so she ______________ worry about doctor's bills.
5. Mrs. Sullivan's oldest son ______________ find a job in order to earn enough money for college.
6. Mrs. Sullivan ______________ make many lifestyle changes after her husband died.
7. She ______________ get married when her children are still at home.
8. Twice a year, Mrs. Sullivan goes away on business, so she ______________ find someone to watch her children.
9. She ______________ make sure that her sons spend time with their uncles.
10. Mrs. Sullivan ______________ try to spend time with other single parents.

Grammar Summary

▶ 1. *Have to/Has to/Had to*

Have to is a modal verb. It shows necessity or obligation.

I **have to order** the invitations.

They **have to reserve** a place for the reception.

She **has to buy** a gown.

We **had to take** a test last week.

▶ 2. *Do not have to/Does not have to/Did not have to*

Do not (Don't) have to shows that an action is not necessary.

I **don't have to rent** a tuxedo.

He **doesn't have to buy** a new pair of shoes.

You **didn't have to walk** to school yesterday.

▶ 3. *Should/Should not*

Should is also a modal verb. ***Should*** expresses advice or an opinion.

You **should have** a small wedding.

You **shouldn't get married** outside.

11 The Greatest and the Smallest

Cheetah

Russia

China

Blue Whale

Sears Tower

Akashi-Kaikyo

London Underground

Nile River

A. Look at the pictures. Then, read and complete each sentence.

1. The fastest mammal in the world is the ______________________________.
2. The heaviest marine mammal is the ______________________________.
3. The most populated country is ______________________________.
4. The tallest building in the U.S. is the ______________________________.
5. The longest suspension bridge is the ______________________________.
6. The longest subway system is the ______________________________.
7. The largest country in the world is ______________________________.
8. The longest river in the world is the ______________________________.

Active Grammar: Superlative Adjectives

A. Write each adjective in the correct column.

comfortable	difficult	fast	expensive
large	small	long	safe
noisy	easy	healthy	big
populated	heavy	sporty	popular
spacious	affordable		

Irregular Superlative Forms
good—the best
bad—the worst
less—the least

One-syllable adjectives	Two-syllable adjectives, ending with *-y*	Two or more syllables, not ending with *-y*
large	noisy	comfortable

B. Write the superlative form of each adjective from the box in Exercise A.

One-syllable adjectives	Two-syllable adjectives, ending with *-y*	Two or more syllables, not ending with *-y*
the largest	the noisiest	the most comfortable

C. Pronunciation. Listen and repeat the superlative adjectives in the chart above.

Comparing Cars

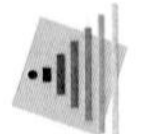

A. Look at the pictures of three cars. Listen and circle the answers.

a subcompact

a sports utility vehicle
(an SUV)

a minivan

1.	(a subcompact)	an SUV	a minivan
2.	a subcompact	an SUV	a minivan
3.	a subcompact	an SUV	a minivan
4.	a subcompact	an SUV	a minivan
5.	a subcompact	an SUV	a minivan
6.	a subcompact	an SUV	a minivan
7.	a subcompact	an SUV	a minivan
8.	a subcompact	an SUV	a minivan
9.	a subcompact	an SUV	a minivan
10.	a subcompact	an SUV	a minivan
11.	a subcompact	an SUV	a minivan
12.	a subcompact	an SUV	a minivan

Explain your answers to a partner.

B. Contrast. Give an example of each type of car. Then, complete the sentences about different types of cars. Some of the sentences are superlative; some are comparative. Use the adjectives in parentheses.

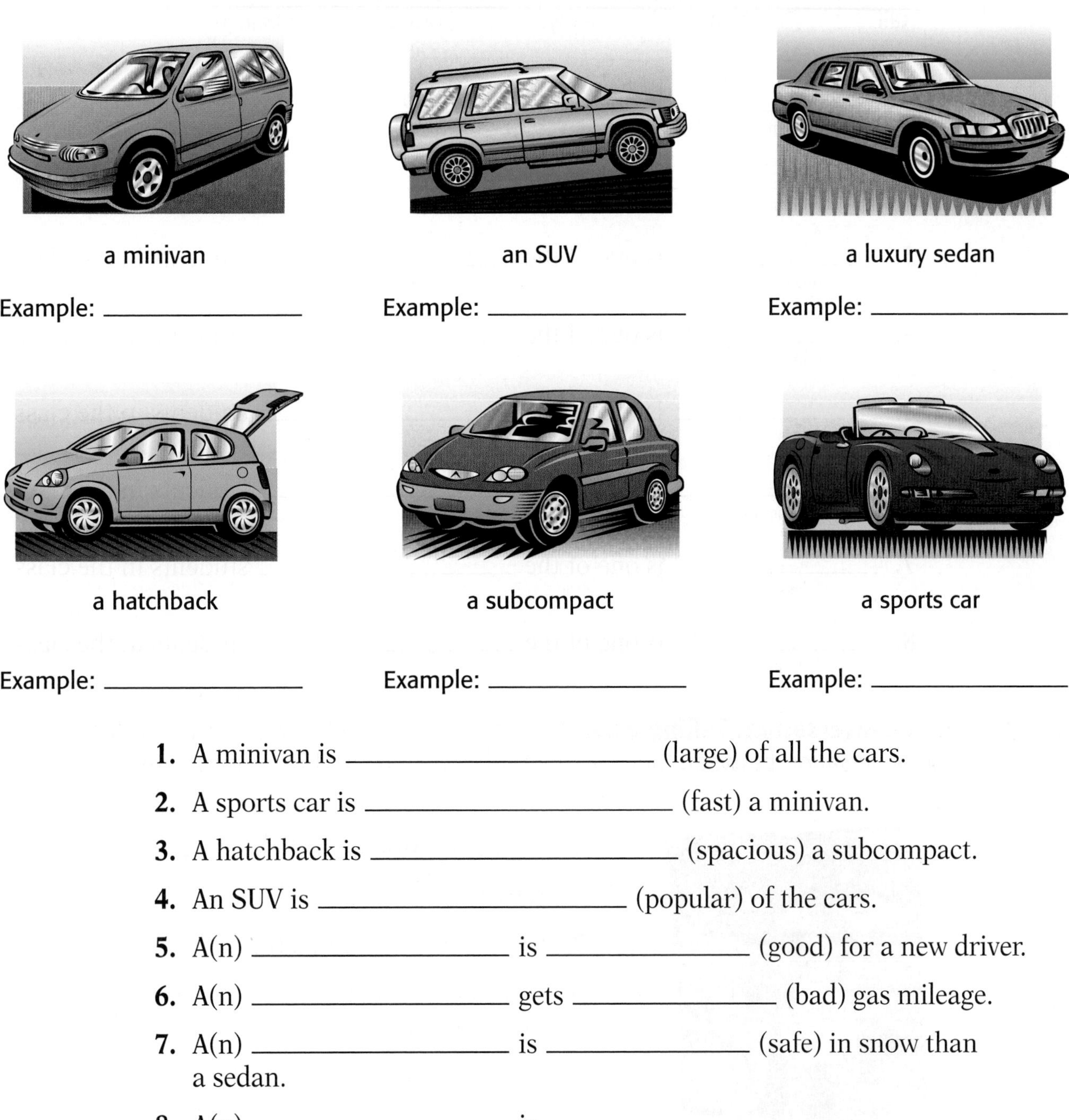

a minivan — Example: ______

an SUV — Example: ______

a luxury sedan — Example: ______

a hatchback — Example: ______

a subcompact — Example: ______

a sports car — Example: ______

1. A minivan is ______ (large) of all the cars.
2. A sports car is ______ (fast) a minivan.
3. A hatchback is ______ (spacious) a subcompact.
4. An SUV is ______ (popular) of the cars.
5. A(n) ______ is ______ (good) for a new driver.
6. A(n) ______ gets ______ (bad) gas mileage.
7. A(n) ______ is ______ (safe) in snow than a sedan.
8. A(n) ______ is ______ (comfortable) car for a family.

Discuss your answers with a group of students.

C. Our class. Sit in a small group of three or four students. Talk about the students in your class.

friendly	serious	athletic	young	studious
tall	funny	early	quiet	talkative

1. ______________ is one of the ___friendliest___ students in the class.
(classmate)

2. ______________ is one of the ______________ students in the class.
(classmate)

3. ______________ is one of the ______________ students in the class.
(classmate)

4. ______________ is one of the ______________ students in the class.
(classmate)

5. ______________ is one of the ______________ students in the class.
(classmate)

6. ______________ is one of the ______________ students in the class.
(classmate)

7. ______________ is one of the ______________ students in the class.
(classmate)

8. ______________ is one of the ______________ students in the class.
(classmate)

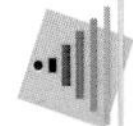

D. A conversation: Selling a car. Monica is trying to sell her car. Listen to the conversation between Monica and her friend, Alison. Then, answer the questions.

1. How does Monica feel about her car?
2. Why is she trying to sell the car?
3. How long has she had the car?
4. How much will it cost to advertise the car on the Internet?
5. How much does a newspaper ad cost for a week?
6. How is she going to sell it?

My Country

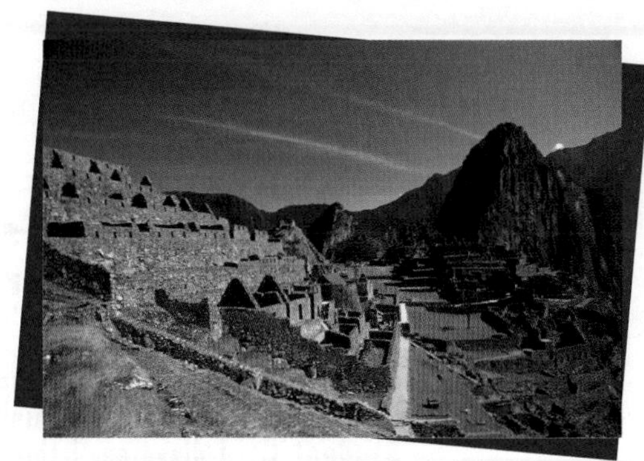

A. Complete the sentences about your country. Use the words in parentheses.

1. Machu Picchu (name of place) is one of the most famous places (famous place) in Peru (native country).
2. ________ (name of place) is one of the ________ (famous place).
3. ________ (name of place) is one of the ________ (historical places).
4. ________ (name of building) is one of the ________ (tall building).
5. ________ (name of beach) is one of the ________ (good beach).
6. ________ (name of dance club) is one of the ________ (popular dance club).
7. ________ (name of restaurant) is one of the ________ (good restaurant).
8. ________ (name of city) is one of the ________ (large city).
9. ________ (problem in your country) is one of the ________ (serious problem).

B. Discuss your sentences with a group of students.

Brand-Name Products

A. Sit in a small group of students. Name three popular brands for each of these products. Then, compare the products. Use the adjectives below the pictures.

> **Student A:** I think (brand-name) aspirin is the safest of the three.
> **Student B:** I disagree. I think (brand-name) aspirin is the safest.
> **Student C:** I disagree. I think (brand name) is safer than (brand name).

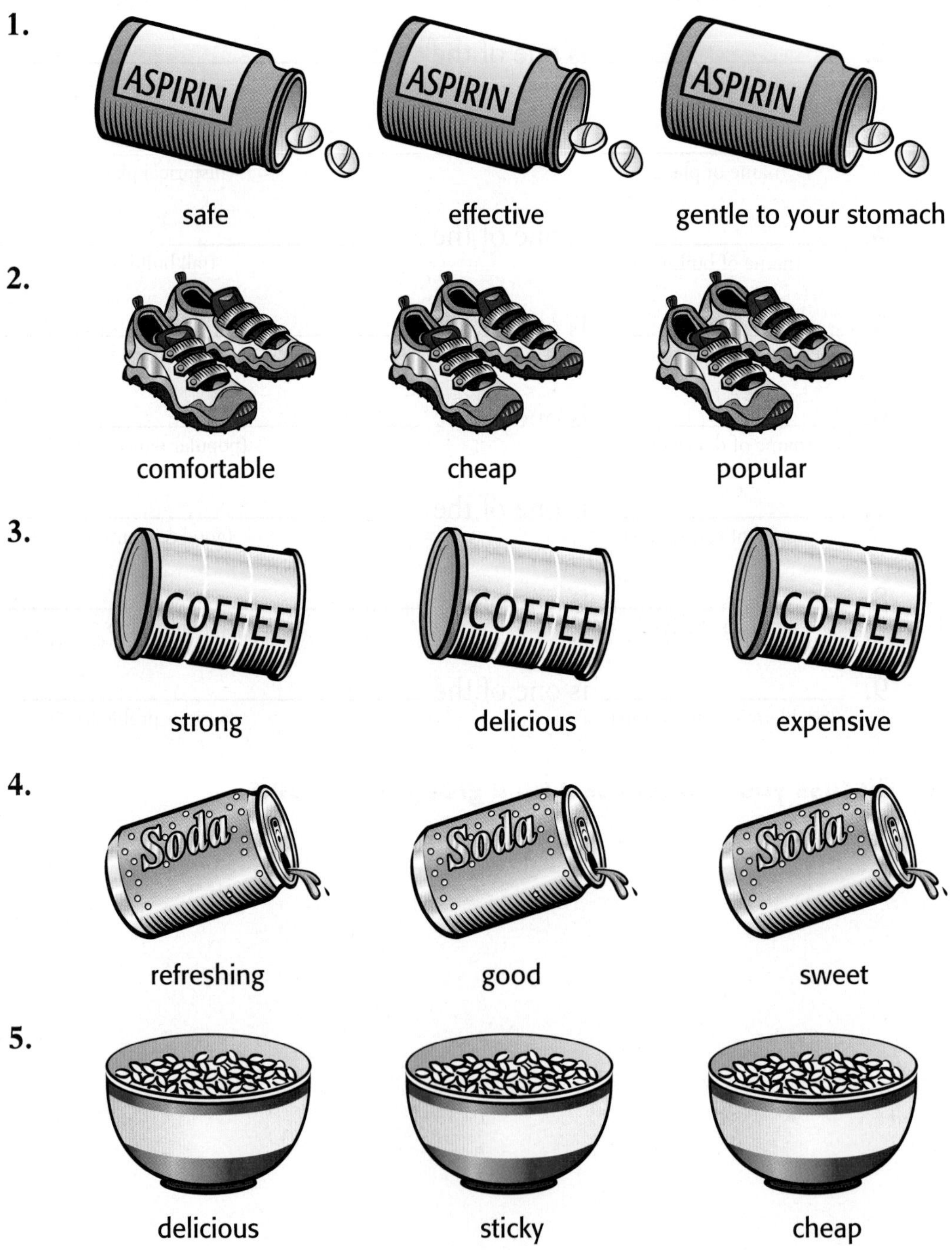

1. safe — effective — gentle to your stomach
2. comfortable — cheap — popular
3. strong — delicious — expensive
4. refreshing — good — sweet
5. delicious — sticky — cheap

Make a TV Commercial

A. Work with a group of three or four students and make a TV commercial. Choose a product for your commercial. You can choose a product that you already know, or you can choose a new product. Use your imagination! Below are a few suggestions.

a dishwashing liquid	a laundry detergent	a breakfast cereal
a new car	a store	a toothpaste
a type of coffee or tea	a computer	

(Draw a picture of your product here.)

This is ______________________________!
(name of your product)

It's the best ______________________________.
(type of product)

It is ______________________________ and
(adjective)

______________________________.
(adjective)

It is one of the ______________________________ for your

______________________________.
(home / life / kitchen/ etc.)

Buy ______________________________ because it is
(your product)

______________________________, ______________________________, and
(adjective) (adjective)

______________________________.
(adjective)

Present your commercial to the class.

The Big Picture: Buying a Computer

A. Listen and complete the information about each computer.

Technical Vocabulary

gigabyte (GB) — This is a unit of computer information
keyboard — You type on a keyboard.
memory — Information is saved in the computer's memory.
screen — You can see images on the computer screen.
user-friendly — A computer that is easy to use is "user-friendly."

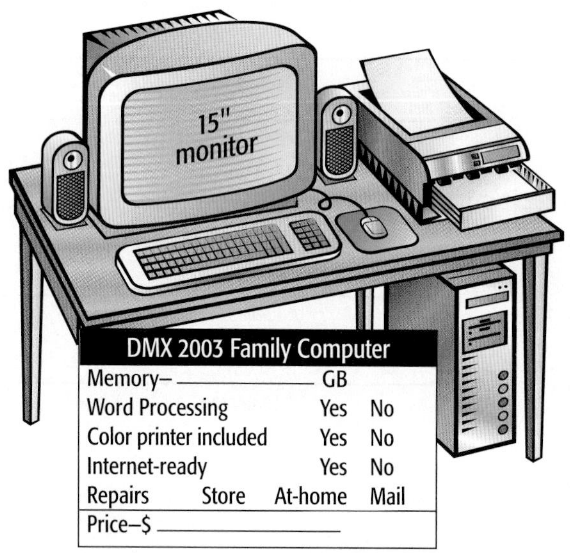

DMX 2003 Family Computer			
Memory– ________ GB			
Word Processing		Yes	No
Color printer included		Yes	No
Internet-ready		Yes	No
Repairs	Store	At-home	Mail
Price–$ ________			

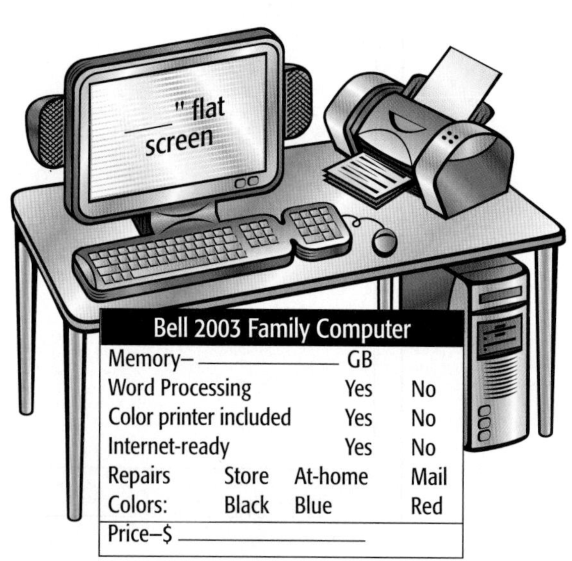

Bell 2003 Family Computer			
Memory– ________ GB			
Word Processing		Yes	No
Color printer included		Yes	No
Internet-ready		Yes	No
Repairs	Store	At-home	Mail
Colors:	Black	Blue	Red
Price–$ ________			

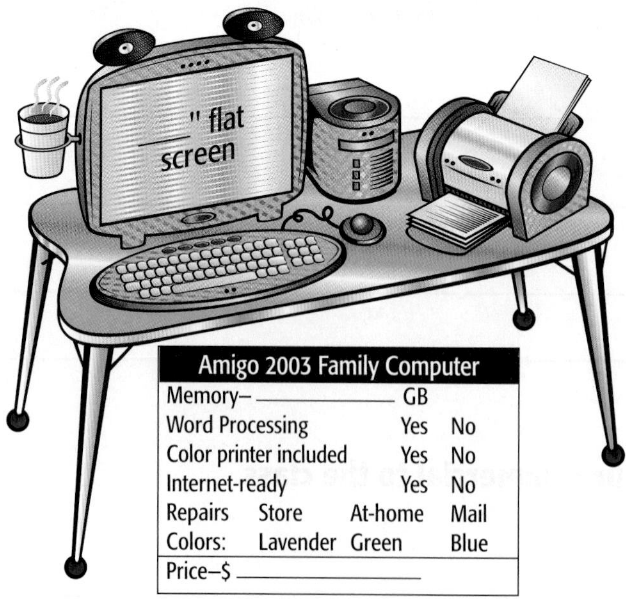

Amigo 2003 Family Computer			
Memory– ________ GB			
Word Processing		Yes	No
Color printer included		Yes	No
Internet-ready		Yes	No
Repairs	Store	At-home	Mail
Colors:	Lavender	Green	Blue
Price–$ ________			

B. Listen again. Complete the sentences with the name of the computer that fits the description.

The DMX	The Bell	The Amigo

1. ________________ is the cheapest.
2. ________________ has the most memory.
3. ________________ has the largest screen.
4. ________________ comes with a color printer.
5. ________________ is faster than both the DMX and the Amigo.
6. ________________ is the least stylish.
7. ________________ is the most user-friendly.
8. ________________ has to be sent back to the company for repairs.
9. ________________ comes in only one color.
10. ________________ and ________________ come in different colors.

C. Complete. Write the correct superlative form of the adjectives.

1. Which computer has ________________________ memory? (large)
2. Which computer is ________________________? (fast)
3. Which computer has ________________________ screen? (wide)
4. Which computer offers ________________________ repair service? (convenient)
5. Which computer is ________________________? (stylish)
6. Which computer is ________________________? (expensive)
7. Which computer is ________________________? (cheap)

Ask and answer the questions with a partner.

D. Make a decision. Look at the features of all three computers. Which computer should the grandparents buy? Explain your answer to a partner. Which computer would you like to buy?

Reading: The Busiest Airports

Culture Note

Many airlines offer frequent flier programs. A frequent flier is a person who frequently flies on one airline. Each time the passenger flies, the airline gives the passenger "miles." The passenger can use the miles to get free flights, to upgrade to business or first class, or to shop.

A. Before You Read.

1. What is the closest airport to your home?
2. What is the busiest airport in your native country?
3. Why is that airport so busy?

Three of the busiest airports in the world are in the United States. LAX is located in Los Angeles, California. O'Hare Airport (ORD) is in Chicago, Illinois, and Hartsfield Atlanta International Airport (ATL) is in Atlanta, Georgia. These three airports are the busiest airports because of the large number of passengers that pass through the airports every year. In addition, the airports move a great deal of cargo (packages, equipment, etc.) through the cargo airlines that also fly from the airports.

Los Angeles Airport, or LAX, was established in 1928. It is now one of the busiest airports in the world with 47 different passenger and cargo airlines that use the airport. In 2001, more than 66 million passengers flew into or out of LAX. About 59,000 employees work at the airport. The employees work at a number of places throughout the airport, including airline counters, coffee shops, bakeries, and one of the 41 stores, where waiting passengers can shop.

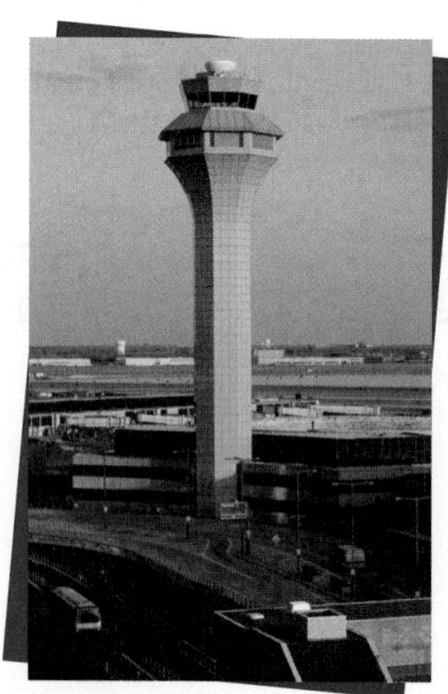

More than 72 million passengers passed through O'Hare in 2001, another one of the busiest airports in the world with 75 airlines using its facilities. O'Hare was established in 1945. Today many frequent fliers know O'Hare because flights often stop in Chicago on the way to other parts of the country or the world. Because so many passengers spend significant time in the airport, O'Hare offers a number of services, such as a hair salon, a children's museum, an athletic club, and a post office. There are 72 different restaurants and stores, which are operated by the airport's 50,000 employees.

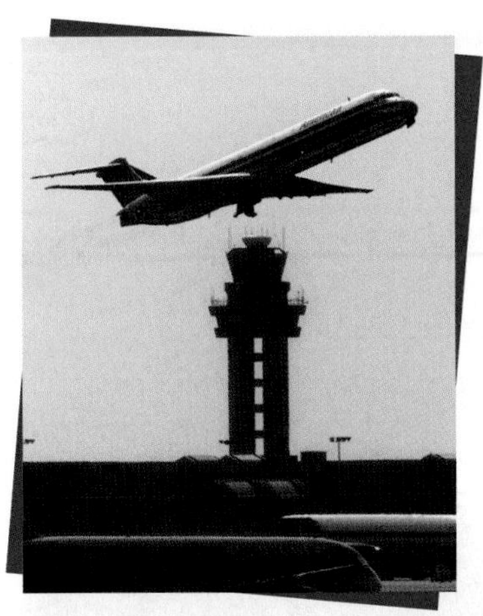

Established in 1925, Hartsfield has become the busiest airport in the world. More than 80 million passengers passed through Atlanta in 2001. Forty-five different passenger and cargo airlines use the airport. Forty-four thousand employees work for the airlines, the 75 restaurants, and 82 shops. In fact, the airport is the largest employer in Georgia. To help people move from terminal to terminal, or from a terminal to one of the 30,000 parking spaces, the airport has an underground people-mover, which connects all of the airport terminals.

B. Reading for details. Scan the reading and complete the chart.

Airport	Number of passengers for 2001	Year established	Number of airlines	Number of employees	Facilities offered
Los Angeles Airport (LAX)					
O'Hare Airport (ORD)					
Hartsfield Atlanta Airport (ATL)					

C. Read each sentence. There is one mistake in the information in each sentence. Find each mistake and correct the information.

1. LAX is the busiest airport in the world.
2. ORD is the oldest airport of the three.
3. ATL employs the most workers of the three airports.
4. ORD offers the least interesting services for its waiting passengers.
5. ATL is the smallest employer in its state.
6. LAX hires the fewest employees.

Writing Our Stories:
An Invitation—Come to Machu Picchu

A. Read.

Dear Friend,

You should come to visit my country, Peru. It is one of the most interesting countries in South America, and it has one of the most unusual places—Machu Picchu. The best time to visit is from May to September. That is the driest period. The busiest time is during our national holiday, July 28th, so it is better to travel before or after that date. If you come in the wintertime, you can experience one of our most exciting festivals, the Festival of the Sun.

Machu Picchu has the most unusual ruins in the world. One of the most famous places there is the Temple of the Sun. It has the finest architecture. Don't miss the Temple of the Three Windows. It has the most fantastic view of the Andes Mountains.

See you in Peru,

Marco

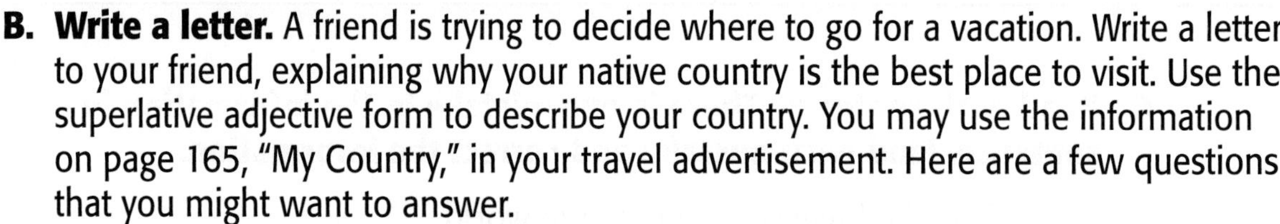

B. Write a letter. A friend is trying to decide where to go for a vacation. Write a letter to your friend, explaining why your native country is the best place to visit. Use the superlative adjective form to describe your country. You may use the information on page 165, "My Country," in your travel advertisement. Here are a few questions that you might want to answer.

- Why should your friend visit your country?
- When is the best time to visit your country?
- What is one of the most popular places to visit? Describe it.
- What is one of the most historic places?
- What is the one of the best beaches, lakes, or rivers? Why is it "the best"?
- What is the most interesting place? Why?
- What is the most fun activity to do in your country?

Remember: When you write your letter, give reasons why your friend should visit the places that you have described. Use *should* to give advice.

C. Commas. Add commas in the correct places.

Use commas (,) in a list of three or more items.
The Amazon, the Nile, and the Yangtze are the three longest rivers in the world.
O'Hare, LAX, and Hartsfield are the three busiest airports.
O'Hare has many restaurants and stores. (No comma)

1. Airport employees work at airline counters stores and restaurants.
2. I need a computer with a modem speakers a flat screen and a printer.
3. My car needs a lot of repairs. It needs new brakes a new clutch and a new radio.
4. In my country, you can listen to the best music at nightclubs restaurants or the university.
5. New York City has the most art museums in the East. For example, you can visit the Museum of Modern Art the Whitney Museum or the Guggenheim.

D. Editing. Read each sentence carefully. There is one adjective (comparative or superlative) mistake in each sentence. Find and correct each mistake.

1. Russia is the ~~large~~ largest country in the world.
2. China is more populated then Russia.
3. The Nile River is more longer than the Yangtze River.
4. The New York subway is much more longer than the Boston subway system.
5. Pablo Picasso was most productive painter. He produced more than 13,000 paintings.
6. The most rich writer in the world is Stephen King, the writer of many mystery novels.

Looking at the Internet

The *Guiness Book of World Records* is published every year. Readers can read the book to find out many interesting and unusual facts.

Search the *Guiness Book of World Records* by typing the title of the book. Put quotation marks (" ") around the title so that you will find only that book. Then, find five interesting or unusual facts. Share the facts with your classmates.

Internet hint: To find an exact title or name, put it in quotation marks.

Practicing on Your Own

A. Food comparisons. Write the superlative form of the adjective in parentheses.

1. Chicken is ______________________ (healthy) meat for your heart.
2. Vanilla is ______________________ (popular) flavor of ice cream.
3. Thai food is ______________________ (spicy) kind of food.
4. Pineapples are ______________________ (sweet) fruit.
5. Cheesecake is ______________________ (heavy) dessert in the bakery.
6. Potato chips are ______________________ (salty) snacks.
7. Iced tea is one of ______________________ (refreshing) drinks in hot weather.
8. Thanksgiving dinner is ______________________ (heavy) meal of the year.

B. Getting the facts. Look at each list. Write a comparative and a superlative sentence about each group.

Popular snacks

1. Potato chips
2. Tortilla chips
3. Nuts
4. Pretzels
5. Popcorn

a. ____

b. ____

Stressful jobs

1. U.S. President
2. Firefighter
3. Senior corporate executive
4. Race car driver
5. Taxi driver

a. ____

b. ____

Grammar Summary

▶ 1. Superlative adjectives

Use the superlative form of the adjective to compare three or more people, places, or things.

The subcompact is **the cheapest** of the three cars.

Use the superlative form of the adjective to compare one person, place, or thing to a larger group.

The Nile River is **the longest** river in the world.

Use the superlative to describe one of a group. Use a plural noun.

LAX is **one of the busiest** <u>**airports**</u> in the world.

▶ 2. Form

a. One-syllable adjectives — Add **the** + ***est***

fast → **the** fast**est**

safe → **the** saf**est**

cheap → **the** cheap**est**

b. Two-syllable adjectives that end with ***y*** → Add **the** and change the ***y*** to ***i*** + ***est***

noisy → **the** nois**iest**

heavy → **the** heav**iest**

friendly → **the** friendl**iest**

c. Adjectives with two or more syllables → Add **the most** + the adjective

expensive → **the most** expensive

athletic → **the most** athletic

delicious → **the most** delicious

▶ 3. Irregular forms

good	**the best**
bad	**the worst**
far	**the farthest**
more	**the most**
less	**the least**

12 Working Parents

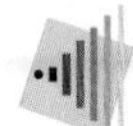

A. Listen as these working parents talk about their lives.

When I get home at night, I'm exhausted.

I read my son a story before he goes to bed.

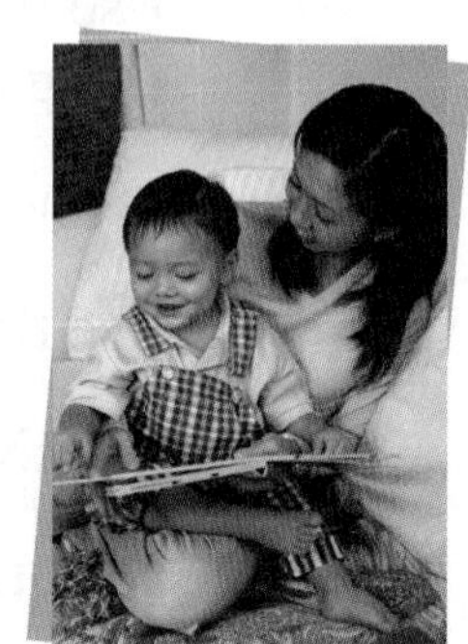

I'm not home when my son gets home from school.

I'm busy every moment until I drop into bed at night!

Before I go to work, I drop my children off at school.

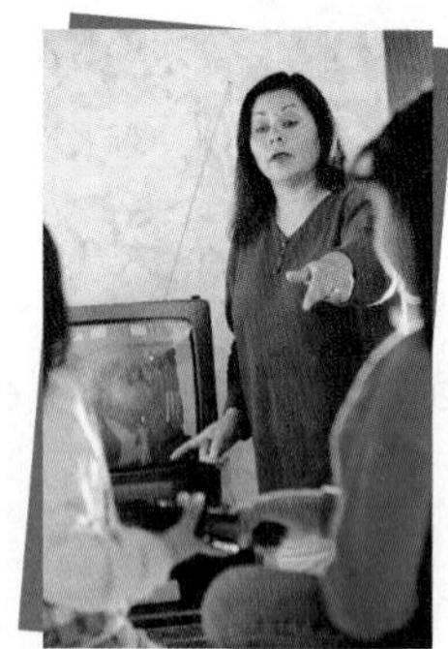

After my kids do their homework, they can watch TV.

My son has to call me as soon as he gets home.

We don't watch TV when we eat dinner.

It was difficult to find a good day care center when I started to work.

Pronunciation: Intonation. Listen and repeat the sentences in Exercise A.

When I get home at night, I'm exhausted.

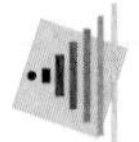

B. Listen to this conversation between two mothers. Then, practice the conversation with a partner.

A: You get a call every day at 3:15.

B: That's my son. He's 12. He walks home after school. He has to call me as soon as he walks in the door.

A: My boys are still little. They stay at day care until I pick them up at 4:30.

B: Big kids, little kids. Childcare is a problem when you're working.

Child Development

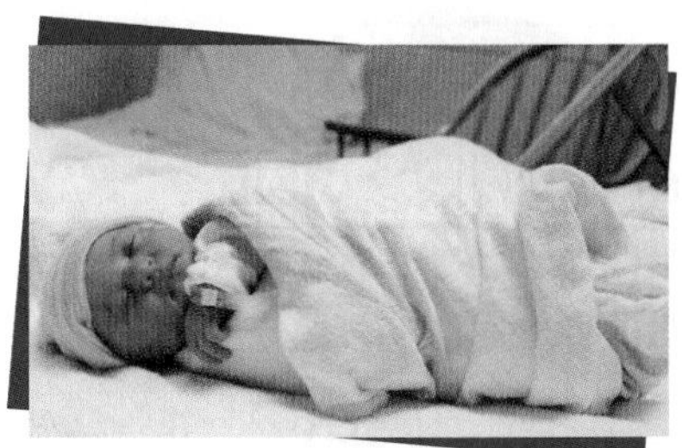
newborn

one-year-old

two-year-old

three-year-old

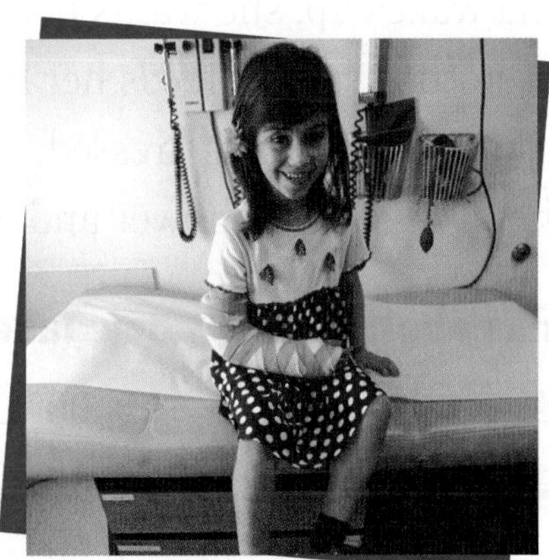
four-year-old

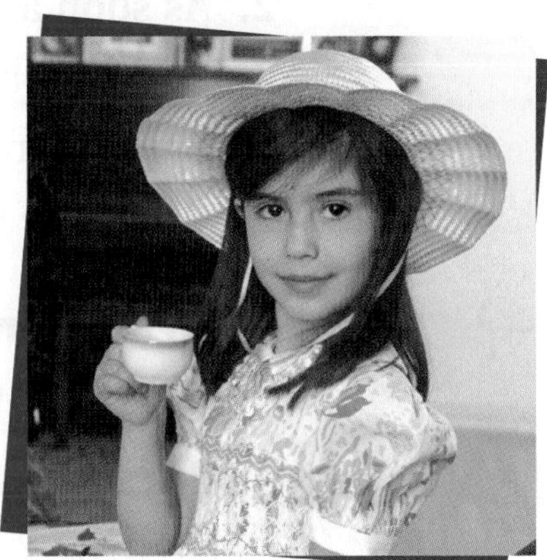
five-year-old

A. Child development. Discuss each activity and talk about a child's development in the early years. Match the activity and age.

A one-year-old is able to ________________.
A one-year-old can ________________.
By the age of one, a child can ________________.

1. walk ______
2. talk in sentences ______
3. ride a bicycle ______
4. cut with a pair of scissors ______
5. walk up and down stairs ______
6. crawl ______
7. say single words ______
8. use the toilet ______

Active Grammar: Present Time Clauses

A. A Stay-at-home mom. Read and discuss the time expressions in these sentences.

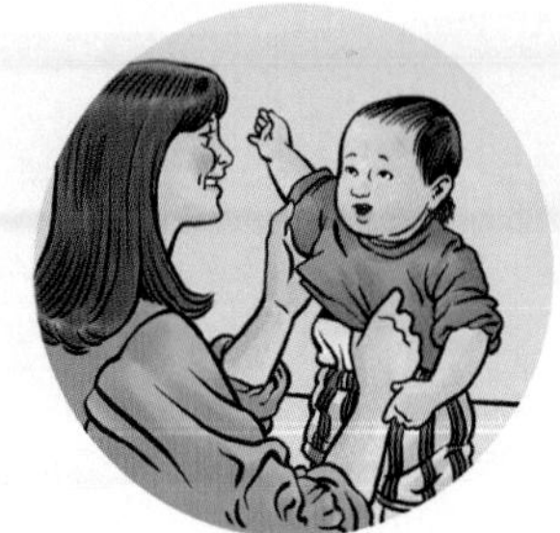

1. Tammy stays in bed **until** she hears Emma wake up.
2. **As soon as** Emma wakes up, she wants her bottle.
3. **After** she has her bottle, Tammy feeds her breakfast.
4. She has breakfast **before** she gets dressed.
5. **When** she watches TV, I take a shower and get dressed.

B. Listen as Tammy talks about Emma's day. Take a few notes.

7:00 ___bottle, breakfast___
8:00 ________________
9:00 ________________
10:30 ________________
12:00 ________________
1:00 ________________
4:00 ________________
5:00 ________________
6:00 ________________
7:00 ________________
8:00 ________________

C. Complete these sentences about Emma's day. Use *before, after, when, as soon as,* or *until.*

1. Tammy is going to stay home ________________ Emma is two years old.
2. ________________ Emma wakes up, she has a bottle.
3. ________________ she has her bottle, she eats breakfast.
4. Tammy cleans the house ________________ she takes Emma to the park.
5. They stay at the park ________________ 12:00.
6. ________________ Emma gets home, she is tired and hungry.
7. She takes a nap ________________ she eats lunch.
8. ________________ we are at the library, we check out five or six books.
9. Emma plays with her father ________________ they eat dinner.
10. Her father reads her a story ________________ she goes to bed.

Active Grammar: Questions

A. Working parents. Maria and George are working parents. Listen to this story about their day. Then, answer the questions.

1. Who leaves the house first? — George does.
2. Who takes Sarah to her aunt's house?
3. Who takes Sam to school?
4. Who takes care of Sarah all day?
5. Who works at home? — Luisa does.
6. Who works outside the home?
7. Who picks up the kids?
8. Who makes dinner? — *Maria does.*
9. Who washes the dishes?
10. Who helps Sam with his homework?
11. Who reads Sarah a bedtime story?
12. Who finally relaxes after the children go to bed? — George and Maria do.

B. Answer these questions about Maria's and George's schedule.

1. What does George do before he goes to work?
2. Does George leave the house before or after Maria does?
3. What does George do before he goes home?
4. How long does he play ball with the children?
5. When does Maria start dinner?
6. What does George do after dinner?
7. When does George help Sam with his homework?
8. When can Sam watch TV?
9. When does Maria read Sarah a story?
10. When can George and Maria finally relax?

 **A. My day.** Sit with a partner and answer these questions about your day.

1. What do you do when you get up?
2. Are you the first one at your home to get up in the morning? Does anyone get up before you?
3. Do you exercise after you get up?
4. Do you eat breakfast before you leave your home?
5. What do you do before you go to school?
6. Who do you talk to before class begins?
7. What do you do as soon as class is over?
8. What do you like to do when you get home?
9. What do you usually do after you eat dinner?
10. What do you do before you go to bed?

B. My teacher's schedule. Listen to your teacher talk about his or her schedule. As you listen, write in the time that your teacher gets up, works, exercises, etc., and complete the chart below. Then, ask your teacher more specific questions about the schedule.

What do you do as soon as you get to work?
Do you correct our papers before you leave school or after you get home?
Do you have a cup of coffee before you leave for work?

Time	Activity
	get up

C. Combine these sentences. Use *before*, *after*, or *when*. Replace the underlined nouns with pronouns.

1. I wash the clothes. I hang the clothes outside to dry.
   After I wash the clothes, I hang them outside to dry.
2. I see money on the sidewalk. I pick the money up.
3. I go to sleep. I read for 30 minutes.
4. I go grocery shopping. I make a list.
5. My children come home from school. I ask my children about their day.
6. My son gets home from school. My son plays with his friends.
7. My daughter is sick. My mother takes care of my daughter.

D. Read each pair of actions. Explain the order in which you usually perform these two actions, using *before* or *after*.

I put on my seat belt. I start the car.
I put on my seat belt before I start the car.
I put on my seat belt after I start the car.

put on my seat belt
start the car

stop talking
the teacher enters the room

get dressed
eat breakfast

return to my car
the parking meter time expires

get paid
pay my bills

turn out the light
get into bed

do my homework
eat dinner

wash the dishes
eat dinner

How do you feel when . . . ?

A. Under each picture, write another adjective from this list that is similar in meaning.

depressed	puzzled	frightened	exhausted
amazed	mad	calm	✔ pleased

happy

pleased

sad

tired

surprised

confused

scared

angry

relaxed

B. Answer these questions. Use the adjectives from Exercise A.

1. How do you feel when you get a parking ticket?
2. How do you feel when you get home after a long day at work?
3. How do you feel when you have a big test?
4. How do you feel when you lose something?
5. How do you feel when you are walking down a dark street alone at night?
6. How do you feel when you miss your family or friends?
7. How do you feel when a person speaks too quickly to you on the phone?
8. When do you feel angry?
9. When do you feel relaxed?
10. When do you feel happy?

Family Responsibilities

A. Use the phrases below to talk about your family or the family of a relative. What are the children's responsibilities?

My son **is supposed to** . . .
My daughter **has to** . . .
My brothers are **supposed to** . . .
My children **have to** . . .

clean his/her room

take care of his/her little brother/sister

take out the garbage

do his/her homework

wash the dishes

call if he/she doesn't come right home after school

help make dinner

set the table

B. Behavior. What behavior do parents expect of a child? of a teenager? Talk about the expectations of your family or a relative's family.

My son is **allowed to** . . .
My children are **allowed to** . . .
My cousins **can** . . .
I **let** my children . . .
My sister **lets** her children . . .

My son isn't **allowed to** . . .
My children **aren't allowed to** . . .
My cousins **can't** . . .
I **don't let** my children . . .
My sister **doesn't let** her children . . .

Children

play with his/her friends after school
cross the street by himself/herself
play in the park alone
walk to school alone
sleep over at his/her friend's house
use the Internet alone

Teenagers

dye his/her hair
get a tattoo
go out on a date
go to the movies with a friend
talk to friends on the phone
go to the mall with his/her friends

The Big Picture: Working Parents

A. Discuss these words and phrases.

look at	put on	wake up	get dressed
jump out of	climb into	drop off	buckle

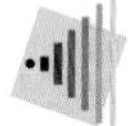

B. Bob and Pat are working parents. Look at the pictures and listen to their morning routine.

C. Complete. Write the correct form of the verb from the box.

put on
get dressed
drop off
jump out of
buckle
get up
watch
wake up
climb into

1. Bob ___gets up___ at 5:45 in the morning.
2. He ______________ bed when the alarm clock rings.
3. He ______________ Pat after he takes a shower.
4. Bob ______________ a video for the boys.
5. The boys ______________ the video.
6. Pat ______________ after she eats breakfast.
7. The boys ______________ their car seats.
8. Pat ______________ the boys in their car seats.
9. She ______________ the boys at the day care center.

D. Answer.

1. Who gets up first?
2. What time does Bob get up?
3. When does he wake Pat up?
4. What does Pat do after she wakes up?
5. What does Bob do before he leaves for work?
6. When does Pat eat breakfast with the boys?
7. When does Pat get dressed?
8. What does Pat do before she starts the car?
9. Where does Pat take the kids before she goes to work?
10. Why aren't Pat's customers annoyed when she is a little late?

E. Complete. Write *before, after, when,* or *as soon as*. For some sentences, more than one answer is possible.

1. ______________ the alarm rings, Bob gets up.
2. Bob takes a shower ______________ Pat gets up.
3. ______________ Bob gets out of the shower, he wakes Pat up.
4. ______________ the boys wake up, they watch a video.
5. ______________ Bob eats breakfast, he leaves for work.
6. Bob kisses everyone good-bye ______________ he leaves for work.
7. ______________ everyone is ready, they leave.
8. The kids always get in their car seats ______________ they get into the car.
9. Pat's customers don't get angry ______________ she's late for work.

Reading: Discipline

A. What is the best way to discipline a young child? Parents discipline their young children in many ways. Discuss each method.

1. I yell at her.
2. I spank her.
3. I send her to her room.
4. I take away a privilege, like watching TV.
5. I talk to her about her behavior.
6. If she's doing something I don't like, I suggest another activity.
7. I give her a time-out for five minutes.

B. Vocabulary. Discuss these words. Then, complete the sentences.

relationship	curious	jealous	praise	privilege	aggressive

1. Young children are often ______________ about new things.
2. She ______________ her son's good behavior so that he will repeat it.
3. My son is too ______________ with other children and often gets into fights.
4. When my daughter doesn't clean her room, we take away a ______________, like watching TV.
5. My daughter is ______________ because her brother gets better grades in school.
6. Children who are three or younger do not understand the ______________ between their behavior and punishment.

C. Read these letters to Dr. Bob, a child psychologist.

Dear Dr. Bob,

I walked into my two-year-old daughter's bedroom and found her coloring on the wall with her crayons. I told her, "No! No! Never write on the wall with your crayons. You can only write on paper." My husband thinks I was too easy on her and that she needed a spanking. What is your opinion?

Debbie

Dear Debbie,

You handled the situation well. Children this age are too little to understand the relationship between their actions and a spanking. Use this as a warning; it's time to babyproof your home. Now that your little one is more active and curious, what else can she reach? Check her room and your home for crayons, paints, medicines, cleaning products, and other items that might attract her.

Dr. Bob

Dear Dr. Bob,

I was visiting my sister, who has two boys, ages seven and five. They were throwing a ball around the living room. She asked them several times to stop, but they didn't listen to her. Finally, one of the boys threw the ball and knocked over a lamp. She yelled loudly at them for several minutes. Then, she sent them to their room. She looked at me and said, "They never listen to me."

Carmen

Dear Carmen,

Your sister needs to be clear to her children what behavior she expects. She should tell her boys, "Don't throw the ball in the house. If you throw the ball again, I'm going to take it." Then, she needs to do what she says. Her boys will soon learn to listen to her.

Dr. Bob

Dear Dr. Bob,

I have a six-year-old son and a four-year-old daughter. My son hits her or pulls her hair several times a day. When my husband sees him do this, he hits him, but the next day, my son will do the same thing again.

Joanna

Dear Joanna,

There is always some sibling fighting when children are growing up. Is he jealous? Do you think he is showing he needs more special time and attention from you or your husband? Try to remain calm. If you feel you must discipline your son, take away a privilege, like TV, for the evening. At other times, praise your son for the good things he does. "I like the spaceship you built." or "Thank you for setting the table. You remembered everything we needed." Your husband might be angry with him, but it doesn't help to hit him. Children who are hit learn that aggression is OK when you are angry. Studies show that children who are hit often are more aggressive and have a more difficult time controlling their anger.

Dr. Bob

Dear Dr. Bob,

Bedtime is always a problem for our three-year-old. We put her to bed, but she cries and refuses to go to sleep. I'm starting to hate this time of night. Any suggestions?

Carlos

Dear Carlos,

It is helpful to have a routine that you use every night. Give her a warm bath and have a warm cup of milk together. Read her a bedtime story. Put her favorite doll or teddy bear in bed with her and give her a kiss goodnight. Before you leave the room, turn on her night-light. It may take a few weeks to get her into the routine, but a calming, quiet time before sleep will relax her and show her it's time to say good night.

Dr. Bob

D. Check (✓) the statements that describe Dr. Bob's ideas on child discipline.

1. It's OK to hit your children when you are angry.
2. Children are more relaxed when their day has a routine.
3. When you are angry at your children, yell at them.
4. Try to anticipate problems in order to prevent them.
5. Be loving and positive with your children.
6. Try to remain calm when your children do not behave.
7. You should not punish children.
8. It's not necessary to talk to your children about their behavior.
9. Try to figure out the reasons for behavior problems.

Writing Our Stories: A Letter of Advice

A. Read Anna's letter to Dr. Bob.

Dear Dr. Bob,

Our three-year-old son has begun to throw temper tantrums. When he doesn't get what he wants, he lies on the floor and screams and cries until he gets his way. The other day in the supermarket, he saw some candy that he wanted. It was 5:00 and I didn't want him to have candy before dinner. But he started to scream and cry so loudly that I was embarrassed and I bought him the candy. How can I stop this behavior?

Anna

B. You are Dr. Bob. Write a response to Anna. Give her specific suggestions about how to handle her child's behavior, both at home and in public.

Dear Anna,

C. Discussion. Sit in a group of three or four students. Each student will read his or her letter of advice to Anna. Discuss your responses. Which suggestions are specific? Which suggestions are the most helpful?

D. Edit. Find and correct the mistakes in these sentences.

1. When my child not listen, I give her a time-out.
2. If my child tries to touch the stove, hit his hand.
3. Young children sometimes cry until they got their own way.
4. After I yell at my children, I felt bad.
5. When children older, they have more serious problems.
6. Before my teenage sons go out, tell them the time to be home.
7. I ask my daughter many questions before she go out.
8. My son have to do his homework before he can talk on the phone.
9. When my children coming home, I talk to them about their day.
10. Children are under a lot of stress when they in high school.
11. If teenagers get regular physical activity, it help them to reduce stress.
12. He not go to sleep until his son comes home on Saturday nights.

www Looking at the Internet

Use your computer at home or go to your school computer lab or the local library. Click **Search** and enter the words ***children and discipline***. Click on one site. Write three suggestions for child discipline that you find on the site.

1. ______________________________

2. ______________________________

3. ______________________________

Name of site: ______________________________

Practicing on Your Own

A. A busy family. Read the story. Then, answer the questions. Use complete sentences.

Mr. and Mrs. Butler have three children—a daughter, Jessica, who is in the eighth grade, and five-year-old twins, David and Joanna. Last year, after 20 years at a telecommunications company, Mr. Butler lost his job. The company downsized, and 1,000 employees were let go. When he lost his job, Mrs. Butler had to go back to work. She's a computer programmer, and now she goes to work five days a week. When there's an important project, she works late at night and even weekends. Mr. Butler stays home and takes care of the children and the house. He's a homemaker now.

When Mrs. Butler leaves for work, she drops the children off at their schools. Then, she drives to work downtown. When she gets to work, she usually gets a cup of coffee and talks with her co-workers. Then, she checks her e-mail and answers her messages. After she answers all her messages, she works on her current projects. When she has a problem, she consults her project supervisor. If she's very busy, she skips lunch or orders out. When everything goes well, she leaves at 6:00, but if there's a problem, she stays late.

At the same time, Mr. Butler takes care of the home. He's getting used to staying home and taking care of the family.

1. How many children do the Butlers have?

   ____

2. When did Mr. Butler lose his job?

   ____

3. What does Mrs. Butler do when there's an important project?

   ____

4. What does Mr. Butler do when his wife is at work?

   ____

5. When does Mrs. Butler have a cup of coffee?

   ____

6. What does Mrs. Butler do before she works on her current project?

   ____

7. If Mrs. Butler is very busy, does she eat lunch?

   ____

8. What time does Mrs. Butler leave work?

   ____

B. Mr. Butler's day. In your notebook, combine each pair of sentences into one longer sentence with the time word in parentheses. Change repeated words to pronouns.

1. Mr. Butler finishes the dishes. Mr. Butler does the laundry. (after)
   After Mr. Butler finishes the dishes, he does the laundry.
2. Everyone leaves. Mr. Butler does the dishes. (as soon as)
3. The twins come home. Mr. Butler reads the classified ads and sends out résumés. (before)
4. Mr. Butler makes lunch. Mr. Butler picks up the twins. (after)
5. Mr. Butler feeds the twins. Mr. Butler and the twins get back home. (when)
6. The twins play in the yard. Mr. Butler calls the twins inside. (until)
7. Jessica gets home. Mr. Butler helps Jessica with her homework. (when)
8. Mr. and Mrs. Butler want to go out for an evening. Jessica baby-sits the twins. (when)
9. The family has dinner together. Mrs. Butler gets home at 6:30. (if)

Grammar Summary

▶ 1. Present time clauses

A time clause begins with words such as **before** or **after**. A time clause has a subject and a verb. In the present tense, both the verb in the main clause and the verb in the time clause are in the present tense.

He does the laundry after he cleans the kitchen.
(main clause) (time clause)

After he cleans the kitchen, he does the laundry.
(time clause) (main clause)

▶ 2. Punctuation

A time clause can come at the beginning of a sentence or at the end of a sentence. When the time clause is at the beginning of the sentence, use a comma (,) to separate it from the main clause.

I read my son a bedtime story before he goes to sleep.
Before my son goes to sleep**,** I read him a bedtime story.

13 Crime

burglar—a person who enters a home to steal from the homeowner

burglary—the crime of entering a home to steal from the homeowner

A. Is your home safe from burglary? Find out how safe your home is by answering the questions below. If the question does not apply to your home situation, circle "N/A" for not applicable. First, look at the pictures of the vocabulary.

Vocabulary

a dead-bolt lock

a peephole

shrubbery

a light timer

a bar

1. Do all of your outside doors have dead-bolt locks?	Yes	No	N/A
2. Did you change all of the locks when you moved into your current home?	Yes	No	N/A
3. Are there peepholes in all of your outside doors?	Yes	No	N/A
4. Do you have outside lights on at night?	Yes	No	N/A
5. Do you use timers to turn your lights on and off when you are away from home?	Yes	No	N/A
6. When you go on vacation, do you stop your mail or have a neighbor or friend pick up your mail?	Yes	No	N/A
7. Do you have an alarm system in your home?	Yes	No	N/A
8. Are there bars in all sliding glass doors in your home?	Yes	No	N/A
9. Is there high shrubbery in front of your windows?	Yes	No	N/A

B. Compare your answers with a partner. What do you need to do to make your home safer?

Active Grammar: Past Time Clauses

A. Listen: A robbery. Jonathan came home and realized that his apartment had been burglarized. Listen to the police officer interview Jonathan about the crime.

Complete the sentences using the verbs from the box. Some of the verbs are negative. Some of the verbs can be used more than once.

leave	find	go	lock	look	open	realize	thank	try

1. When Jonathan ____left____ his apartment, it was 8:30.
2. Jonathan ________________ his door when he ________________ his apartment.
3. Before Jonathan ________________ to bed last night, he ________________ the windows.
4. Jonathan thinks that he ________________ the windows before he ________________ to work.
5. Jonathan ________________ that something was wrong as soon as he ________________ to put his keys on the table.
6. When Jonathan ________________ for the TV, he ________________ that it was gone.
7. When Jonathan ________________ the refrigerator, he ________________ his leftover Chinese food.
8. Jonathan ________________ the police officer before she ________________.

Time clauses: Time clauses can come at the beginning or at the end of a sentence.

I locked my door **before** I went to work. (time clause) **Before** I went to work, I locked my door. (time clause)

They turned off the alarm **as soon as** they entered their home.

As soon as they entered their home, they turned off the alarm.

She changed the locks **when** she rented her new apartment.

When she rented her new apartment, she changed the locks.

I installed new locks **after** a burglar broke in.

After a burglar broke in, I installed new locks.

B. Look at the pictures and complete the sentences with *before, after, as soon as,* or *when.* There is more than one possible answer.

1. The thief hid behind a tree ___before___ the couple parked their car.
2. The couple parked their car ______________ they found a good parking space.
3. ______________ the couple left the car, they put the packages in the trunk.
4. ______________ the couple put the packages in the trunk, they locked the car.
5. The thief checked for other people ______________ the couple left.
6. ______________ the thief approached the car, he looked around again.
7. ______________ the thief touched the car, a large dog appeared in the back seat and scared the thief.
8. The thief ran away ______________ he saw the dog.

Active Grammar: Past Continuous Tense

A. Listen to the story two times. Then, complete the sentences. Some of the verbs can be used more than once.

I He She It	was	**watching** a movie. **walking** in the park. **driving** to work. **locking** the door.
You We They	were	

feel	run
drive	see
jump	✓ start
pay	walk
realize	come

1. Andrew ___was starting___ his car when he ________________ that his briefcase was in the house.
2. Frank ________________ down the street.
3. Andrew went back into the house, but the car ________________.
4. Frank ________________ an opportunity, ________________ into the car, and ________________ away.
5. Andrew ________________ out of his house when he ________________ Frank drive away with his car.
6. Andrew ________________ very foolish.
7. Frank ________________ so quickly that he ________________ attention to the fuel gauge.
8. The car ________________ out of gas only six blocks from Andrew's house.

B. Describing a suspect. Look at the picture below. You will have one minute to memorize the features of this person. Pay attention to the color of his clothes, his height, his weight, etc. Does he have any particular facial characteristics (a beard, a moustache, a scar, etc.)?

Now turn to page 246 in the Appendix.

C. Discussion. Talk about the questions in a small group.

1. Were you or someone in your family ever the victim of a crime? Explain what happened.
2. Did you ever witness a crime? Explain what you saw.
3. Is crime a problem in your city or town?
4. Was crime a problem in the place where you grew up?
5. Is the police department doing anything special in your neighborhood?
6. Do people in your neighborhood worry about robberies? What do they do to prevent them?
7. Do you worry about a robbery?
8. How do you keep your valuables safe?

Before and After

A. Choose eight of the phrases. Use *before* or *after* and write about an event in your life.

came to this country	Before I came to this country, I was working in an office.
got a visa	After I got a visa, I came to this country.

came to this country	fell in love	graduated from high school
got a visa	found a job	enrolled in English classes
became a citizen	found an apartment	got my driver's license
bought a house	got divorced	graduated from college
got married	had a baby	got robbed

B. Read your sentences to a partner.

C. Pronunciation: Stress of content words. Listen and repeat. Pay attention to the content words in **bold print**.

1. Before I **left** my **home,** I **locked** the **door.**
2. When we **went** on **vacation,** we **stopped** the **mail.**
3. She **turned on** the **alarm** before she **left** her **apartment.**
4. They **closed all** of the **windows** before they **left.**
5. I **called** the **police** as soon as I **saw** the **broken door.**
6. I **dialed 911** when I **heard** a **noise downstairs.**
7. After their **house** was **robbed,** the **elderly couple bought** a **dog.**

Practice saying the above sentences with a partner.

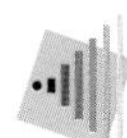

D. Listen and underline the content words. Then, practice the sentences.

1. Before I get into my car at night, I always look in the back seat.
2. After I opened the door, I turned off the alarm.
3. I locked my doors after I got into the car.
4. When we went on vacation, we used traveler's checks instead of cash.
5. While I was walking down the street, someone tried to steal my wallet.
6. We were watching TV when we heard a window break.

Culture Note

Many travelers use traveler's checks instead of cash when they go on vacation. If someone steals a traveler's check, the company can replace it. If you lose cash, you cannot get the money back.

Active Grammar: Time Clauses with *while*

> ***While*** means "at the same time." ***While*** is also used with past time clauses.
> 1. ***While*** I was walking down the street, I was listening to music.
> 2. I was walking down the street ***while*** I was listening to music.
>
> ***Note:*** There is no difference in meaning between (1) and (2).

A. Complete the following sentences.

1. While I was coming to school today, I was listening to the radio.
2. While the teacher was returning tests, the students ______________________________.
3. While the class was listening to the teacher, I ______________________.
4. I was working while ______________________________.
5. While I was driving to work, I ______________________.
6. ______________________________ while I was studying.
7. ______________________________ while I was watching TV.

B. Time clauses: Interrupted actions. Look at each set of pictures and read the sentences below. Then, read the combined sentences.

I was reading.

I heard a noise.

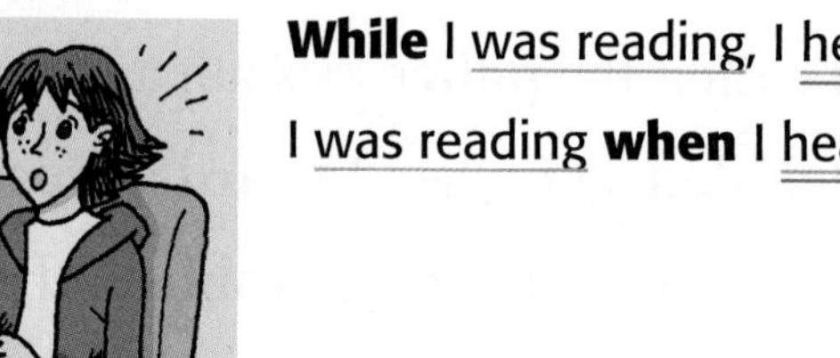

While I was reading, I heard a noise.

I was reading **when** I heard a noise.

Natalie was walking her dog.

A man stole her wallet.

Natalie was walking her dog **when** a man stole her wallet.

While Natalie was walking her dog, a man stole her wallet.

C. With a partner, look at each pair of pictures. Complete the sentences. Write each sentence two ways.

1. a. Tyler was walking down the street when ______________________.
   b. While Tyler ______________________, he ______________________.

2. a. Grace ______________________ when a police officer pulled her over.
   b. A police officer ______________________ while she ______________ ______________________.

3. a. While Luke was trying to open the door, ______________________.
   b. Luke ______________________ when ______________________.

4. a. While Erica and Sean ______________________, an elderly woman tried to steal Erica's purse.
   b. An elderly woman ______________________ ______________________.

In your notebook, write two more sentences with time clauses.

The Big Picture: A Robbery at the Jewelry Store

A. Vocabulary. Match each vocabulary word with the correct picture from the story below. Write the number of the picture on the blank provided.

______ arrest	______ block	______ fist	______ take off
______ mask	______ break into	______ get out of	______ climb into
______ put on	______ chase	______ handcuff	______ pick up

B. Last night, Spike and Tina tried to rob a jewelry store. Look at the pictures and listen to the story.

C. Retell the story.

D. Answer the questions about the robbery in Exercise B.

1. What did Spike put on while he was going to the store?
2. How did Spike break the window?
3. What was Tina doing while Spike was in the store?
4. What did Spike do as soon as he got into the store?
5. What did Spike steal?
6. When did Spike see the pizza?
7. What happened when he picked up a slice of pizza?
8. When did the alarm ring?
9. When did the police officer get out of the car?
10. What did the police officers do after they arrested Spike and Tina?

E. True or False. Read each statement and look at the pictures. Circle *T* for True or *F* for False.

1.	Spike put on gloves after he broke the window.	T	F
2.	Spike climbed into the store after he broke the window.	T	F
3.	While Spike was looking around the store, the police arrived.	T	F
4.	When Spike saw the pizza, the alarm rang.	T	F
5.	Before Spike left the store, he took some jewelry.	T	F
6.	As soon as Spike saw the police car, he tried to run away.	T	F
7.	Spike took off his mask and hat while he was running away.	T	F

F. Complete each sentence with *before, after, when, while,* or *as soon as.*

1. Spike put on gloves ______before______ he went into the store.
2. Spike took some jewelry ____________________ he got into the store.
3. Spike looked around ____________________ he entered the store.
4. The alarm rang ____________________ Spike dropped his bag.
5. ____________________ Tina was sitting in the car, Spike was robbing the store.
6. Tina started the car ____________________ she heard the alarm.
7. The police officers handcuffed Spike and Tina ____________________ they put them into the police car.

Reading: The Booking

A. Before You Read. Match each vocabulary word on the left with the definition on the right. All of the words are in bold print in the reading below.

__b__ **1.** offense

_____ **2.** NCIC

_____ **3.** FBI

_____ **4.** bail

_____ **5.** restitution

_____ **6.** fingerprints

_____ **7.** weapons

_____ **8.** probation

_____ **9.** arraignment

a. money or work that a guilty person does to pay a victim back for a crime

b. a crime

c. 

d. a court meeting with a judge; at this time, the judge will set bail, explain the charge, and will ask the arrested person to plea "guilty" or "not guilty"

e. money paid to the court to stay out of jail; the money will be returned if the arrested person appears at the trial

f. Federal Bureau of Investigation

g. a gun, a knife, a bat, fists, etc.

h. National Crime Information Center

i. a specific period of time when a guilty person must stay out of trouble; if the person gets into trouble again, he or she may go back to prison

B. Read.

After the police arrived at the police station with Spike and Tina, there were a lot of procedures to complete. First, the police officers put Spike's and Tina's names into a computer. A nationwide service called **NCIC** (National Crime Information Center) has computerized information on all criminals. The police wanted to find out if Spike and Tina were using their real names, and they also wanted to know if they had been in trouble before. There was no information on Tina, but the police found out that Spike had been arrested two years ago for burglary.

Then, the police took Tina's and Spike's **fingerprints.** They kept one copy of prints for their own police department, sent one copy to the state, and sent another copy to the **FBI.** After the police took the prints, they took pictures of Spike and Tina for the files. Before Spike and Tina signed the fingerprints form, the police reread them their rights. After the police were sure that Spike and Tina understood their rights, Tina and Spike signed the forms. Their signatures were also useful as handwriting samples.

When Spike and Tina finished the paperwork, the police told them to empty their pockets and to remove their belts and shoelaces. Spike and Tina were both allowed to make one telephone call. When Spike called his lawyer, an answering machine picked up, so the police allowed Spike to call his brother. Tina called her mother. Because it was late at night, and the court was closed until the next morning, Tina and Spike had to spend the night in jail.

The next morning, Spike and Tina went to meet a judge for the **arraignment.** The judge set **bail** for Spike and Tina. Spike and Tina both pleaded "not guilty." Spike didn't use any **weapons** in the burglary, so the judge set his bail at $1000. This was Tina's first **offense,** so her bail was set at $750. Tina's mother paid her bail, and Spike's lawyer arranged to pay ten percent of his bail. They promised to appear in court in four weeks.

Four weeks later, Spike and Tina had to go to court. Spike was wearing a suit and Tina was wearing a simple dress because they both wanted to make good impressions on the judge. Tina was lucky. Because she did not have a criminal record, the judge gave her six months **probation** and 200 hours of community service. She will work at the jewelry store, cleaning the inside and outside of the store.

Spike was lucky, too. Spike did not use any weapons in the burglary and no one was hurt, so the judge sentenced him to one year of probation and 500 hours of community service. Spike will have to work at a local boy's club, helping the counselors and talking about crime prevention. Also, Spike will have to pay **restitution** to the owner of the jewelry store for breaking the window. Spike will pay the owner $1000. Spike did not have a regular job before, but now he has to find a job to pay his restitution.

C. Sequencing. Put the following statements in order from 1 to 10. Write the numbers on the blanks.

_____ **a.** The police officers took Spike's and Tina's fingerprints.

_____ **b.** Spike and Tina had their arraignment.

_____ **c.** Spike and Tina made phone calls.

__1__ **d.** Spike and Tina tried to rob a jewelry store.

_____ **e.** The judge gave them probation and community service.

_____ **f.** The judge set bail.

_____ **g.** The police checked their records.

_____ **h.** The police arrested Spike and Tina.

_____ **i.** Spike and Tina were released on bail.

_____ **j.** Spike and Tina spent the night in jail.

Writing Our Stories: A Moving Van

A. Read.

In July 2001, my grandparents and a neighbor were talking in the living room. It was a Saturday night at about 9:00. My grandfather was looking through the window, and he saw a large green truck in the street. Ten minutes later, he saw two men. The men were wearing dark brown uniforms. They were putting a sofa, two armchairs, and a coffee table in the truck. Then, he saw them putting two TVs, a computer, and a stereo in the truck. He asked my grandmother and the neighbor, "Are Maria and Pablo moving?"

As soon as the neighbor saw the men, she said, "They're thieves!"

My grandfather went out of the house and got into his old car, and the neighbor got into the car, too. My grandmother stayed in the house.

My grandfather and the neighbor went after the thieves, but the thieves' truck was faster than my grandfather's car, so they couldn't catch them.

When the owners of the house, Maria and Pablo, came back from the beach, my grandfather said, "I'm sorry. I saw what happened, but I couldn't stop them. My car is too old."

Maria and Pablo said, "Fortunately, you didn't catch the thieves. Don't worry. The insurance will pay for everything and more."

My grandfather was surprised. He said, "I will never risk my life again for problems that aren't mine."

Nora

B. Editing: Capital letters, a review. Read each sentence. Many of the words should be capitalized. Add the capital letters.

1. A thief smashed a window on north avenue yesterday.
2. Officer stephen taylor arrested two men in front of national bank.
3. A 21-year-old woman from summit was robbed while she was walking home.
4. The woman was walking on main street at 12:46 A.M.
5. Three teenagers were arrested when they tried to break into a chicago high school early sunday morning.

Culture Note

In most cities, 911 is the police emergency number. You should use 911 only in an emergency, such as a robbery, a violent crime, a medical emergency, or a fire.

C. Complete the police report about the crime in Exercise A. Use your own personal information (name, address, etc.) to complete the form.

Police Report	
Today's Date ___ /___ /___ Mo Day Year	**Date of Incident** ___ /___ /___ Mo Day Year
Please provide the following information about where the property was taken.	
Address: ______________________________ Street Address City State Zip code	
Name: ______________________ Last Name First Name MI	**Date of Birth:** ___ /___ /___ Mo Day Year
Work Phone: ( ) - __________	**Home Phone:** ( ) - __________
E-mail: ______________________________	
Employer / School ______________________________	
Use the space below to describe the incident (what happened) and the lost property. **Be sure to include: Who What When How Where**	

Looking at the Internet

There are many Web sites about crime prevention (how to stop crime) on the Internet. Search the following topics:

"Home Safety" "Home Security" "Crime Prevention" "Preventing Burglary"

Tell your classmates one way to prevent crime.

Write the Web site address.

URL: http:// ______________________________

Practicing on Your Own

A. Sentence combining. Combine each pair of sentences with a past time clause using the word in parentheses. Change repeated subjects to pronouns.

1. The police officers arrived at the police station. The officers had many procedures to complete. (when)

   When the police officers arrived at the police station, they had many procedures to complete.

2. The police officers were filling out paperwork. Spike and Tina were becoming worried. (while)

   ____

3. The police officers brought Spike and Tina to the police station. The police officers checked their records. (after)

   ____

4. Spike and Tina listened carefully. The police were rereading Spike and Tina their rights. (while)

   ____

5. Spike and Tina made phone calls. The police officers gave Spike and Tina permission. (after)

   ____

6. Spike's lawyer didn't answer. Spike called his brother. (when)

   ____

7. Spike and Tina could go home. Their families paid their bail. (as soon as)

   ____

Grammar Summary

▶ 1. Past continuous tense

The past continuous shows that an action was in progress in the past.

I **was walking** down the street.
You **were talking** on the telephone.

We **were going** on vacation.

She **was buying** her groceries.
It **was raining** hard.

They **were taking** a break.

▶ 2. Past time clauses: Simple past

A time clause begins with words such as **before, after, as soon as,** and **when.** A time clause has a subject and a verb. In the past tense, both the verb in the time clause and the verb in the main clause are in the past tense.

I locked my door **before** I went to work. (main clause) (time clause)
Before I went to work**,** I locked my door. (time clause) (main clause)

Note: If the time clause is at the beginning of a sentence, use a comma(**,**) **after** the time clause. If the time clause is at the end of a sentence, no comma is necessary.

▶ 3. Past time clauses—Past continuous with *while* and *when.*

a. *Simultaneous actions.* Two actions are happening at the same time in the past. Use the past continuous.

I **was walking** down the street **while** I **was listening** to some music.
The police **were interviewing** witnesses **while** the TV reporters **were reporting.**

b. *Interrupted action.* One action was in progress when another action happened. Use the past continuous in the main clause. Use the simple past in the time clause with **when**. Use **while** in a past continuous time clause.

We **were watching** TV **when** we **heard** a noise in the basement.
I **was walking** my dog **when** someone **stole** my wallet.

While we **were watching** TV, we **heard** a noise in the basement.

14 Careers

A. Look at the photos. Then, write the jobs.

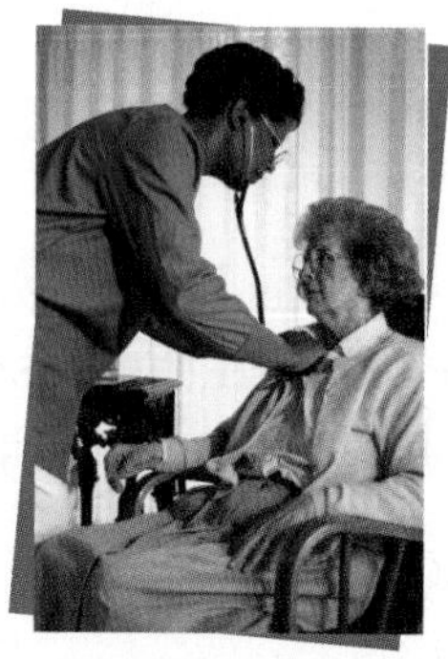

B. Which jobs from Exercise A would you like to have? Talk about the jobs with a partner.

> I would like to <u>be</u> an accountant.
> I would like to <u>work</u> in an office.
> I would like to <u>have</u> a job with a possibility of promotion.

1. Which job would you like to have?
2. Where would you like to work, in an office or outside?
3. Would you like to have a job that requires travel?
4. Would you like to have a job that allows you to supervise other people?
5. What kind of salary would you like to earn?

C. Occupations. Read the list of occupations. Put them into categories according to the level of education required. Ask your teacher about any occupations that are new to you. Some occupations may fit in more than one category.

Occupations	Level of Education Required
carpenter	**Professional Degree**
computer engineer	**1.** ____________
cook or chef	**2.** ____________
dental hygienist	**3.** ____________
dentist	**Bachelor's Degree (Four-year college)**
electrician	**1.** ____________
emergency medical technician (EMT)	**2.** ____________
hair stylist	**3.** ____________
home health aide	**4.** ____________
lawyer	**Associate's Degree (Two-year college)**
licensed pratical nurse (LPN)	**1.** ____________
machine operator	**2.** ____________
manicurist	**3.** ____________
physician	**Vocational Training**
physical therapist	**1.** ____________
plumber	**2.** ____________
registered nurse (RN)	**3.** ____________
respiratory therapist	**4.** ____________
social worker	**Learn on the Job / Short-term training**
secondary school teacher	**1.** ____________
	2. ____________
	3. ____________
	4. ____________
	5. ____________
	6. ____________

Check your answers in the Appendix on page 245.

Active Grammar: Future Time Clauses

If I **lose** my job, I **will look** for another one.
When I **get** a promotion, I **will buy** a new car.
After I **start** my new job, I'**m going to be** happier.

Culture Note

When people apply for new jobs, they often have to give the company a *résumé*. A résumé describes their education and work experience. Another name for a résumé is a *curriculum vitae*, or *CV* for short. It is a good idea to type your résumé.

A. Last month Maria lost her job as an accountant when her company moved overseas. Listen and complete her options and plans.

1. If she finds a part-time job, she ______won't earn______ enough money.
2. Before she looks for another job, she ____________________ her résumé.
3. When her résumé is ready, she ____________________ many copies.
4. After she mails her résumé, she ____________________ for answers.
5. If she gets a rejection, her family ____________________ her feel better.
6. When she goes on an interview, she ____________________ a new suit.
7. If she is confident during the interview, she ____________________ a good impression.
8. If she makes a good impression, the company ____________________ her.

B. Matching. Match each clause on the left with the appropriate main clause on the right.

__c__ 1.	If I do well in my English course,	a.	he will need to take a physical exam.
____ 2.	After Julia completes her engineering degree,	b.	I will get a better job.
____ 3.	When Frank becomes a nurse,	c.	I will become an interpreter.
____ 4.	Before Rick applies to the police department,	d.	she'll enter a community college.
____ 5.	If my supervisor gives me a good evaluation,	e.	I will research the company.
____ 6.	When I finish my degree,	f.	she'll design automobiles.
____ 7.	After Laura finishes high school,	g.	I will get a promotion.
____ 8.	Before I go to the job interview,	h.	he will have to give medication.

C. Read and complete the sentences. Bernato wants to own his own restaurant. Use the present tense in the time clause, and use a future tense (*will* or *be going to*) in the main clause. Use the verbs from the box. Some of the verbs are negative.

apply	be	decide	discuss	save
hire	look for	open	take	

1. If he ____decides____ to open a restaurant, he __is going to discuss__ his plans with his family.
2. If he ________________ enough money, he ________________ for a bank loan.
3. Before he ________________ his own restaurant, he ________________ a few business courses.
4. When he ________________ ready to buy a restaurant, he ________________ a good location.
5. Before Bernato ________________ the restaurant, he ________________ his employees.

Active Grammar: Modals—*May* and *Might*

May and ***might*** are modals that express possibility.

	Meaning
I **will take** a vacation in January.	definite; sure
I **may take** a vacation in January.	possible; maybe
I **might not travel** far.	possible; maybe
He **is** sick.	definite; sure
He **may be** sick.	possible; maybe
He **might be** sick.	possible; maybe

A. Miguel was laid off from his job. What is he going to do next? Look at the pictures and talk about the possibilities. Use *may* or *might* and the words from the box. Some of the verbs are negative.

apply for
buy
go back to
move in with
stay
work with

B. Ask and answer the questions with a partner. Use *may* or *might* in your answer.

What are you going to do next week?
I don't know. I **might take** a vacation.

1. What are you going to do on your next vacation?
2. What will you do if you lose your job?
3. What are you going to do if you go back to your country?
4. Where will you go this weekend?
5. What are you going to do after class?
6. What are you going to eat for dinner?
7. What are you going to do after you become fluent in English?

C. Look at each picture. Make a statement about each situation. Use *may* or *might*.

> If they win the lottery, they **might go** to Hawaii.

D. Pronunciation: Stress and intonation. Listen and repeat each question. Pay attention to the stress and intonation.

1. What are you going to do if you win the lottery?
2. What will you do after you finish this class?
3. What is he going to do before he starts school?
4. Where are they going to live after they get married?
5. If she gets a promotion, what is she going to buy?
6. When he finishes college, where will he work?
7. Before I apply for the job, what forms will I have to complete?

Practice reading the above questions to a partner.

Should—A Review

A. A job interview. There are certain things that a person should and shouldn't do during a job interview. Read each action. Put each action under the correct category. Then, discuss your choices.

chew gum	wear lots of jewelry
dress neatly	make eye contact with the interviewer
wear heavy perfume or cologne	speak in a very soft voice
arrive a few minutes early	wear a baseball cap
send a thank-you note after the interview	research the company
send a present to the interviewer	ask questions during the interview
bring a family member	arrive a few minutes late

Should	Shouldn't
	chew gum

B. Look at the picture. Each person is waiting for a job interview. How can they improve their chances for employment? Use *should* or *shouldn't.*

C. An interview. Sharon Taylor is applying for a job as an office manager in a large medical office. This job will be a good career move for her. Before listening to her interview, review the vocabulary. Ask your teacher about any new words.

applicant	was hired	to be responsible for	to schedule
application	to hire	responsibility	to file

computer skills:
- database—a collection of information
- spreadsheet—an accounting program
- word processing—writing documents on a computer

D. Sharon Taylor's job interview. Listen and answer the questions.

1. Ms. Taylor has
   a. no experience. b. good experience. c. three years of experience.
2. Ms. Taylor worked as a
   a. nurse. b. manager. c. receptionist.
3. Where did she work?
   a. At a hospital. b. At a nursing home. c. At a school.
4. When did she begin working as an administrative assistant?
   a. Two years ago. b. This year. c. Last year.
5. What was she responsible for?
   a. Taking messages. b. Scheduling meetings. c. Hiring new staff.
6. Ms. Taylor has no experience
   a. With computers. b. Designing newsletters. c. Supervising staff.
7. When will she receive an answer about the job?
   a. After the interviews are finished. b. When she gets home c. Next month.

E. Discuss the interview with a group of students. Do you think that Mr. Parker will hire Ms. Taylor? Why or why not?

The Big Picture: Career Choices

A. Ronaldo Silva is looking for a new job and maybe a new career. Listen to Ronaldo discuss his decision. What are the advantages and disadvantages of each choice?

B. Listen and circle the job that fits the description.

1. Large company Own business Both
2. Large company Own business Both
3. Large company Own business Both
4. Large company Own business Both
5. Large company Own business Both
6. Large company Own business Both
7. Large company Own business Both
8. Large company Own business Both

C. Match the two parts of each statement.

h	1. After Ronaldo works for one year at the company,	a.	he may miss activities with his family.
____	2. Ronaldo's wife will handle the bills	b.	he will have to hire a few employees.
____	3. When Ronaldo goes on a business trip,	c.	if he does not have enough money to rent a store.
____	4. Ronaldo will receive a promotion,	d.	if he becomes one of the top twenty salespersons.
____	5. Before Ronaldo opens his store,	e.	when she has free time.
____	6. If Ronaldo takes the new job,	f.	he will have to travel.
____	7. Ronaldo will apply for a bank loan	g.	he may need to use his wife's insurance.
____	8. If Ronaldo starts his own business,	h.	he may receive a promotion.

D. Sentence combination. Read the pairs of sentences. Combine each pair into a longer sentence with a future time clause. Use the time expression in parentheses and change repeated subjects to pronouns.

> Ronaldo takes the new job. Ronaldo will discuss his decision with his family. (before)
> ***Before Ronaldo takes the new job, he will discuss his decision with his family.***

1. Ronaldo takes the new job. Ronaldo will give his employer two weeks notice. (if)
2. The company hires Ronaldo. The company will give him a company car. (after)
3. The company will give Ronaldo his tickets. Ronaldo has to take a trip. (when)
4. Ronaldo will have two weeks vacation. Ronaldo takes the new job. (if)
5. Ronaldo will fill out a loan application. Ronaldo wants to start a business. (if)
6. Ronaldo's family will have a party. The new store opens. (when)
7. Ronaldo will install an alarm system. Ronaldo opens the store. (before)
8. Ronaldo may open a second store. The first store is very successful. (if)

E. What should Ronaldo do? Discuss your answer with a group of students.

A. Before You Read.

1. What information should you include on a résumé?
2. What information shouldn't you include on a résumé?
3. Should you type your résumé?
4. If you have a period of time when you didn't work, should you put that information on your résumé?
5. What kind of paper should you use for your résumé?

B. Read Kenneth Phillips's résumé.

Kenneth M. Phillips
937 Cactus Lane
Sparks, Nevada 89431
Tel: (775) 555-6347 e-mail: kmphillips@callhome.net

> Include your name, address, telephone number, and e-mail address (if you have one).

Career Objectives: To pursue a career in sales in telecommunications, television, or radio; to use my experience and interpersonal skills to increase sales. Available: June

> What kind of career are you looking for?

Education: New York University. B.S. Marketing, June 2002
Desert View High School. June 1998

> What schools did you attend? When did you graduate?

Work Experience:

Jan. 2002—Present — **Salesman,** Cellular Communications. Responsible for selling cellular telephone plans to companies; in charge of Southwest region sales.

Jan. 2001—Dec. 2001 — **Administrative Assistant,** Cellular Communications. Assistant to Head of Sales Dept.; scheduled meetings; trained new staff; did research for Sales Dept.

> Describe your jobs and what your responsibilities were at each job; most people write their résumés in reverse chronological order (from now to the past).

May 2000—Dec. 2000 — **Temporary Employee,** KJZ FM Radio Station; sold advertising time to local companies.

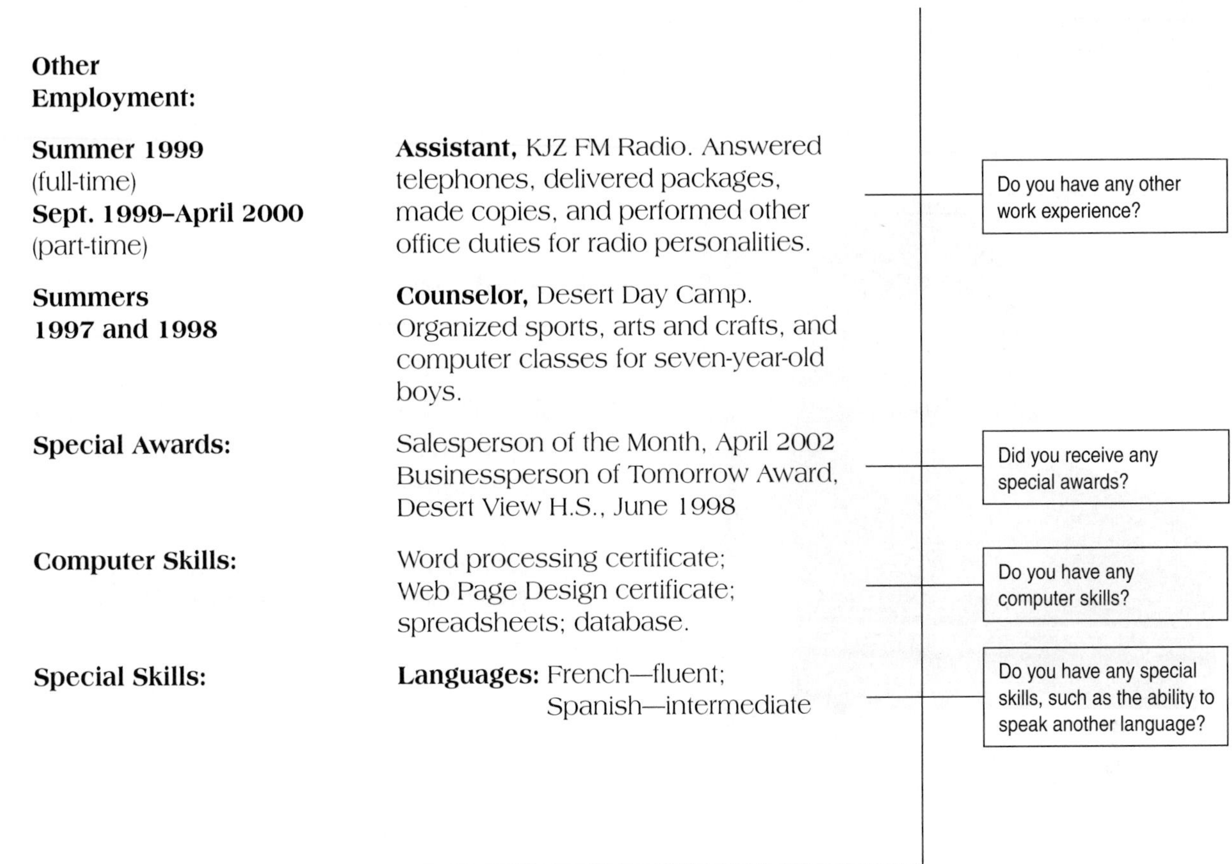

Other Employment:

Summer 1999 (full-time) **Sept. 1999–April 2000** (part-time)	**Assistant,** KJZ FM Radio. Answered telephones, delivered packages, made copies, and performed other office duties for radio personalities.
Summers 1997 and 1998	**Counselor,** Desert Day Camp. Organized sports, arts and crafts, and computer classes for seven-year-old boys.
Special Awards:	Salesperson of the Month, April 2002 Businessperson of Tomorrow Award, Desert View H.S., June 1998
Computer Skills:	Word processing certificate; Web Page Design certificate; spreadsheets; database.
Special Skills:	**Languages:** French—fluent; Spanish—intermediate

C. After You Read. Review the résumé. Answer the following questions.

1. What kind of job is Kenneth looking for?
2. What field is Kenneth's degree in?
3. What jobs did he have at Cellular Communications?
4. Does Kenneth have experience as a supervisor?
5. Does Kenneth have good computer experience?
6. Did Kenneth receive any awards in high school?
7. Does Kenneth speak another language?
8. Kenneth is applying for a promotion to become Director of Sales at Cellular Communications. Would you give him the job? Why or why not?

Writing Our Stories: Cover Letter

A. Read. Danielle Lee is a college student in her junior year. She is studying optometry and is looking for a summer job. She wants a position that will give her on-the-job experience in optometry. Read Danielle's cover letter.

optometry—the profession of examining and prescribing eyeglasses and contact lenses.

March 20, 20__

Dr. Mitchell Jones
Eye See U Optometry
1351 Rainier Boulevard
Seattle, Washington 98109

Dear Dr. Jones:

I am a junior at the University of Washington and am looking for a summer job. I am majoring in biology and plan to become an optometrist. I have a 3.75 grade point average and am fluent in Korean and Chinese. I am looking for a summer job as a receptionist or a secretary in an optometrist's office in order to gain experience in the field of optometry. I can work seven days a week, and I can also work evenings.

In addition to a full-time schedule at the university, I am working part time in the university's library. I work ten hours a week at the circulation desk. I check out books and answer questions about the library. I have been working in the library for two years, but the library does not need me during the summer, so I need a job with more hours. I also work in the Admissions Office. I give tours to prospective students and their families. I work in Admissions about six hours a week and sometimes on Saturdays. Last summer I worked full time at the Seattle Diner as a waitress. I was responsible for setting and clearing tables, taking orders, serving customers, and making coffee. This summer, I would like a job related to my career.

I hope to hear from you soon.

Sincerely yours,

Danielle Lee

B. Danielle's résumé. Use the information from the cover letter to complete the résumé.

Danielle Lee
1501 Kenyon Street
Seattle, Washington 98109
Tel: (206) 555-5996 e-mail: dlee@callhome.net

Career Objectives: To pursue a career in ______________
____

Available: ______________

What kind of career is she looking for?

Education: University of Washington, ______________

Ranier High School ______________

What degree will she receive? When will she graduate?

Work Experience:

______ – **Present** ______ , ______
Job Company

____
Responsibilities

____
Responsibilities

______ – ______ ______ , ______
Job Company

____
Responsibilities

____
Responsibilities

Summer ______ ______ , ______
Job Company

____
Responsibilities

____
Responsibilities

Describe her jobs and what her responsibilities were at each job.

Special Skills: ______________________

____

What special skills does Danielle have?

C. Write your résumé.

Practicing on Your Own

A. Complete. Look at each picture. Complete each main clause. Use the future tense, or *may* or *might.* There is more than one possible correct answer.

1. If it rains, the family ________________________.
2. If it doesn't rain, the family ________________________.

3. After the test is over, the students ________________________.
4. The students ________________________
   when they come back to class tomorrow.

5. If Paul gets the promotion, ________________________.
6. Paul ________________________
   if he doesn't get the promotion.

B. Sentence combining. Combine each pair of sentences with a future time clause using the groups of words. Change repeated subjects to pronouns. Remember to place the comma in the correct position.

1. if / it / rain — we / come home / early
   If it rains, we will come home early.
2. before / I / go home — I / stop / at the supermarket
   ____
   ____
3. I / get (negative) / the job — if / I / have (negative) / a good interview
   ____
   ____

4. I / make / many copies after / I / type / my résumé

____

____

Looking at the Internet

There are many career and job-related Web sites on the Internet. One very helpful Web site is the "Occupational Outlook Handbook." This Web site describes careers and their outlook (future employment possibilities). Search the Internet for "Occupational Outlook Handbook." Research a career. Share the information with your classmates. What education is necessary for the career? What salary can you expect? Is the outlook good?

Grammar Summary

1. *Would like to* ***Would like to*** expresses desires; it is a polite form of *want.*

I **would like to** work in a hospital.	We **would like to** hire you.
You **would like to** apply for this job.	
He **would like to** change careers.	They **would like to** take a vacation.

2. Modals: *May* and *Might* ***May*** and ***Might*** express possibility.

I **may go** to Hawaii for my vacation.	I **might go** to Hawaii for my vacation.
You **may get** the job.	You **might get** the job.
We **may interview** three people.	We **might interview** three people.
He **may not** apply for the job.	She **might not** apply for the job.
It **may not** rain today.	It **might not** rain today.
They **may not** work full time.	They **might not** work full time.

3. Future time clauses

A time clause begins with words such as *if, before, after, as soon as,* and *when.* A time clause has a subject and a verb. In the future tense, the verb in the time clause is in the **present** tense and the verb in the main clause is in the **future** tense or is a modal, such as ***may*** or ***might.***

I **will type** my cover letter	**before** I mail it.	If I **get** an interview,	I **may buy** a new suit.
(main clause)	(time clause)	(time clause)	(main clause)

Note: If the time clause is at the beginning of a sentence, use a comma **after** the time clause. If the time clause is at the end of a sentence, no comma is necessary.

15 City Life

A. Look at the picture. Write the number of each job next to the correct person.

1. clothing shop owner
2. construction worker
3. doorman
4. waiter
5. sanitation workers
6. window washer
7. customers
8. parking violations officer
9. hot dog vendor
10. dog walker
11. firefighters
12. delivery person
13. mail carrier
14. travel agent
15. taxi driver
16. businesswoman

B. Who is . . . ? Listen and write the answers to these questions. Use the occupations on page 224.

1. The customer is.
2. ______
3. ______
4. ______
5. ______
6. ______
7. ______
8. ______
9. ______
10. ______

Active Grammar: *For and Since*

A. Write these words under the correct column.

For	**Since**
For shows an amount of time: for a few minutes for three weeks for two years	*Since* tells when an action started: since 2:00 since 1998 since Sunday since she began her new job

8:00	I came to the U.S.	an hour
ten minutes	a long time	2002
I started school	an hour	more than five years
a year	three days	July
Monday	this morning	six months
	she lost her job	

For	**Since**
ten minutes	8:00
__________	__________
__________	__________
__________	__________
__________	__________
__________	__________
__________	__________

B. Circle *for* or *since* in these sentences.

1. She has been trying on sunglasses **for / since** an hour.
2. He has been washing windows **for / since** 9:00 this morning.
3. They have been waiting for the bus **for / since** thirty minutes.
4. She has been walking dogs **for / since** early this morning.
5. The travel agent has been helping that customer **for / since** two hours.
6. The mail carrier has been walking this same route **for / since** ten years.
7. The doorman has been working at that building **for / since** 1990.
8. The construction worker has been remodeling that store **for / since** April.

Active Grammar: Present Perfect Continuous

A. Listen and complete these sentences about the picture on pages 224-225.

I You We They	have	been	working	since 8:00.
He She It	has			for two hours.

The **present continuous** describes what a person is doing.
The **present perfect continuous** tells *how long* a person has been doing that action.

Katie is delivering mail.
She **has been delivering** mail for two hours.
She **has been working** for the post office since 1997.

1. Larry ______________________ windows since 8:00 this morning.
2. Janet ______________________ sunglasses for an hour.
3. They ______________________ for the bus for a long time.
4. The parking violations officer ______________________ tickets for two hours.
5. The travel agent ______________________ Mrs. Johnson since she sat down.
6. The firefighters ______________________ the fire truck for 30 minutes.
7. The dog walker ______________________ in the park for 20 minutes.
8. The hot dog vendor ______________________ on that corner for ten years.
9. They ______________________ in the restaurant since noon.
10. The sanitation workers ______________________ trash since 6:00 A.M.
11. These people ______________________ busy all morning.

B. Look at the picture on pages 224–225. Write five more sentences using the present perfect continuous.

1. ____
2. ____
3. ____
4. ____
5. ____

What have you been doing?

A. Pronunciation: *'ve been, 's been.* Listen and repeat.

1. She's been looking for a job.
2. We've been planning a vacation.
3. They've been learning how to use a digital camera.
4. He's been painting his house.
5. I've been enjoying my new boat.
6. She's been reading a good book.
7. I've been dating a wonderful guy.

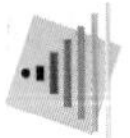

Listen and repeat. Then, practice this conversation with a partner.

A: Hi, Raj. How's it going?
B: Pretty boring. I've been putting in a lot of overtime. How about you? What've you been up to?
A: We've been looking at apartments. We might move to the city.
B: Good luck!

B. A busy weekend. There are three items in each group. What do you think each person has been doing? Use a contraction in your answer.

paint
easel
brushes

I think she's been painting a picture.

helmet riding gloves a tire repair kit	sleeping bags tent backpack	shovel watering can seeds	computer keyboard modem
ball bat glove	vacuum cleaner mop dust cloth	suitcase passport tickets	film camera flash

Now, fill in each list with three related items that a person is using. Can the other students guess what each person has been doing?

1. ______	1. ______	1. ______
2. ______	2. ______	2. ______
3. ______	3. ______	3. ______

C. Present continuous and present perfect. Ask and answer questions about these pictures.

What is ________________ doing?

How long has he/she been ________________? *or*

How long have they been ________________?

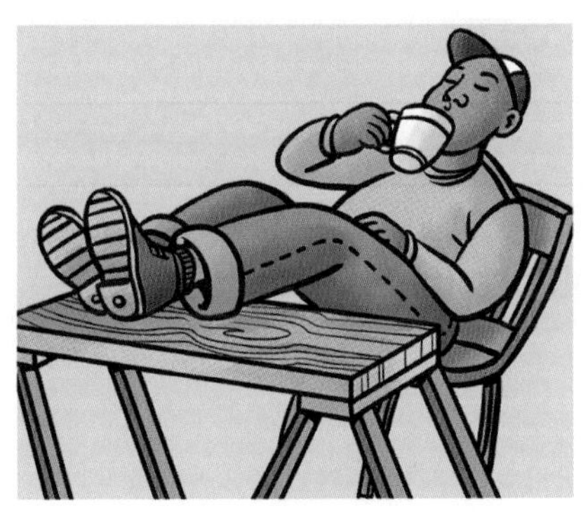

D. Complete this information about yourself.

1. I live in ________________. (city)
2. I work at ________________.
3. In my free time, I ________________.
4. I like to play ________________.
5. I study at ________________.
6. In order to stay healthy, I ________________.

Now read each fact about yourself to your partner. Your partner will ask you a *How long* question for each response.

A: I live in Minneapolis.
B: How long have you been living in Minneapolis?
A: I have been living here for two years.

Tense Contrast

A. *So.* Match the two parts of each sentence.

d	**1.** I got laid off,	**a.** so I've been painting and decorating it.
____	**2.** I broke up with Marie,	**b.** so I've been traveling around the country.
____	**3.** I bought a new house,	**c.** so I've been reading the Personal Ads.
____	**4.** I got engaged last month,	**d.** so I've been looking for a job.
____	**5.** I bought an RV,	**e.** so I've been studying a lot.
____	**6.** I started college,	**f.** so we've been planning the wedding.

Complete these sentences.

7. I joined a health club, so ______________________________.

8. I bought a camera, so ______________________________.

9. I just retired, so ______________________________.

10. I ____________________, so______________________________.

B. Tense meanings. Read the sentences. Circle the sentence that has the same meaning.

1. She worked at the travel agency for six years.

a. She is still working at the travel agency.

b. She doesn't work at the travel agency any more.

2. She's been delivering the mail since 9:00.

a. She's finally finished work for the day.

b. She's still delivering the mail.

3. Janet has been trying on sunglasses for an hour.

a. She is still trying on sunglasses.

b. She left the store.

4. They waited for the bus for 40 minutes.

a. They have been waiting for 40 minutes.

b. The bus finally came.

5. Pablo washed windows from 8:00 to 4:00. It's now 4:30.

a. He's washing windows.

b. He finished washing windows.

C. Andre's Café. Read the information. Label the people in the picture.

Andre is the owner and the chef at Andre's Café. He's been cooking and managing the restaurant for ten years. The food is delicious, so the restaurant is full for lunch and dinner every day.

Andre opened the restaurant at 11:00 this morning. He has four employees. It's lunchtime and the kitchen is busy. Andre is standing at the stove and grilling sandwiches. Ted is his assistant and he's been working at the restaurant for six months. When Ted began to work, he was very thin. Ted loves Andre's cooking, so he's always eating. He has been gaining a lot of weight. Victor is a waiter. He's been working with Andre since the restaurant opened. He's picking up an order.

Carol is Andre's sister. She's been working with her brother for ten years. Carol is very talkative. She's been talking with Ann for an hour. They've been talking about the new beauty parlor that is going to open next door. Ann is Andre's girlfriend. She's been going out with Andre for three months. She's only been working at the restaurant for one month. Right now, she's making salads. She had better be careful. She's using a sharp knife and she isn't paying attention to her work.

D. Student to student dictation.

Student A: Turn to page 244.

Student B: Write the questions Student A dictates. When you finish, change pages.

1. ______________________________
2. ______________________________
3. ______________________________
4. ______________________________
5. ______________________________
6. ______________________________

Now, ask one another your questions!

The Big Picture: Harry, the Doorman

A. Listen to Harry, the doorman, talk about the tenants in the apartment building.

B. Read each comment by Harry. Who is he speaking to?

1. Good morning! Beautiful day for a walk!
2. You're better off without her!
3. Don't worry. I didn't see anything. I didn't hear anything.
4. Good luck today!
5. You have another delivery at the front desk. They're beautiful!
6. Happy Birthday!
7. I'm a city person, too. I love all that the city has to offer.
8. Excuse me, sir. The landlord will be in the building at 3:00 and he would like to speak with you.

C. Complete these sentences using the present perfect continuous.

receive	feel	walk	argue	send	travel	look	complain

1. Leena ______has been looking______ for a job.
2. Mr. Wilson ____________________ letters from credit card agencies.
3. Mr. and Mrs. Shapiro ____________________ around the world.
4. Some of the neighbors ____________________ about a dog barking.
5. Silvia's new boyfriend ____________________ her flowers.
6. Mr. and Mrs. Alvarez ____________________ about where to live.
7. Ms. Chan ____________________ in the park.
8. Many people ____________________ at the apartment to rent.
9. Manuel ____________________ depressed.

D. Listen again. Then, answer these questions about the tenants in the apartment.

1. Why is Manuel depressed?
2. When did his girlfriend leave him?
3. Why didn't Harry like his girlfriend?
4. How old is Ms. Chan?
5. When did she retire?
6. How far does she walk every day?
7. What has Leena been doing?
8. What is she wearing today?
9. When did Silvia meet her new boyfriend?
10. What has he been sending her?
11. Which apartment have people been looking at?
12. How much is the rent?

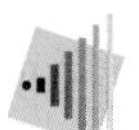

E. Listen and circle the letter of the correct answer.

1. **a.** No, he didn't. **b.** No, he isn't.
2. **a.** Yes, he does. **b.** Yes, he has.
3. **a.** She got a dog. **b.** She is getting a dog.
4. **a.** No, he hasn't. **b.** No, he doesn't.
5. **a.** He received an offer in the country. **b.** He will receive an offer in the country.
6. **a.** She wants to live in the city. **b.** She wanted to live in the city.
7. **a.** They argued. **b.** They have been arguing.
8. **a.** He lived in Apartment 4A. **b.** He lives in Apartment 4A.
9. **a.** He has been receiving cards. **b.** He received cards.
10. **a.** He was a doorman for ten years. **b.** He has been a doorman for ten years.

Reading: Las Vegas

A. Before You Read.

1. Find Nevada on a map of the United States. What part of the country is it located in?
2. What do you know about the geography of this area?
3. What do you think the weather is like?
4. What do you know about Nevada? About Las Vegas?

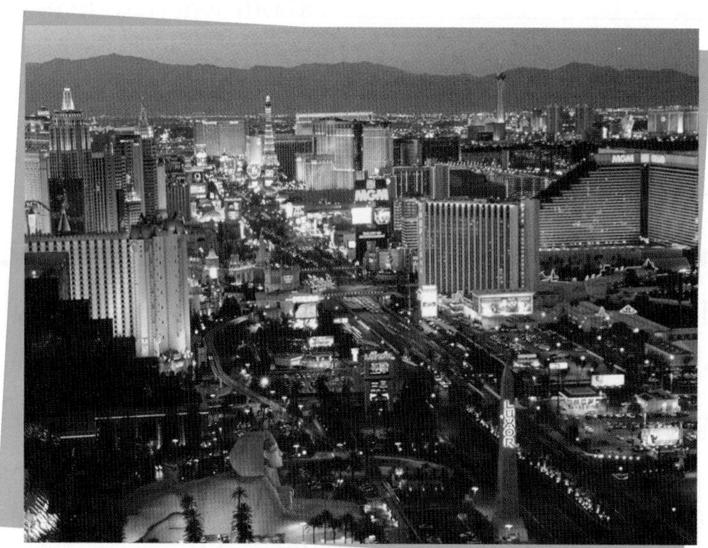

The population of the United States grows larger every year. Between 1990 and 2000, the population of the United States **increased** by 33 million people. The state that has been growing the fastest is Nevada. From 1990 to 2000, Nevada grew 55%. The city that has been receiving the most new residents is Las Vegas. Las Vegas, located in the desert in southern Nevada, grew 112%. In 1990, there were 450,000 people living in Las Vegas. Today, that number is over one million.

Why are so many people moving to Las Vegas? First, it is easy to find a job. Tourism is the number one industry in Las Vegas, so there are many **service jobs.** Construction workers are building thousands of new homes, buildings, and schools. The children need teachers. People need to shop for food, clothing, and cars, so the stores are looking for clerks and cashiers. About one-third of the new residents are from California, where it is more difficult to find a job. Second, Nevada has no income tax. Most states have an income tax of 2%, 4%, 5%, or more. Third, many people like the weather. Even though it's very hot in the summer, often above 100°, the other seasons are beautiful. There are over 250 days of sunshine each year. Finally, housing is still **affordable,** with the price of a new home at about $139,500. People moving from California and the Northeast find that this is reasonable in comparison to homes in their states.

Las Vegas is a tourist city. It is the gambling capital of the world, with more casinos than any other city. One long street, named "The Strip," has more than twenty large casinos. These hotels are very large, some with 3,000 or more rooms, and they offer theaters, stores, restaurants, pools, and health clubs. People walk or drive along The Strip enjoying Egyptian pyramids, an erupting volcano, giant amusement rides, replicas of the Eiffel Tower and New York City, and dramatic light shows.

Las Vegas is also the wedding capital of the United States. It is easier to get married in Las Vegas than in any other city in the United States. You don't need a blood test. You don't need to wait for a week or ten days for a marriage license. It's possible to get married the same day you apply for a marriage license.

Las Vegas also has problems. Because it is located in the desert, there is not enough water. Las Vegas only receives four inches of rain a year. Even though water is expensive, residents have not been careful in **conserving** water. Next, Las Vegas has serious air pollution problems. Las Vegas is surrounded by high mountains, some as high as 10,000 feet. These mountains hold in the pollution from the cars and the nonstop construction projects. At times, there are **warnings** not to exercise outdoors. Finally, as the city **expands,** people are traveling farther to work and the average commute time has been **increasing.** Some new residents are finding the same big city problems that they wanted to leave behind.

B. These words are in bold print in the reading. Discuss their meanings.

increase	service job	affordable
conserve	warning	expands

C. Circle the letter of the correct answer.

1. One example of a service job is
   a. teacher. **b.** carpenter. **c.** desk clerk.
2. One way to conserve water is to
   a. take a short shower. **b.** water your lawn every day. **c.** keep your car clean.
3. An affordable price for a house is
   a. $110,000. **b.** $300,000. **c.** $850,000.
4. The population of that city has been increasing. It used to be 50,000; now it is
   a. 40,000. **b.** 50,000. **c.** 60,000.
5. When a city expands, traffic
   a. becomes lighter. **b.** stays the same. **c.** becomes heavier.
6. There are warnings not to exercise when
   a. there is not enough water. **b.** the pollution is too high. **c.** the traffic is heavy.

D. The pros and cons. Complete these lists with one- or two-word answers.

People are moving to Las Vegas because of

1. jobs
2. ______
3. ______

Some of the problems in Las Vegas are

1. ______
2. ______
3. ______

Writing Our Stories: The Pros and the Cons

A. Read these two paragraphs. One writer would like to move to New York City. The second writer is thinking about leaving New York City.

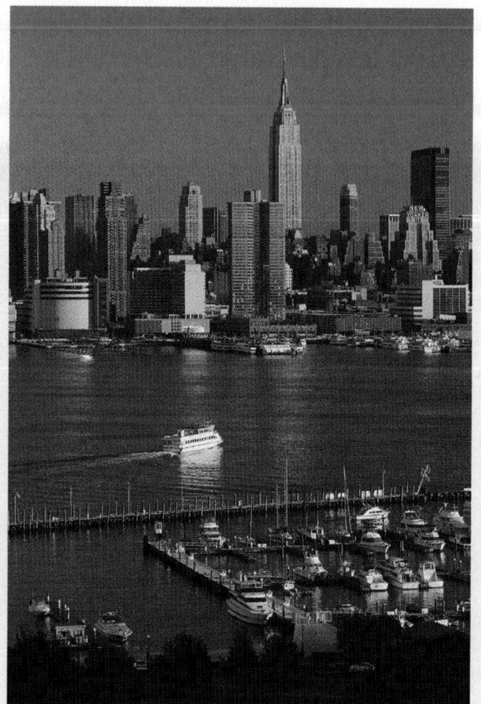

I'm thinking about moving to New York City. First, there's always something happening in New York. There are concerts, museums, and sports. I could watch my favorite team, the New York Mets. Next, it's easy to get a job in New York and the salaries are high. My friend is a waiter in a nice restaurant and he makes about $400 a week. Finally, I would feel more at home because there is a Thai community in the city. There are Thai grocery stores, Thai restaurants, and Thai social clubs. I'm going to live with my friend in New York for a month. If I find a job, I'm going to move there.

I live in New York City and I'm thinking about moving to the suburbs. First, the rents in New York are very expensive. My wife and I and two children live in a one-bedroom apartment. The rent is $1,200 a month. Next, the traffic is impossible. Sometimes it takes me an hour to get to work. And finally, life here is too busy and too fast. The streets and sidewalks are always crowded. People are always in a hurry, too busy to stop and say "Hello." I'm going to look for a job in a smaller city or town.

B. Looking at the paragraphs.

1. Circle the words *first*, *next*, and *finally*.
2. Underline the reasons each person gives for moving or staying.

C. Discussion. Sit in a group and discuss these questions. Use some of the reasons below and add your own ideas. Give a specific example for each reason.

1. What city do you live in now?
   What do you like about it?
   What don't you like about it?
2. Where would you like to live? Why?

> **Reason:**
> **The schools are good.**
> **Example:**
> **The teachers write a weekly class note to the parents. The schools offer music, art, and after-school programs.**

traffic	jobs	family
weather	crime	houses/apartments
schools	recreation	

D. Move or stay? Choose one of these sentences and write a short paragraph about your plans. List three reasons for your choice and give examples. Use *first*, *next*, and *finally* for your reasons.

☐ I live in ______________________ and I am going to stay here.

☐ I live in ______________________, but I'm thinking about moving.

☐ I would like to live in ______________________.

E. Edit. Circle and correct the eight grammar mistakes.

I live in Miami, Florida, and I'm (I) going to stay here. First, I have a lot of family in this area. My mother, father, and my two sister live in Miami. We see them every weekend. Next, I have a secure job. I have working at a delivery company since ten years and I'm manager there. Finally, I am from Cuba and there is a large Cuban community in Miami. I can go to Cuban restaurant, enjoy Cuban music, and see my Cubans friends. At the same time, my children is comfortable in both English and Spanish and they know their culture. I'm planning to stay here and enjoy this beautiful city.

Looking at the Internet

Click on **Search**. Type the name of your city and state. What information can you find?

Practicing on Your Own

A. Complete. Write the present perfect continuous form of the verbs. Circle ***for*** or ***since***.

sit	shop	wait	direct	live
study	watch	take	deliver	

1. Harry has been watching the people on the street **for / since** 8:00.
2. The police officer ______________ traffic **for / since** an hour.
3. Nelson ______________ for the subway **for / since** 15 minutes.
4. No one ______________ in Apartment 5A **for / since** three months.
5. Yelena ______________ in traffic **for / since** 30 minutes.
6. Ali ______________ packages **for / since** 7:00.
7. Nita ______________ a break **for / since** her boss left the office.
8. Paula and Katie ______________ **for / since** the store opened.
9. I ______________ English **for / since** ______________.
10. I ______________ in this country **for / since** ______________.

B. Complete the questions.

George put up the umbrella of his hot dog stand about ten minutes ago. As usual, Sam is his first customer. He buys a hot dog every morning at 11:00. He's been coming to George's hot dog stand since the day it opened, ten years ago.

1. How long has George's stand been open this morning?

   ____

2. What does he sell?

   ____

3. How long has George been selling hot dogs on this corner?

   ____

4. What is Sam doing?

   ____

Gloria has been working at Dog Watchers for six months. She walks dogs in the park all day. When she began this job, she weighed 150 pounds. Because of all the exercise, she has been losing weight. She now weighs 125 pounds and she feels great!

1. How long ______________________________

______________________________?

She has been working for this business for six months.

2. How much __________ she __________ when she began this job?

She weighed 150 pounds.

3. Why ______________________________?

She has been losing weight because of all her exercise.

4. How much ______________________________?

She weighs 125 pounds.

Grammar Summary

▶ 1. Present perfect continuous

The present perfect continuous talks about an action that started in the past and continues in the present. The action is not yet complete. It tells how long the action has been in progress.

He **has been washing** windows since 8:00.

They **have been waiting** for the bus for twenty minutes.

I You We They	have	been	working	since 8:00.
He She It	has			for two hours.

▶ 2. *For* and *since*

For shows an amount of time.

for three hours

for ten days

Since tells when an action started

since 2:00

since he came to the United States

▶ 3. *How long* questions

How long **has** she **been looking** for a job?

How long **have** they **been living** in the city?

Appendix A

Unit 3: Pets

Page 37

E. Student to student dictation.

Student A: Read the questions below. Student B will write each question next to the appropriate answer on page 37.

How far does she live from the city?

Do you listen to the news every day?

Are you a creative person?

How many children does he have?

How often does she call her sister?

How much English do you speak?

Where is she from?

Student B: Read the questions below. Student A will write each question next to the appropriate answer on page 37.

Are you talkative?

How far does he live from work?

How much coffee do you drink?

Where do his parents live?

How many tickets does she need?

How often does he go to the gym?

Do you have a computer?

Unit 4: The States

Page 57

E. Student to student dictation.

Student A: Dictate these questions to Student B. Student B will write them on page 57.

1. How many Native Americans are there in Montana?
2. How many Indian reservations are there?
3. How much snow is there in the Rocky Mountains?
4. How much industry is there in Montana?
5. How many rivers are there in Montana?

Student B: Dictate these questions to Student A. Student A will write them on page 57.

1. How many large cities are there in Montana?
2. How many farms and ranches are there?
3. How much tourism is there in Montana?
4. How much traffic is there in Montana?
5. How many tourists visit Montana every summer?

Unit 5: Computers and the Internet Page 66

C. Student to student dictation: Computer use.

Student A: Read statements 1 to 8 to Student B.

1. They are making airline reservations.
2. He is studying vocabulary words.
3. They are sending photos of the baby to their parents.
4. He is reading about his favorite tennis players.
5. He is listening to the news in Italian.
6. He is buying a tennis racquet online.
7. They are ordering a baby stroller.
8. They are planning each day's activities.

Student B: Read statements 9 to 16 to Student A.

9. He is ordering tennis tickets for the U.S. Open.
10. They are checking the prices of hotels.
11. They are printing a map of the city.
12. He is reading an Italian newspaper.
13. They are designing their baby announcements.
14. He is checking the dates and times of tennis matches.
15. They are making a list of the immunizations that their baby needs.
16. He is sending an e-mail to his friend in Italian.

Unit 6: A Healthy Lifestyle Page 85

tarea

D. Student to student dictation: A hospital visit.

Student A: Read these questions to Student B.

1. How are you feeling?
2. Are you going to need an operation?
3. How long are you going to stay in the hospital?
4. When are you going home?
5. What other tests are you going to need?

Student B: Read these questions to Student A.

1. When is Dr. Green going to talk with you?
2. When are they going to take X rays?
3. Are you finally going to stop smoking?
4. When is the nurse going to give you your medication?
5. When are you going to know the test results?

Unit 7: People and Places Page 100

B. Student to student dictation.

Student A: Read these five sentences about the two children to Student B.

1. Jose is not as young as Hans.
2. Jose's hair is not as curly as Hans'.
3. Jose is as friendly as Hans.
4. Jose likes soccer as much as Hans.
5. Jose is not as tall as Hans.

Student B: Read these five sentences about the two children to Student A.

1. Hans is not as old as Jose.
2. Hans' hair is not as curly as Jose's hair.
3. Hans is not as short as Jose.
4. Hans is as popular as Jose.
5. Hans' family is not as big as Jose's.

Unit 8: Moving Page 121

D. Student to student dictation

Student A: Ask Student B these questions. Your partner will circle the correct answer.

1. Who lived in the United States first?
2. How long did Jiang live with his uncle?
3. Where did he work at first?
4. Where did he first study English?
5. Who did he rent a small studio apartment with?
6. Where did he meet his wife?
7. How many times did he move?
8. Where does he work now?
9. When did he meet his wife?
10. Where does he live now?

Student B: Ask Student A these questions. Your partner will circle the correct answer.

1. Who stayed in China?
2. How long did he work in the shoe factory?
3. Where did he find a better job?
4. Where is he studying now?
5. Who helped him with his English?
6. Where did he continue his education?
7. How many jobs did he have?
8. What does he want to do in the future?
9. When did he get married?
10. Where did he live when he first came to the United States?

Unit 9: Natural Disasters Page 132

D. Student to student dictation: The heat wave.

Student A: Ask Student B these six questions. Student B will circle the correct answer.

1. Were you living in Texas in 1998?
2. Was that the summer of the bad heat wave?
3. How long did the heat wave last?
4. How many people died?
5. Did you have air-conditioning?
6. How did you stay cool?

Student B: Read these questions to Student A. Student A will circle the correct answer.

1. Did you live in Texas in 1998?
2. Were you here for the heat wave?
3. How hot was it?
4. Why did so many people die?
5. Was your house air-conditioned?
6. Did you go to the beach?

Unit 10: Wedding Plans Page 150

B. Student to student dictation.

Student A: Listen to Student B read statements 1–4. Give your opinion. Say "I agree" or "I disagree." Then, read statements 5–8 to Student B. Listen and check (✓) Student B's opinion. Discuss your opinions.

Statement	Agree	Disagree
5. Money is the most appropriate gift for a couple.		
6. The groom's family should help pay for the wedding.		
7. The couple should agree about having children before they get married.		
8. The couple should send thank-you cards for all wedding gifts.		

Unit 15: City Life Page 231

D. Student to student dictation.

Student A: Read these questions to Student B.

1. How long has Andre been managing his restaurant?
2. Why is the restaurant always busy?
3. What is Andre doing?
4. How long has Ted been working at this restaurant?
5. Why is he always eating?
6. Has Ted been gaining weight?

Student B: Read these questions to Student A.

1. What is Victor doing?
2. How long has he been working with Andre?
3. Who is Carol?
4. Who has she been talking to?
5. How long has Ann been working at the restaurant?
6. How long has she been going out with Andre?

Appendix B

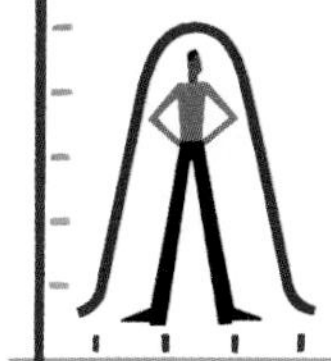

Unit 2: The Average American Page 16

Exercise A

1. one **2.** one **3.** one **4.** three **5.** 80
6. 74 **7.** drive **8.** 25 **9.** cereal

Unit 14: Careers Page 209

Exercise C

Professional Degree

dentist
lawyer
physician

Bachelor's Degree (Four-year college)

computer engineer
social worker
physical therapist
secondary school teacher

Associate's Degree (Two-year college)

registered nurse
dental hygienist
respiratory therapist

Vocational Training

hair stylist
manicurist
licensed practical nurse
emergency medical technician

Learn on the Job/Short-term Training

carpenter
cook or chef
electrician
home health aide
machine operator
plumber

Appendix C

Unit 13: Crime Page 196

B. Describing a suspect.

Describe the man you just saw. Answer the questions with a partner.

1. How tall was he?

   a. tall **b.** medium height **c.** short

2. How much did he weigh? ________ pounds

3. What was he wearing?

   He was wearing ________________________________

   ____

4. What was his race?

   a. Caucasian (white) **b.** African-American **c.** Hispanic / Latino
   d. Asian **e.** other

5. He was . . .

   a. light-skinned. **b.** dark-skinned.

6. What color were his eyes?

   a. black **b.** dark brown **c.** brown **d.** blue **e.** green **f.** hazel

7. What shape was his face?

   round oval square

8. Did he have any facial hair?

   a. a beard **b.** a moustache **c.** a beard and a moustache **d.** none

9. What else do you remember about the suspect?

   ____

Audio Script

Unit 1: The First Week

Page 3

A. Listen as Gloria interviews Kenji about his life in the United States. Take notes as you listen. Then, talk about Kenji.

Gloria: Hi, Kenji.
Kenji: Hi, Gloria.
Gloria: I'd like to interview you for class.
Kenji: Sure. Go ahead.
Gloria: Kenji, what country are you from?
Kenji: I'm from Japan.
Gloria: How long have you been here in the United States?
Kenji: For six months.
Gloria: Is your family here in the United States?
Kenji: No, my family is in Japan. I came here alone to study English. In Japan, I have my mother and father and one sister.
Gloria: Where do you live?
Kenji: In the student dorms, right here on campus.
Gloria: Are you a new student?
Kenji: Yes, this is my first semester here at school.
Gloria: Do you work?
Kenji: No, I don't.
Gloria: Are you married?
Kenji: No, I'm not. I'm only 21 years old. That's too early to get married.
Gloria: What are your interests?
Kenji: I'm a swimmer. I was on the swim team in high school in my country. They have a great pool here on campus and I swim four or five times a week. And I like photography. I have a digital camera and I'm sending lots of pictures of California back to my family in Japan.
Gloria: What kind of music do you like?
Kenji: I like rock.
Gloria: Do you have a computer?
Kenji: Yes, I have a laptop.
Gloria: Thank you, Kenji.

Unit 2: The Average American

Page 17

B. Charlie. Listen to Charlie describe himself and his lifestyle. Take notes. Compare Charlie to the average American male.

Hi. My name's Charlie Johnson, and I'm supposed to tell you a little about myself. I'm 32 years old, and I'm single. That's right, I'm not married yet. I'm 6'2" tall, and I weigh about 210 pounds. I guess I could lose a little weight. I'm a computer programmer at a large company. I really like my job. It's interesting, and I can be creative. My hours are long—about ten hours a day. Sometimes, I have to come in on weekends—but the best part is the salary—$60,000 a year. Yeah, it's good. I live in the city in a one-bedroom apartment. I like it because it's in a good location. It's near public transportation, and that's good for me. I don't have a car, but that's OK. I can walk to work or take a bus. And, I have a roommate. He spends most of his time sleeping and lying on the couch. He's my cat, Floppy.

Page 20

B. Which sound do you hear? Circle the correct sound.

a. wears	**e.** drives	**i.** studies
b. washes	**f.** earns	**j.** lives
c. sleeps	**g.** uses	**k.** likes
d. takes	**h.** goes	**l.** watches

Page 24

The Big Picture: The Shaw Family

B. Listen and complete the information on the pictures about the Shaw family.

1. This is the Shaw family. Mike Shaw is 42 years old. He is a high school math teacher. Like other public school teachers, he works nine months a year. His hours are 7:30 to 3:00. He earns $55,000 a year and gets excellent benefits. His wife, Maria Shaw, is 39 years old. She is a software engineer. She works at a bank from 9:00 to 5:00. She earns $65,000 a year and she has good benefits, too. She's expecting her second child in about a month. She had her first child when she was 31.
2. Mike Shaw drives to work. It only takes him 20 minutes to get to work. Mrs. Shaw commutes to work. It takes her 40 minutes by train to get to work. At home, she drives a minivan.
3. The Shaws live in a house with their son, Mark. He's eight years old. Mike's parents also live with them. Mark likes living with his grandparents. And the Shaws have two pets—a cat and a dog. Their house cost $175,000, and it's old. It has three bedrooms, a living room, a kitchen, a den, and a small yard.
4. The family eats out every Friday night. After a long, busy week, they like to take a break from cooking.

5. Every summer, they take a vacation for a week or two. They like to go to the beach.
6. Like many American families, they spend most evenings at home. Maria, Grandma Shaw, and Mark usually sit in the living room and watch TV or rent a movie. There's another TV upstairs, but everyone likes to sit together in the living room. Grandpa Shaw usually falls asleep in the chair. It's a relaxing evening for everyone except Mike. Mike sits at his desk and corrects his students' homework.

Unit 3: Pets

Page 38

A. Interview: A dog owner.
Listen. Then, answer the questions.

A: That's a beautiful dog. She's a Lab, isn't she?
B: Yes, she's a Lab. Her name is Lucky.
A: How old is she?
B: She's seven.
A: Can I pet her?
B: Yes, she's very friendly.
A: How often do you walk her?
B: Three times a day. My husband walks her in the morning and in the evening. Just a short walk, maybe around the block. And in the afternoon, I take her for a long walk in the park, about 40 or 50 minutes. I love it and I need the exercise.
A: How often do you feed her?
B: She only eats once a day, in the evening.
A: How is she with the children?
B: She loves them. They play with her after school and she watches TV with them. And at night, she sleeps in my son's room on his bed.
A: Do you need to comb her every day?
B: No, I brush her maybe two times a week.
A: Is she a good watchdog?
B: I'm afraid not. She's too friendly. She doesn't bark at the letter carrier. And when a stranger comes to the door, she just wags her tail.

Page 38

C. Interview: A cat owner.
Listen. Then, complete the questions.

A: Your cat has a beautiful coat. It's jet black. What's her name?
B: Midnight
A: How old is she?
B: She's 14.
A: Fourteen. Isn't that old for a cat?
B: Yes, she isn't very active anymore. She sleeps a lot. During the day, she sits in the front window and watches the birds. And after I come home, she just sits in my lap when I watch TV.
A: Where does she sleep?
B: Well, she has her basket. And she sleeps on the sofa.
A: Does she ever go outside?
B: No, never. She stays inside.

Page 40

The Big Picture: The Humane Society

B. Listen and complete the information on the card on the right.

Dad: There are a lot of dogs in here. About 50 . . . 60.
Mom: Look at this one. A Lab. They're great with children. This one looks very old.
Dad: Hmm-hmm.
Boy: Dad, Mom, here's one. Look how big he is!
Dad: Too big. He's bigger than you!
Mom: A lot of these dogs are strays. I guess they just picked them up on the street.
Girl: I like this one. He likes me, too.
Dad: He *is* friendly. He's a boxer.
Boy: I like his color, a nice soft brown.
Mom: Let's see. Let me read the card. Well, first of all, it's not a *he*. It's a *she*. Her name is Daisy. She's good with children. And she's good with other animals. She's here because her owner moved into an apartment and couldn't keep her. So, of course she is housebroken. And she has her rabies immunization.
Boy: She's licking my hand!
Dad: She's only been here for two days. Look. She's wagging her tail.
Mom: Let's ask them to take her out of the cage for a few minutes.
Girl: Mom, Dad, can we keep her?
Dad: Maybe. We'll see. We'll see.

C. Listen to the conversation between the manager of the Humane Society and Mr. and Mrs. Vento. Complete the form as you listen.

Interviewer: Mr. and Mrs. Vento, who will be responsible for the dog?
Mrs. Vento: We all will. I'm home a lot, so I'll take her for a long walk in the afternoon. But we expect the children to help, too.
Jake and Susan: Yes! Yes!
Interviewer: How many children do you have?
Mr. Vento: Two. This is Jake and this is Susan. Jake is eleven and Susan is eight.
Interviewer: Do you have your own home?
Mr. Vento: Yes. We have a house.
Interviewer: And where will you keep the dog when you aren't at home?
Mr. Vento: We are planning to keep the dog inside.

Interviewer:	How many hours a day will the dog be outside?
Mrs. Vento:	Probably three or four.
Interviewer:	Do you have a fenced yard?
Mrs. Vento:	No, we don't. We'll tie her outside.
Interviewer:	Is this your first pet? Have you ever owned a dog or a cat in the past?
Mr. Vento:	Yes. We had another dog before this, a mixed breed, Peanut. He died last year. He was 13.
Interviewer:	Where did you get Peanut?
Mrs. Vento:	From my brother. His dog had puppies and we took one of them.
Interviewer:	Any other pets?
Mrs. Vento:	No, just our dog, Peanut.
Interviewer:	Did you ever adopt from a Humane Society before?
Mr. Vento:	No, we haven't. But our neighbors got a dog here about two years ago and they're very happy with her. She's very good with their children.

Unit 4: The States

Page 50

B. Listen: Mark your own location on the map. Point to each location on the map.

The United States

This is a map of the United States. The United States is a large country on the continent of North America. There are three countries in North America: Canada, the United States, and Mexico. The United States is in the middle. Canada is to the north and Mexico is to the south.

The United States reaches from the Atlantic Ocean on the east to the Pacific Ocean on the west. To the south is the Gulf of Mexico.

There are 50 states. Forty-eight states are joined together. Two states, Hawaii and Alaska, are separate. Hawaii is a group of islands in the Pacific Ocean, and Alaska, the largest state, is far to the northwest.

When you look at the map of the United States, you see that many of the major cities are on the coast. These cities all have excellent seaports. On the east coast, you can see Boston, New York, and Miami. New Orleans is on the Gulf of Mexico. On the Pacific Ocean, you can find San Diego, San Francisco, and Seattle.

There are two major mountain ranges in the United States; both run from north to south. In the east, the Appalachian Mountains are an older, lower mountain range. In the west, the Rocky Mountains are a younger and much higher mountain range. Snow covers the tops of these mountains most of the year.

This map of the United States shows the east, the central area, and the west.

The east is light green. This is an area of coastal plains and low mountains. From Boston to Washington, D.C., is a line of large cities and towns.

The central area is blue. In the northern part are the five Great Lakes, lying on the border between Canada and the United States. The Mississippi River begins in the north and flows south to New Orleans and into the Gulf of Mexico. There are many farms and ranches in the central and southern areas.

The west is yellow. The geography of the west is very dramatic, with high mountains, valleys, and deserts. There are many beautiful national parks in this part of the country, such as the Grand Canyon in Arizona and Death Valley in California. Millions of tourists visit the national parks every year.

Page 56

The Big Picture: Montana

B. Look at the map and listen to the information about Montana. Then, make statements using the words.

Montana

Montana is the fourth largest state in the United States. It is located in the northern part of the country. On the north, it shares a border with Canada. Montana is divided into two geographic areas. The Rocky Mountains are in the western part of the state. The Great Plains cover the eastern part. Several important rivers run through Montana. The Missouri River, the second longest river in the United States, begins in Montana.

The western part of Montana receives a lot of rain and snow. Because Montana is so far north, it has very cold winters. There are often heavy snowstorms. In the other seasons, there is a lot of rain. Because the Rocky Mountains are so high, they stop the rain clouds, and the eastern part of the state is dry.

With fewer than 800,000 people, Montana has one of the lowest populations in the United States. There are about 50,000 Native Americans living in Montana. Many of the Native Americans live in the state's seven Indian reservations, while others live in small towns and cities throughout the state. Towns and cities are small and far apart.

Thousands of tourists visit Montana every summer and fall to enjoy the beautiful scenery, to hike in the mountains, and to fish in the rivers and lakes. Some tourists stay at the many large horse ranches in the Great Plains. In the winter, skiing in popular.

Unit 5: Computers and the Internet

Page 71

C. Listen to these conversations. Then, answer the questions.

Conversation 1

A: Gloria's on the phone again.
B: Who's she talking to?
A: Her boyfriend. He lives in Oregon. And a few minutes ago, she was talking to her sister in Michigan.
B: Isn't that expensive?
A: No, she has a great calling plan. She pays $75 a month for 3,000 minutes. She can talk to anyone, anytime, anywhere in the United States.
B: Three thousand minutes!? Who can use 3,000 minutes?
A: Gloria can! She's on the phone an hour or two a day.

Conversation 2

A: Steve! Look at the camera! Smile!
B: Mom! The game is starting!
A: OK. I got a good picture of you.
C: Is that a digital camera?
A: Yes. I'm taking pictures of the game today. I send lots of photos to my parents in Arizona. They only see their grandchildren once or twice a year.
C: How do the pictures turn out? Are they as good as a regular camera?
A: This camera takes great pictures. When I get home, I put them on the computer. The pictures I like, I keep. And the ones I don't like, I can just delete.
C: That sounds too complicated for me.
A: It really isn't. The first time, you need someone to show you how to do it. After that, it's easy.

Conversation 3

A: What is that called again?
B: It's a PDA, a personal digital assistant. Most people just call them hand-helds.
A: What do you use it for?
B: For this business, everything. I have the name and phone number of every beauty salon in the state. I have all my clients' names and addresses and phone numbers here. And, this part here, it shows my schedule for the day. And in this part here, I can enter orders. See, here? Your order is 20 bottles of shampoo, 15 bottles of conditioner, the hair color you need. I check the items you need and write the number.
A: How much are those?
B: Some are about $200, but this one has a lot of features. It was $599.

Page 72

The Big Picture: Cruiseaway.com

B. Listen to the information about the Internet company cruiseaway.com.

Cruiseaway.com is a travel site for cruises. People go to the site and find information on over one hundred cruise companies that offer cruises worldwide. They can look at photos of the ships, they can see the maps of different routes, they can check prices and dates, and they can make cruise reservations, all online. Cruiseaway.com designed, organized, and programmed the Web site, but the employees do not work with tourists directly. If tourists need more information, they call the specific cruise line directly.

Crusiseaway.com is typical of many small Internet companies. It's a small office with only a few employees. The office is informal and relaxed. Most of the employees are young, and most of the programmers are male. The typical clothing is jeans and a T-shirt. The employees work long hours, so the coffee pot is always on. There are sodas in the refrigerator, and snacks on the tables. Toys and games are popular. There are stress balls near the computers and remote control cars on the floor.

Today is a typical day at Cruiseaway.com. Megan and Samip are programmers. Megan is designing a Web page for a new cruise line. She's playing with a stress ball. Samip is sitting near her and drinking a can of soda. He's debugging the site; in other words, he's checking for errors and fixing them. Michael is on the phone. He's talking to one of the cruise companies about adding a new ship and several new vacations. Antonio, another programmer, is taking a break. He's drinking a cup of coffee and playing with a remote control car. He's directing the car under the computer table. Lee is just arriving at work. He usually doesn't arrive until 10:00, but he works until 8:00 at night. Most of the employees work nine or ten hours a day. When they are working on a big project, they work eleven or twelve hours a day. When the programmers are not at work, one always wears a beeper. If the site goes down, even in the middle of the night, that person has to drive to work immediately and get the site up and running again.

Unit 6: A Healthy Lifestyle

Page 84

C. Discuss the new vocabulary. Then, listen to the conversation between Mr. West and the doctor. Answer these questions.

D: These are the X rays, Mr. West. Jimmy has a broken leg. It's a bad break. The nurse is putting ice packs on his leg now because it's swollen quite a lot. We need to wait for the swelling to go down, so we're going to keep him in the hospital for two days, and then, we'll put the cast on. When was his last tetanus shot?
M: Not for a long time, maybe seven or eight years ago.
D: I'm going to give him a tetanus shot.

M: How long is he going to need the cast?
D: For children, it's usually six to eight weeks.
M: He's in a lot of pain.
D: We're going to give him something for the pain in a few minutes. Is he allergic to anything?
M: No, he zsn't.
D: He's going to need painkillers for a few days.
M: Can he go to school?
D: Don't worry. He will be back in school next week. But he's going to need crutches.

Page 88

The Big Picture: The Accident

B. Listen to the story. Then, complete the sentences with the new vocabulary.

There was a bad accident at the intersection of Maple and Central Avenue about 10 minutes ago. A **witness** who saw the accident immediately called 911. The police and two ambulances were at the scene of the accident a few minutes later.

Luis is lying by the side of the road. His arm is cut very badly. One emergency medical worker is applying a **pressure bandage** to stop the **bleeding.** The other technician is talking to him and taking his **blood pressure.** She's telling Luis that the bleeding is under control and that she is going to start an **IV.** Then, they are going to take him to the hospital.

Two other emergency workers are with the woman on the **stretcher.** She is pale and confused. She doesn't know her name and she can't answer any questions. One worker is covering her with a **blanket.** Because the front **windshield** of her car is broken, the workers think that she might have a **concussion.**

The police officer is directing traffic at the scene. Traffic is moving very slowly because everyone wants to look at the accident.

Page 89

E. Listen and circle the correct answer.

1. Is Luis hurt?
2. Does he have a bad cut on his leg?
3. Is the technician going to start an IV?
4. Is the woman confused?
5. Does she know her name?
6. Is she going to need an X ray?
7. Is the police officer directing traffic?

Unit 7: People and Places

Page 97

B. Pronunciation: Listen and repeat the comparative adjectives in the chart above.

shorter than	lazier than	more athletic than
shyer than	friendlier than	more handsome than
smaller than	healthier than	more talkative than
taller than	heavier than	more interesting than
thinner than	prettier than	more quiet than
bigger than		more beautiful than
longer than		more serious than
		more hardworking than

Page 98

D. Two brothers. Listen and complete the sentences about Jack and Julian.

1. Jack is more serious than Julian.
2. Jack is heavier than Julian.
3. Jack is shyer than Julian.
4. Jack is shorter than Julian.
5. Julian is more sociable than Jack.
6. Julian is more athletic than Jack.
7. Julian is healthier than Jack.
8. Julian is taller than Jack.

Page 99

A. Like father, like son. Listen and complete the sentences.

Father (Charles):
My name is Charles, and this is my son, Roger. Roger is only 16, but he's as tall as I am. We're both 5'11". My son is not as athletic as I am. He plays video games all the time, but I play basketball and exercise five days a week.

Son (Roger):
My dad is not as well dressed as I am. He's still wearing clothes from his college days. My dad is as talkative as I am. We both like to talk a lot. My dad is definitely not as handsome as I am. I think I am much better looking.

Father (Charles):
Roger is as hardworking as I am. He studies hard, and he belongs to many school clubs. I'm very proud of him.

Page 104

The Big Picture: Two Cities

A. Listen and complete the information about two cities—Austin, Texas and Boston, Massachusetts.

According to the *Places Rated Almanac,* Austin, Texas, is one of the best places to live in the United States. Austin is the capital of Texas, and it has a population of 656,562 and an unemployment rate of 5.2 percent. The residents pay the state tax of 6.25 percent. The average income for Austin residents is $27,300. There are eight different colleges and universities in Austin, and twelve hospitals. In terms of cultural activities, residents can visit three art museums and listen to two different symphony orchestras. Austin has no professional sports teams, but there are teams in other cities in Texas.

Boston, Massachusetts, is also a good place to live. Boston is smaller than Austin—it has a population of 589,141. The unemployment rate in this high-tech city is 4.2 percent, and the state tax is 5 percent.The average income of Bostonians is $37,700. One thing that visitors notice when they go to Boston is the number of colleges and universities. College students seem to be everywhere. That's because there are 64 colleges and universities in this small city. There are also 65 different hospitals. In terms of cultural activities, Boston is a great city. There are eleven art museums and twenty-five symphony orchestras. Boston is not only a great place for culture but also for sports. Boston has one hockey team, one basketball team, one baseball team, one football team, and one soccer team—five professional sports teams.

B. Listen and circle the correct city.

1. Which city is larger?
2. Which city has lower unemployment?
3. Which city has higher taxes?
4. Which city's residents earn more income?
5. Which city offers more educational opportunties?
6. Which city has more hospitals?
7. Which city has fewer cultural events?
8. Which city is better for a sports fan?

Unit 8: Moving

Page 116

D. Finding an apartment. Put your pencil down and listen twice to Miguel and Ana's story about finding their new apartment. Then, complete the story with the verbs from Exercise A.

We were lucky in finding our current apartment. Before this, we lived in a different town, but we weren't happy there. The area wasn't safe, and last month someone broke into our apartment and stole our TV and stereo. We talked to friends and looked in the paper, but we didn't find anything. Then one day we got in the car and drove around in a neighborhood we both liked. We were on a quiet street a few blocks from town when we saw a two-family house with a sign in the window, "Apartment for Rent, Inquire Within." We rang the doorbell. The owner was home and he showed us around the apartment. It was sunny and clean with lots of room. We signed a lease that day and gave him one month's rent and a security deposit. We were very lucky! The owner told us, "I just put the sign in the window this morning!"

Page 120

The Big Picture: Jiang

A. Listen to this conversation between Jiang and a friend from business class. As you listen, add more information to the timeline.

Friend: What country are you from?
Jiang: I'm from China.
Friend: When did you come to the United States?
Jiang: In 1999.
Friend: Did you come alone?
Jiang: Yes, I did. My family stayed in China, but I had an uncle here. He sent us many letters about how wonderful life is here, so I decided to come to the United States. I was only 23 years old.
Friend: Did you live with him?
Jiang: Yes, I lived with him for about a year. He helped me find a job in a shoe factory, but I hated it. The work was hard and everyone spoke Chinese. I thought, "How am I ever going to learn English?" I was upset about English. I didn't understand anything and I had no idea how to speak it.
Friend: So how did you learn English? You speak it very well.
Jiang: Well, I saved a little money and moved to a studio apartment with a friend that I met at the factory. And I started English classes at college. I studied very hard. And I found a better job, at a small store that sold and repaired appliances. The owner was American and he helped me with my English, too.
Friend: How long did you work at that store?
Jiang: I'm still there today. The owner gave me more and more responsibility. I still repair appliances, but I help customers, too. I like business. After I finished my English classes, I began taking business classes.
Friend: Is that where you met your wife, at college?
Jiang: Yes, she was a student there, too. We met in 2001 and we got married in 2002. That's when we moved here, near the college. We are still working and going to school. We hope to start a small business of our own some day.

Unit 9: Natural Disasters

Page 129

B. Before you listen, match each question to the event on page 128. Then, listen and write the answers to the questions.

1. **A:** How deep was the water?
   B: The water was six feet deep.
2. **A:** How strong was the wind?
   B: The wind was 100 mph.
3. **A:** How high was the temperature?
   B: The temperature was over 100° for two weeks.
4. **A:** How much snow was there?
   B: There was 3 feet of snow.

5. **A:** Was there any rain?
   B: No, there was no rain for three months.
6. **A:** How high were the flames?
   B: The flames were over 100 feet high.
7. **A:** How strong was the earthquake?
   B: It was 6.2 on the Richter scale.
8. **A:** Was there a lot of fire and lava?
   B: Yes, there was.
9. **A:** How many tornadoes were there?
   B: There were two funnel clouds.

Page 136

The Big Picture: The Hurricane

B. Listen to the conversation. Then, use these cues to describe what this couple did before the hurricane, during the hurricane, and after the hurricane.

A: That was a really bad hurricane you had last month!

B: I know. It was our first hurricane since we moved here to North Carolina. We thought it was terrible, but the old-time residents told us it was just an average one.

A: How much warning did you have?

B: Warning?! That's all we got. Twenty-four hours a day, all day. For about a week. The radio, the TV, the newspapers. The news was nonstop.

A: So, what did you do to get ready?

B: Well, we had to get everything out of the yard. We put the yard furniture, and the barbecue grill, the garbage cans, everything, into the garage. If we didn't, they could fly through a window during the hurricane. And we bought lots of food—canned food—in case we didn't have power for cooking. We had to buy batteries for flashlights and radios. And they us told to buy water, lots and lots of water. And we filled the bathtub with water, too. We also bought a power saw.

A: A power saw?

B: Hm, hm. Hurricanes knock down trees. And in a bad hurricane, two or three trees might fall in your yard. Everyone around here has power saws to cut them up.

A: How bad was the hurricane?

B: I thought it was terrible. The rain was so heavy we couldn't see out the windows. The wind was about 80 miles an hour and it reached 100 miles an hour at times. It knocked down the power lines and we didn't have electricity for two days. We were lucky, only one tree came down in the back yard. But our neighbor had a tree come down right though his roof into one of the bedrooms upstairs. He had water all over, in all the rooms, because the rain was so heavy and it rained for hours.

A: So, did you evacuate?

B: No, we stayed in the house. For this storm, most people stayed in their homes.

A: Were you scared?

B: I was so scared! Most of the time, I stayed in the bathroom. I thought, any minute, something was going to come flying through a window or that a tree was going to fall on our house. My husband was more relaxed. He lit candles and listened to the news.

A: So, are you glad you moved to North Carolina?

B: Well, we really like it here, but these hurricanes . . . I don't know. Maybe we'll get used to them.

Unit 10: Wedding Plans

Page 146

B. Jennifer and Brian have just become engaged. It's November, and they plan to get married in late August. Listen to the timetable for some of their plans. Match the month and the task.

First, Jennifer and Brian have to announce their engagement. They want to tell their family and closest friends. In early December, they have to reserve the ceremony site and a place for the reception. It's important to reserve early. Later the same month, Jennifer has to order the dresses for herself and for the bridesmaids. Selecting the right dress sometimes takes a long time. Jennifer and Brian have to book the band in January because they have a favorite band, but it's very popular. In February, they have to start planning the honeymoon. They'll get a good price if they reserve early. Planning the guest list will take time. They have to start planning in March. In April, they have to order the invitations. In May, Jennifer will start getting nervous about her dress. She has to go for the final wedding gown fitting. Jennifer and Brian want to use a good florist, so they also have to reserve the florist in May. In early June, they are going to mail the invitations because they want to make sure all of their friends can attend. In July, Brian and Jennifer will go to City Hall to apply for the marriage license. Now, all that's left is the wedding.

Page 148

C. Pronunciation: *Have to/has to.* Listen and circle the correct modal.

1. They have to tell their parents.
2. We have to make honeymoon reservations.
3. She has to tip the disc jockey.
4. They have to order invitations.
5. You have to have a photographer.
6. He has to rent a tuxedo.
7. The bride has to contact a caterer.
8. I have to set a date.

Page 150

A. Decisions, decisions. Leslie and Mitch are getting married. They have many decisions to make about their wedding and reception. Listen to their conversation and circle the correct answer. Discuss the couple's decisions.

Mitch: Let's keep the reception simple. I don't want a big wedding, just something small, something affordable.

Leslie: That would be nice, but what are we going to tell our parents? They expect a big wedding. We'll have to limit the guest list. Maybe we should just invite our brothers and sisters, and aunts and uncles.

Mitch: But I have to invite my cousins!

Leslie: Don't you have a lot of cousins?

Mitch: Yeah, I do, but we're very close. I have to invite them.

Leslie: Well, then, we should have a bigger wedding.

Mitch: I guess you're right. Now, when are we going to get married? A spring wedding would be nice. We could get married in April or in May.

Leslie: We'll never be ready for a spring wedding. We have to plan for a summer wedding. How about a garden wedding in August?

Mitch: August is good, but it's going to be hot. What will we do if it rains? We should get married inside.

Leslie: Aww. You're right. It'll be too hot. Let's get married inside.

Mitch: Should we have the ceremony and the reception in the same place? Maybe we should get married in a wedding hall. That will be easy for everybody.

Leslie: But, Mitch, I want to get married in my family's church.

Mitch: But, honey, that's pretty far from here, about 75 miles!

Leslie: I know, but my whole family lives near there. Your sister lives near there, too.

Mitch: All right, but we should find a reception hall somewhere in the middle.

Leslie: OK, let's look around.

Page 152

The Big Picture: Where's My Dress?

B. Listen to the interview. Circle *True* or *False*.

Interviewer: Okay, Freddy, when did you get married?

Freddy: I got married on August 4, 1984.

Interviewer: Where did you have the ceremony?

Freddy: The ceremony was at my wife's church.

Interviewer: How many attendants did you have in your ceremony?

Freddy: Let's see. In the ceremony, we had 21 attendants, and there were about 500 people in the church.

Interviewer: Five hundred people in the church? That is a big wedding. So, who was in your wedding party?

Freddy: My wife, Louise, is an only child, but her father has 15 brothers and sisters. I have a relatively big family, too. Most of the people in the wedding party were our relatives.

Interviewer: Fifteen brothers and sisters? Wow! So, who was your best man?

Freddy: My best man was my friend, Carl. We grew up together.

Interviewer: Who was Louise's maid of honor?

Freddy: She had both a matron of honor and a maid of honor. They were both close friends.

Interviewer: What did Louise wear?

Freddy: Well, it's kind of an interesting story. She had a dressmaker. He told her how much the wedding gown would cost, and she gave him the money, but she never saw him again. He left with all the money. When she told me, I said, "Where is he?" I was going to go with her father to get the money. But she wouldn't tell me the address. This was one week before the wedding.

Interviewer: One week before the wedding? What did she do? Did she call the police?

Freddy: No, she didn't want to. Oh, and he took all of the bridesmaids money, too, so we had to do everything again. You know that Louise's a singer, right?

Interviewer: Right.

Freddy: Well, Louise was working in a Broadway show at the time. One of the guys who was in the show said, "I'll make your dress for you." This was only one week before the wedding, and he made the dress. It was absolutely beautiful.

Interviewer: Wow! That's an amazing story. So, did her family pay for this?

Freddy: Yes, she had to pay for the wedding dress twice, and for the bridesmaids dresses twice. First of all, the bridesmaids paid for their own dresses, but after the dressmaker ran off with the money, she felt bad, so she paid for them.

Interviewer: That is an incredible story. How long have you been married now?

Freddy: We've been married for 18 wonderful years.

Page 161

C. Listen and repeat the superlative adjectives in the chart above.

the largest	the noisiest	the most comfortable
the smallest	the easiest	the most populated
the fastest	the heaviest	the most spacious
the longest	the healthiest	the most difficult
the safest	the sportiest	the most affordable
the biggest		the most expensive
		the most popular

Page 162

A. Look at the pictures of three cars. Listen and circle the answers.

1. Which car is the smallest?
2. Which car is the cheapest?
3. Which car is the most expensive?
4. Which car is the most comfortable?
5. Which car is the fastest?
6. Which car is the safest in bad weather?
7. Which car is the easiest to park?
8. Which car is the most difficult to park?
9. Which car is the most economical?
10. Which car is the best for a large family?
11. Which car is the least economical?
12. Which car would be the most practical car for you and your family?

Page 164

D. A conversation: Selling a car. Monica is trying to sell her car. Listen to the conversation between Monica and her friend, Alison. Then, answer the questions.

Alison: Hi, Monica. I hear you're selling your car.
Monica: Yeah, I am.
Alison: Why are you selling it? You love that car!
Monica: I know, but it's beginning to cost me more and more money. A little repair here, a little repair there. Costs are adding up.
Alison: How long have you had the car?
Monica: Eight years.
Alison: Eight years? That's a long time. So, are you going to put an ad in the paper?
Monica: I'm not sure. I heard that you can sell a car on the Internet.
Alison: That's right. My brother sold his car that way. It took about 3 weeks.
Monica: How much was the ad?
Alison: It cost about $40 for two weeks. Then, he renewed it for another week for free.
Monica: That's a pretty good deal, but I think I'll put an ad in the paper and put a sign inside the car.
Alison: I guess that'll be the easiest way. It might be the fastest way to sell it, too. Will it be cheaper?
Monica: I think so. It'll cost $20 to advertise for a week.
Alison: Twenty dollars? That's not bad. Well . . . good luck selling your car.
Monica: Thanks.

Page 168

The Big Picture: Buying a Computer

A. Listen and complete the information about each computer.

Mr. and Mrs. Bennett are in an electronics store. They're looking for a computer. Mrs. Bennett wants to communicate with her grandchildren who live far away. She also wants to share recipes with her friends in other towns. Mr. Bennett wants to use the Internet. He wants to check on his investments and get more information on his favorite hobby—woodworking. He's a retired carpenter. The Bennett's grandson, Kevin, is helping them.

Kevin: So, Grandpa, what do you think of this computer? It's the DMX 2003.
Grandpa: What do you think?
Kevin: Well, let's see. It has 8 gigabytes of memory, so it'll be pretty fast. It has a regular keyboard, and it comes with a word processing program and a good black-and-white printer, too. For $950, that's a very good buy.
Grandpa: What about if I need repairs?
Kevin: There are many stores in the area that sell this computer. You can take it to the store in your neighborhood.
Grandpa: Can I use the Internet with this computer?
Kevin: You can, but in order to get the low price, you'll have to keep the same Internet company for three years.
Grandpa: Three years? Hmm. The screen looks kind of small. Oh, yes. It says here it's only 15". Is there one with a bigger screen?
Kevin: Sure, let's look at this one. It's a Bell computer. That's a good company, and they offer at-home repairs.
Grandma: At-home repairs? What does that mean?
Kevin: That means that someone will come to your house and fix the problem.
Grandma: I like that. That's really convenient, but what about the memory?
Kevin: It has 10 gigabytes of memory. That's impressive. Plus it has a 17" flat screen monitor.
Grandpa: Does it come with any software?
Kevin: Yes, it does. It comes with software for photos and a simple word processing program. It's Internet-ready, too.
Grandma: Internet-ready?
Kevin: Yeah, Grandma. You can use the Internet and e-mail right away.
Grandma: That's good for me.
Grandpa: What about a printer?

Kevin: The printer is extra, so it's $1,150 with a printer.

Grandma: What's that cute one over there?

Kevin: Oh, that's the newest computer. It's called the Amigo.

Grandma: That's a strange name for a computer.

Kevin: It's supposed to be very user-friendly. The Amigo even has a cup holder.

Grandpa: Alright, let's talk about the features. How much memory?

Kevin: It has 8 gigabytes, like the first computer, but that's good. It's a fast computer, but it's slower than the Bell. It comes with a color printer, a word processing program, and it has mini speakers.

Grandma: Is it . . . what did you call it . . . Internet-ready?

Kevin: Let's see. Yes, it's Internet-ready, and it has the largest screen, 19".

Grandpa: What about repairs?

Kevin: Hmm. You'll have to send the computer back to the company if you have any problems.

Grandma: That's not very convenient. And, this one's the most expensive, $1,300.

Grandpa: This is a tough decision. I don't know which one to buy.

Unit 12: Working Parents

Page 178

B. Listen as Tammy talks about Emma's day. Take a few notes.

I am a homemaker. My little girl, Emma, is one and a half years old, and she keeps me busy all day. I'm planning to stay home until she is two years old. Emma wakes up at 7:00. She likes a bottle right away. After her bottle, I give her breakfast. Then, I get her dressed. At 8:00, she watches her favorite TV program in my bedroom, so I can take a shower and get dressed. She plays and follows me around the house from 9:00 to 10:30. I clean the house, wash the dishes, and do the laundry. At 10:30, I put her in her stroller and we walk to the park. There are lots of other mothers and fathers with their children in the playground. Emma likes to sit on the swings and play in the sandbox. I have a chance to relax and talk to other parents. We are home by 12:00. I give Emma lunch and a bottle. Then, she's ready for her nap. She sleeps from 1:00 to 3:00. When she wakes up, we play quietly for an hour. Then, I put her in her car seat. We go food shopping or I take her to the library. She loves books and I check out five or six books a week. We are home by 5:00. When we get home, I start dinner. Emma plays on the kitchen floor with the pots and pans. My husband walks in the door at 6:00 and Emma can't wait to see him. He plays with her until dinner. We have dinner at 7:00. After dinner, I give Emma a bath. Then, my husband reads her a bedtime story. She's in bed by 8:00.

Page 179

A. Working parents. Maria and George are working parents. Listen to this story about their day. Then, answer the questions.

My husband—his name is George—and I have two children. Sam is nine—he's in third grade—and Sarah is four. She doesn't go to school yet. Well, both George and I work, but we are very lucky. My sister, Luisa, lives in the same town, about a mile from here.

George leaves the house first and he takes our daughter, Sarah, to my sister's house. I leave about an hour later, and I drop Sam at school. After school, Sam walks over to his aunt's house and stays there for the afternoon. My husband picks up the kids at 5:00 and takes them home. If it's nice out, he plays ball with the kids until I get home. I get home at 6:00 and start dinner. After dinner, George does the dishes and I give the kids their baths and showers. Then, George helps Sam with his homework and I read a story to Sarah. We put Sarah to bed at 8:00. When Sam finishes his homework, he can watch TV or play on the computer. He goes to bed at 9:00.

Page 184

The Big Picture: Working Parents

B. Bob and Pat are working parents. Look at the pictures and listen to their morning routine.

Pat and her husband Bob have two children, Timmy and David. Timmy is three years old and David is five. The mornings are always busy because Pat and Bob are working parents. At 5:45 the alarm clock rings, and Bob jumps out of bed. He uses the bathroom first and takes a shower. When he goes back into the bedroom, he wakes up Pat. After Pat gets up, she wakes up the children, then, starts to make breakfast. Bob puts on a video for the boys because they're sleepy, and the video gives them a chance to wake up slowly. Bob gets dressed and eats breakfast. Before he leaves for work, he kisses the children and Pat good-bye. After Bob leaves, Pat eats breakfast with Timmy and David. After breakfast, she gets dressed and gets the boys ready for the day. Then, she takes them out to the car, and the boys climb into their car seats. Pat buckles the boys into their car seats, then drives to the day care center, which is about 15 minutes from the house. As soon as she drops off the boys, Pat drives to work. She's a hairstylist. She's often a little late for work, but her customers understand, because they are mothers, too.

Page 193

A. Listen: A robbery. Jonathan came home and realized that his apartment had been burglarized. Listen to the police officer interview Jonathan about the crime.

Police officer: Wow! The burglar really made a mess.

Jonathan: Uh, Officer, . . . my apartment always looks like this.

Police officer: Oh, excuse me. Now, where were we? What time did you leave this morning?

Jonathan: I left at 8:30.

Police officer: Did you lock the door?

Jonathan: Yes, I'm sure I locked the door when I left. I was in a hurry, but I know that I locked the door.

Police officer: Did you lock the windows, too? The windows are open now.

Jonathan: Of course, I did. Well, maybe I didn't. I don't remember. I was late for work, and it was very hot when I went to bed last night. I opened the windows before I went to bed, but I overslept. Maybe I forgot.

Police officer: OK, sir. What time did you come home?

Jonathan: I came home at 6 P.M.

Police officer: When did you notice that something was wrong?

Jonathan: Well, as soon as I walk in the door, I usually put my keys on a table by the door. Well, the table was gone, and the keys fell on the floor!

Police officer: What else?

Jonathan: I went to turn on the TV, but it was gone. And so was my stereo, my DVD player, and all of my CDs! That was a great collection! I can't believe someone stole all of my CDs!

Police officer: Now, we'll have to dust for fingerprints. Did you touch anything else besides the door when you came in?

Jonathan: I opened the refrigerator, and my leftover Chinese food was gone, too.

Police officer: Are you sure that you didn't eat it?

Jonathan: I'm positive! I was saving that food for dinner tonight!

Police officer: I'll call the detectives and they will check for fingerprints. Then, you'll have to fill out a report.

Jonathan: Thank you, Officer.

Page 195

A. The car robbery. Listen to the story two times. Then, complete the sentences. Some of the verbs can be used more than once.

Andrew was late for work and in a hurry. He was starting his car when he realized that his briefcase was still in the house on the kitchen table. At the same time, Frank was walking down the street. Andrew got out of the car and returned to his house. Andrew didn't turn off the ignition, so the car was still running. Frank saw an excellent opportunity. He jumped into the car and drove it away. Andrew was coming out of the house with his briefcase when he saw Frank driving away. Andrew felt very foolish. Fortunately, Frank was driving so quickly that he wasn't paying attention to the fuel gauge. The car ran out of gas only six blocks from Andrew's house.

Page 200

The Big Picture: A Robbery at the Jewelry Store

B. Last night, Spike and Tina tried to rob a jewelry store. Look at the pictures and listen to the story.

1. This is Spike, and he's a burglar. Last night he tried to rob a jewelry store, but the police caught and arrested him. Spike likes to break into homes, jewelry stores, and cars, but he is not good at his profession.
2. Late last night, Spike and his girlfriend, Tina, drove downtown. While Tina was driving, Spike put on a mask, a black hat, and a pair of gloves.
3. When they arrived at a jewelry store, Tina parked on the side of the store, where it was dark. Spike got out of the car.
4. Spike broke a window with a towel and his fist. He didn't make a lot of noise.
5. As soon as he broke the window, he climbed into the store.
6. After he got into the store, he looked around at the jewelry. He decided to take some expensive watches, necklaces, and rings. He put the jewelry into his bag.
7. While he was robbing the store, Tina was waiting in the car. She was watching for the police.
8. Spike was getting ready to leave when he saw some leftover pizza on a table. "I'm a little hungry," he thought. When Spike picked up the pizza, he dropped his bag of jewelry.
9. As soon as the bag fell on the floor, an alarm rang.
10. When Spike heard the alarm, he grabbed the bag and left the store. When Tina heard the alarm, she started the car to drive away.
11. When Spike got out of the store, he saw a police car coming down the street, and he began to run.
12. As soon as the police saw Spike, one officer got out of the car and chased him. The other officer stayed in the car.
13. The other officer blocked Tina's car before she could drive away.

14. While Spike was running, he took off his mask and hat, but he forgot to take off his gloves.
15. Spike stood on a corner with a group of other men, but as soon as the police officer saw his gloves and the necklace in his pocket, he arrested Spike.
16. The police officers then arrested Tina. They handcuffed both of them and put them in the back of the police car.

Unit 14: Careers

Page 210

A. Last month Maria lost her job as an accountant when her company moved overseas. Listen and complete her options and plans.

1. If she finds a part-time job, she **won't earn** enough money.
2. Before she looks for another job, she **will write** her résumé.
3. When her résumé is ready, she **is going to make** many copies.
4. After she mails her résumé, she **will wait** for answers.
5. If she gets a rejection, her family **will help** her feel better.
6. When she goes on an interview, she **will wear** a new suit.
7. If she is confident during the interview, she **will make** a good impression.
8. If she makes a good impression, the company **is going to hire** her.

Page 215

D. Sharon Taylor's job interview. Listen and answer the questions.

Mr. Parker: Good afternoon, Ms. Taylor. Please, have a seat.
Ms. Taylor: Thank you.
Mr. Parker: So, Ms. Taylor, your experience is good. You worked for two years at County General Hospital. Could you tell me more about your job at that position?
Ms. Taylor: Well, I was a receptionist for two years.
Mr. Parker: But, your résumé says that you were an administrative assistant.
Ms. Taylor: That's true. I was promoted last year to administrative assistant. The doctors told me that they were pleased with my work.
Mr. Parker: What were you responsible for in your new position?
Ms. Taylor: Well, I made appointments, filed patients' records, and scheduled meetings. I've taken a few computer courses, so I also did word processing. I prepared all of the doctors' letters, and the monthly newsletter to patients. I also helped with the spreadsheets
Mr. Parker: That's good. Do you have any experience supervising employees?
Ms. Taylor: Not really. I trained the new full-time receptionist, and I trained the weekend receptionist, but I didn't hire any new staff.
Mr. Parker: Well, Ms. Taylor, your experience seems appropriate for this job. You have the kind of experience we're looking for, but we will be interviewing three more applicants this week. We'll probably have an answer for you next week.
Ms. Taylor: Thank you, Mr. Parker. It was nice meeting with you.

Page 216

The Big Picture: Career Choices

A. Ronaldo Silva is looking for a new job and maybe a new career. Listen to Ronaldo discuss his decision. What are the advantages and disadvantages of each choice?

I have a decision to make. Right now, I'm a salesman at a small telephone company. I sell cellular telephone plans, and, to tell you the truth, I'm pretty good at it. I have had the job for five years, and this year, I'll make $40,000. But, I'm bored, and I'm thinking about making a change. I'm not sure what to do. I had a job interview last week at a large telecommunications company. The company was looking for someone with my experience. I know a lot about the cellular-phone business, and I would like more variety in my work. The large company offers good benefits, including medical and dental insurance. I would sell both national and international cellular-phone plans. I would also receive a promotion after one year if I become one of the top twenty salespersons. The company is located only thirty minutes from my home, so I won't have to move. But, there's a disadvantage to the new job. I would have to take frequent business trips to other offices to visit customers. I might also have to go overseas five or six times a year to visit our international customers.

I have another idea. I'm thinking about opening my own business. There's a nice-sized store available downtown. I'm thinking about renting it. It's right in our neighborhood. If I'm my own boss, I'll be more independent. I can select my own employees, and my wife, who is an accountant, will take care of the bills and the payroll on the weekend. I won't have to travel unless I want to, and I can set my own working hours. In my store, I would like to sell cellular phones and all their accessories and telephone cards. I might sell pagers and hand-held computers, too.

But, you know, there's a lot of risk in opening your own business. I'll need a bank loan, and I'll have to pay for my own medical insurance. My family might have to use my wife's insurance plan for a while. She may have to keep her job in the beginning. This is a very important decision for me and for my family.

B. Listen and circle the job that fits the description.

1. He'll have good benefits.
2. He'll sell cellular-phone plans.
3. He'll receive a promotion after one year.
4. He'll be more independent.
5. He'll have to travel often.
6. He'll sell telephone cards.
7. He won't have to move.
8. He'll set his own working hours.

Unit 15: City Life

Page 225

B. Who is . . . ? Listen and write the answers to these questions. Use the occupations on page 224.

1. Who is trying on sunglasses?
2. Who is collecting garbage?
3. Who is delivering a package?
4. Who is washing the windows in the apartment building?
5. Who is making plane reservations?
6. Who is walking the dogs?
7. Who is delivering mail?
8. Who is selling hot dogs?
9. Who is writing parking tickets?
10. Who is remodeling the hair salon?

Page 227

A. Listen and complete these sentences about the picture on pages 224–225.

1. Larry has been washing windows since 8:00 this morning.
2. Janet has been trying on sunglasses for an hour.
3. They have been waiting for the bus for a long time.
4. The parking violations officer has been writing tickets for two hours.
5. The travel agent has been helping Mrs. Johnson since she sat down.
6. The firefighters have been washing the fire truck for 30 minutes.
7. The dog walker has been walking in the park for 20 minutes.
8. The hot dog vendor has been working on that corner for ten years.
9. They have been sitting in the restaurant since noon.
10. The sanitation workers have been collecting trash since 6 A.M.
11. These people have been busy all morning.

Page 232

The Big Picture: Harry, the Doorman

A. Listen to Harry, the doorman, talk about the tenants in the apartment building.

Hello. My name is Harry and I'm the doorman at the Plaza, an expensive apartment building downtown, across from the park. I've been opening and closing the door at the Plaza for ten years. I stand here at the door all day, watching people come and go, talking to everyone. I know a lot about the people who live in the building.

Manuel is the young man in Apartment 1A. He's very depressed because his girlfriend moved out a few days ago. Manuel has been sitting in his apartment looking out the window. I didn't like her very much. She never talked, never even said "Hello." This is Ms. Chan, Apartment 1B, walking into her apartment. She's in great shape. She's 82 years old, but she walks two miles every day. She's been walking every day since she retired 17 years ago.

Denise lives in Apartment 2A and just got a dog. She brought it into the building late at night. No pets are allowed in the building. Some of the neighbors have been complaining to the landlord and saying that they hear a dog barking at night. But me, I say, "Dog? Barking? No, I don't know anything about a dog." Leena is the tenant in Apartment 2B. She lost her job last month and she's been looking for a new one. That's her right now. She's walking out of the apartment building. She has a job interview at 12:00.

There has been a lot of arguing in Apartment 3A for the past few months. Mr. Alvarez is tired of city life. He has a job offer in a small town in the country. Mrs. Alvarez loves the excitement of the city with the restaurants, and shows, and museums. She wants to stay in the city. Silvia lives in Apartment 3B. A few weeks ago she met a nice young man at a party. He's been sending her flowers twice a week.

It's Danny birthday today. Danny lives in Apartment 4A, and he has lots of family and friends. He's been receiving cards and packages all week. Mr. Wilson, in Apartment 4B, has been having financial problems. He didn't pay his rent last month or the month before. He's been receiving letters from different credit agencies, too.

There isn't much happening on the fifth floor. Apartment 5A is empty. Lots of people have been looking at the apartment, but rents in the city are very high. That apartment is renting for $3,000 a month. The apartment has been empty for three months. Apartment 5B is quiet, but it's not empty. Mr. and Mrs. Shapiro have been traveling. They're on a cruise around the world and they'll return at the end of the month.

Page 233

E. Listen and circle the letter of the correct answer.

1. Did Mr. Wilson pay his rent last month?
2. Has Mr. Wilson been having financial problems?
3. What did Denise get?
4. Does the landlord know that Denise has a dog?
5. Where did Mr. Alvarez receive a job offer?
6. Where does Mrs. Alvarez want to live?
7. What have they been doing?
8. Where does Danny live?
9. What has Danny been receiving?
10. How long has Harry been a doorman at the Plaza?

Skills Index

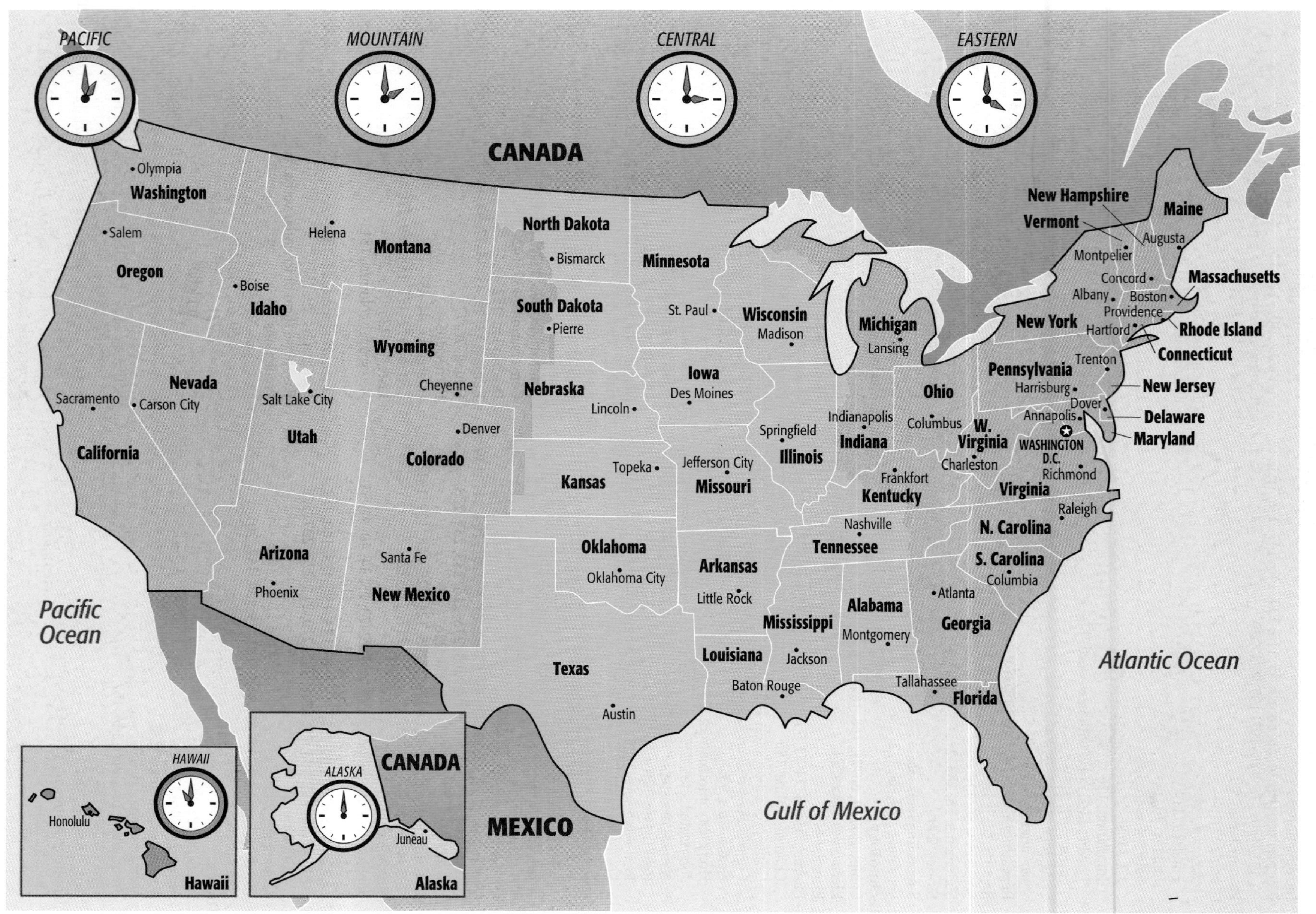

PACIFIC
MOUNTAIN
CENTRAL
EASTERN
CANADA
Olympia
Washington
Salem
Oregon
Boise
Idaho
Helena
Montana
Wyoming
Cheyenne
Sacramento
Carson City
Nevada
California
Salt Lake City
Utah
Denver
Colorado
Arizona
Phoenix
Santa Fe
New Mexico
North Dakota
Bismarck
South Dakota
Pierre
Nebraska
Lincoln
Kansas
Topeka
Oklahoma
Oklahoma City
Texas
Austin
Minnesota
St. Paul
Iowa
Des Moines
Missouri
Jefferson City
Arkansas
Little Rock
Louisiana
Baton Rouge
Wisconsin
Madison
Illinois
Springfield
Mississippi
Jackson
Michigan
Lansing
Indiana
Indianapolis
Kentucky
Frankfort
Tennessee
Nashville
Alabama
Montgomery
Ohio
Columbus
Georgia
Atlanta
Florida
Tallahassee
W. Virginia
Charleston
Virginia
Richmond
N. Carolina
Raleigh
S. Carolina
Columbia
Pennsylvania
Harrisburg
New York
Albany
New Hampshire
Vermont
Maine
Augusta
Montpelier
Concord
Massachusetts
Boston
Providence
Rhode Island
Hartford
Connecticut
Trenton
New Jersey
Dover
Delaware
Annapolis
Maryland
WASHINGTON D.C.
Pacific Ocean
Atlantic Ocean
Gulf of Mexico
MEXICO
HAWAII
Honolulu
Hawaii
ALASKA
CANADA
Juneau
Alaska